Transnational Spaces and

Social Networks, Border Regions

Angela Pilch Ortega and Barbara Schröttner (eds.)

# Transnational Spaces and Regional Localization

## Social Networks, Border Regions and Local-Global Relations

Waxmann 2012
Münster / New York / München / Berlin

**Bibliographic information published by die Deutsche Nationalbibliothek**
Die Deutsche Nationalbibliothek lists this publication in the Deutsche Nationalbibliografie; detailed bibliographic data are available in the internet at http://dnb.d-nb.de.

This book has been printed with the help from

UNI GRAZ Karl-Franzens-Universität Graz

URBI Umwelt-, Regional und Bildungswissenschaftliche Fakultät der KFU Graz

BM.W_F[a] Bundesministerium für Wissenschaft und Forschung in Wien

Das Land Steiermark → Wissenschaft Amt der Steiermärkischen Landesregierung, Abteilung Wissenschaft und Forschung

AlfredSchachnerGedächtnisFonds Alfred-Schachner-Gedächtnisfonds in Graz

ISBN 978-3-8309-2521-7


Postfach 8603, 48046 Münster

www.waxmann.com
info@waxmann.com

Cover Design: Anne Breitenbach, Tübingen
Cover Picture: Martin Bauer, Graz – www.martinbauerphoto.com
Setting: Stoddart Satz- und Layoutservice, Münster
Print: Hubert & Co., Göttingen

Printed on age-resistant paper, acid-free as per ISO 9706

FSC www.fsc.org MIX Papier aus verantwortungsvollen Quellen FSC® C016439

Printed in Germany

# Contents

# Acknowledgements

We are very thankful to the authors for inspiring thought and insight in their remarkable research into the topic of transnationalism. Their differing regional perspectives and interdisciplinary points of view have truly enriched the content of this volume. We thank Martin Bauer for his attractive cover image. We furthermore would like to acknowledge the support of the publisher and those who provided financial backing.

# Introductory Thoughts on Transnational Spaces and Regional Localization

*Angela Pilch Ortega and Barbara Schröttner*

Globalization has encouraged worldwide mobility, intensified migration and supported growing interconnectness through new technologies; it has therefore substantially contributed to the development of so-called transnational spaces. Relatedly, societies are increasingly heterogeneous, less limited by physical boundaries and more spatially and socially spread out. This collected edition focuses on transnational spaces which should not be understood as locations on a map or as sealed containers, but instead as relational social areas which are composed of various relationships. Transnationalization increases liberation and/or emancipation from place because social relations overcome physical space and local, regional and national boundaries. As a consequence, a reconfiguration of social, cultural, political and economic scopes of action is occurring. Nevertheless, place does not lose its relevance as an organizing and structuring principle – instead it gains relevance because social relations and other interactions still have a territorial reference. Because globalization encourages the crossing of borders in various ways, goods and capital nowadays move freely around the globe; the market for many services has become global. However free trade is mainly the domain of those countries which have sufficient power in the global order. Unequal social availability is increasingly connected to access to information technology which is in turn linked to economic resources and competence (i.e. the digital divide). As this edited volume illustrates, international and transnational companies, anonymous market forces and unfettered free trade represent only one aspect of transnationalism because the realization of transcultural and transnational spaces is also initiated, carried out and enforced by social actors.

In recent decades, a substantial change in the social structures of interactions and networks has been observable. Through these changes, the participation of social actors transforms individual and collective living environments, resulting in alteration in the social order, and in addition it implies a greater transnational and cosmopolitan orientation. This book draws attention to the fact that social networks developing out of these processes change the attitudes and practices of individuals as well as the social structures of communities and societies, both on the regional and global level. Transnational spaces also function as platforms for global social movements such as the anti-globalization movements which seek to work against hegemonic claims to power. A multitude of social movements and networks which are more or less strongly cross-linked have also arisen on the regional level. Both transnational social networks and regional civic networks act within a multitude of fields such as human rights, gender issues, the rights of gays and lesbians and civil rights in general, environmental protection, nuclear disarmament, peace activism, etc. Transnationalization from the bottom-up has its own logic, but can largely be analyzed based on various basic social conditions. The aims of social movements are therefore often similar: to gain more influence in decision making processes on the local, regional, global and transnational level and to free individuals and communities from oppressive restrictions imposed by authorities which impact lifestyle choices, individual behavior and political views. It is worth noting that new transnational experiences and fields of action are also shaped by inequality and power relations. As many social movements and social networks show, they are in part successful in resisting the exploitative practices of transnational policies, companies and organizations; there is an exchange of information and knowledge, and the formation of solidarity alliances. It is possible to emphasize that social actors take up the task of re-appropriating global space and freeing it from the confines of geographical space. Local, regional, national and transnational anti-globalization movements, social networks and solidarity communities are thus at least partially opposed to the practices of transnational companies, organizations and institutions.

This volume reveals that for people in general and particularly for migration movements, new borders have been established in many places all over the world. The biographies of global actors and migrants reference this alteration of space. Within these spaces, experiences of transnational acting and interacting are being biographically gathered and developed. Some of the articles in this book show that migrants establish relationships in different geographical places and maintain these relationships through new technologies which facilitate other forms of communication; this allows for the continuation of social interactions across physical borders. In this context it appears that the overlapping of virtual spaces with social locations entails new challenges which have to be mastered in the organization of everyday life. Taking this reality into consideration, it should be noted that through migration, streams of people deal with issues such as diversity, contradictoriness, virtual distance and proximity. Additionally this collected edition calls special attention to border regions and their social configurations. Borders appear for instance as narratives which can have an enormous impact on social structures. In order to better understand this development, it is important to note that migration movements play an important role within border regions as a number of articles in this edition show.

This book further deals with different aspects and various tensions having to do with local and global change, interplay and interdependence. Globalization leads to development that often ignores regional needs, supports the continuation of postcolonial power and maintains hegemonic dominance. Various aspects of these tension-filled fields are highlighted, such as the tendency of essentialism concerning issues of language; the impact of global hegemonic forces on marginalized world views; public schooling and the environments of international and transnational students.

It can be concluded that transnational spaces can in no way be regarded as a homogeneous phenomenon. There are many things to consider. How and under which conditions do they develop? How do people create their own transcultural references in their everyday lives and how do these references support the transformation of regionally embodied structures and practices? What impacts do power relations and hegemonic forces have on transnational spaces? The content of the selected articles is to be found in the following three sections: first, *Transnational Space and Social Networks*; second, *Migration and Border Regions* and third, *Spaces of Tensions: Local – Global*. These three main themes allow for concentration on specific issues which are shaped, influenced and affected by transnational processes. The authors of this volume come from various scientific disciplines and diverse national backgrounds, and they start their analyses from different understandings and conceptions of transnationalism. The book offers diverse theoretical perspectives on the phenomenon of transnationalism and raises important questions concerning this topic. Moreover, you'll find critical reflection on power relations within these transnational spaces, opening up new and innovative fields of action, giving regional insights into diverging modes of transnationalization and supporting innovative scientific research approaches in this field.

In the introductory article *(Re)Contextualization of Global and Local Place. Emergent Transnationalism and the Role of Cultural Diversity,* **Barbara Schröttner** shows that developments caused by globalization and transnationalism challenge the existing concept of the nation-state. Developments such as global interconnectedness and interdependencies come about through increasing cross-national flows and networks remove power from the national context. In her writing, the author reflects on the fact that these developments strongly transform the form, meaning and impact of nation-states. Schröttner offers a theoretical perspective on the role of national space in the 21st century, arguing that the national sphere is growing in strength through transnational activities. This consolidation of the nation-state can be, for example, explained by the rise of civil society actors which operate on a translocal and transnational level. The author reveals that through the process of restructuring the local, national and international space people are forced to transform their relations to space and their sense of identity. In her theoretical discourse about an emerging transnationalism, she concentrates not only on space as a static concept and the nation state as a container; instead the author describes place as a relational structure and dynamic phenomena which generates new references to life and leads to new allocations of meaning.

Part I of the publication, entitled **Transnational Space and Social Networks**, is a collection of five chapters which examines the characteristics and conditions of different types of social networks such as transnational family networks and related challenges; digital networks and the impact of new media on transnational spaces; and private or professional cross-border networks and their influence on the identity building processes.

In the first article, *Transnational Social Relations – A Challenge of Everyday Life?*, **Angela Pilch Ortega** focuses on transnationalization processes from the bottom up in relation to biographies and social networks. In this respect the author emphasizes that "transnational spaces are understood to be relational social areas which are created by social actors in their daily lives" (29). She argues that biographies reference transnational articulations. These articulations highlight the transnational orientations and strategies of social actors who are confronted with heterogeneous overlapping social areas. The author offers insight into some of the challenges which appear when people interact with "different knowledge, diverging perspectives and varying reference systems" (24). She further shows that the conditions and possibilities for participation in transnational spaces are not equal among participants. Pilch Ortega reveals that transnational activities require specific resources, competencies and capacities. As a consequence, the author emphasizes that transnational acting initiates complex learning processes in everyday life which can lead to excessive demands on people. The article *Transnational Spaces, Hybrid Identities and New Media* by **Alexander Unger** aims to clarify "the role of new technologies within (...) parlous transformation" (37). The author focuses on new media and its relevance for transnationalization processes. In this regard he suggests that it is "important to consider the macro level of encompassing societal transformation as well as the micro level of everyday social practices" (40). Unger emphasizes that the World Wide Web not only fosters the movement away from the national and de-regionalization processes but also opens up possibilities for staying in contact in spite of geographical distance. Furthermore the author focuses on issues such as transnational identities and hybridization. In his analysis, Unger shows that the utilization of ethno-portals can have differing effects on individual understandings and identity conceptions. He points to the fact that individuals are not only victims of globalization processes but that they are also creators who are able to form individual everyday life practices. The article *Social Networks and Identity Building Processes through Transnational/Cross Regional Experiences of Experts in Southern Europe* by **Estrella Gualda, António Fragoso, Emilio Lucio-Villegas, Teresa González Gómez** and **Vània Martins** focuses on the frontier region of two cities in the south of Spain and Portugal. In their work they address the issue of identity building of people who are involved in cross-border cooperations and social networks because of activities in their professional or personal life. Based on open-ended interviews and a structural module for analyzing social networks, the authors look at the influence of transnational activities and experiences on identity building processes. The results of their research indicate the dominance of regional orientations in identity building processes. The authors argue in this regard that "it is possible that we are witnessing a movement of implicit or explicit resistance that (...) is opposed to those who want to connect outside their original territory" (59). In their article *The Role of Transnationalism, Personal Networks and Social Networks in the Migratory Projects of a Small Cameroonian Community in Huelva,* **Estrella Gualda** and **Carmen Márquez** present an empirical study about the life paths of Cameroonian immigrants living in Spain. Through a social network analysis and analysis of several life histories, the authors focus on the influence of social networks on migration projects and integration processes. They examine "how far transnational networks influence and configure the immigrants' lives" (62). The results of their study show the importance of geographical proximity in daily life. Additionally the authors emphasize the tendency to reproduce and reinvent social structures of the countries of origin in the destination country; this is reflected in the exemplary cases of their investigation. In her writing entitled *How to Share Space? Inside/Outside/Along/Within/Together,* **Elke Krasny** reflects on different cultural policies for sharing space. Her analysis is based on the assumption that transnationalization produces 'other' spaces with new cultural and social meanings. The author emphasizes that the idea of sharing is archaic, idealized and highly politicized. In her article she presents the biographies of three social actors with different "scenarios" of sharing space. From her perspective the text itself references a shared space. Drawn from narrated life histories, Krasny reflects on and gives insights into differing life constructions, strategies of dealing with transnational spaces and diverging policies of sharing space. The author aims to present the relational aspects of space and exchange structures and reveals the inherent problems and also the potential benefits of sharing transnational space.

Part II is entitled **Migration and Border Regions** and is a compilation of six chapters linking the theme of transnationalization to questions of migration and border regions. The theoretical and empirical analyses cover border regions and urban spaces such as "inner and outer borders" in Kosovo and in Cyprus, the 'British Isles', the south border region separating Mexico and Guatemala, refugee camps in Western Sahara and the urban space of Cologne in Germany.

In her investigation, *A Transnational Politics of Mobility. Thinking From and Across Borders*, **Jennifer M. Murphy** introduces a study which concentrates on the question of how to critically address the uneven transnational movements of peoples across borders and the unequal rules that govern and sanction this mobility. Murphy's article is based on the assumption that any theoretical discussion about transnational mobility has to be built on the theoretical concept of the "coloniality of power" (91). The author argues that only if we take this concept into consideration, can a transformative "transnational politics of mobility" (90) be realized and territorially fixed notions of nation can be met. Murphy considers that it is compulsory to reconstitute the predominant epistemologies of the global and the local. Moreover, the author claims that it is necessary to question the colonial project, the hegemonic imaginary and the technologies of power. Only then, as the author critically asserts, is it possible to manage transnational space and movement. In the article *Borders are Narratives. Habitual Involvement in Ethnic and Social Spaces,* **Rudolf Egger** focusses on relationships between "inner and outer borders" in Kosovo and in Cyprus against the background of fundamental changes due to the European integration processes over the last decades. His analysis shows that beside powerful economic forces which attempt to overcome 'old' borders, the emerging new maps are not well connected to the heterogeneous ethnic and economic situation in these regions. The author reveals in his analysis the presence of an ethnically encoded memory space which has an enormous impact on the development of social structures. Egger gives insights into strategies for dealing with issues of being 'separated' and the development of 'new' identities. Referring to his research in Kosovo in which he analyzed life histories, he presents biographical research as a useful method for reconstructing narratives in order to identify and understand the dominant forces and values in a society. His analysis suggests different strategies for dealing with the past and diverging modes of the production of the present. In his analysis about *Imagining and Re-imagining Transcultural Spaces – The 'Mitteleuropa' Discourse and Deconstructing the 'British Isles'*, **Fergal Lenehan** offers thoughts on the influence of linguistic processes and nomenclature which are essential for the formation and transformation of transcultural spaces that can be inclusive and thus can lead to the imagining and creation of new or revived spaces. These revitalized spaces include macro-regional transcultural spaces beyond the confines of the nation-state and yield a sense of belonging as well as a sense of place outside the nation-state. Lenehan suggests that linguistic processes and spatially oriented discourses also function as a force of separation through deconstructing established trans-cultural notions. As a consequence, they can undermine conventional transcultural spatial notions such as the 'British Isles' discourse of the 1990s and the 2000s shows. As the central theme the author introduces the 'Mitteleuropa' discussion of the 1980s as an example of an inclusive transcultural spatial imagining. He shows that the discourse on 'Mitteleuropa' aspired to realize a transnational sense of belonging, based upon the linguistic reality itself and the related intrinsic idea of a distinct transcultural space. In his analysis *Presencia Centroamericana en la Frontera Sur de México: un Espacio en Construcción Transnacional*, **Germán Martínez Velasco** focuses on social interactions in the Mexican border region between Chiapas and Guatemala. This border region has been influenced by various historical events; among them was the geographical allocation of the territory of Chiapas to Mexico which led to a political and geographical reassignment of Guatemalan people to Mexico. Another historical event was the Guatemalan civil war which brought with it a wave of refugees and led to the settlement of many Guatemalan people in the rural area of Chiapas. Additionally, a continuing (trans)migration movement from Central America to the US is observable. Some of these (trans)migrants decide to stay in the border region of Chiapas. In his empirical study, Martínez Velasco offers insights into the configuration of these transnational spaces in which mainly migrants take part. Drawn from an empirical long-term study the author highlights the often precarious social conditions of migrants living in this south Mexican border region. He further looks at strategies for dealing with such transnational social relations. Martínez Velasco points out social borders between different groups of actors which are often enforced through ethnic policies. Additionally he points to the hegemonic dominance of a stated Mexican culture and the social vulnerability of migrants and former refugees in this region. The study about *National Identity Formation in Transnational Spaces: The Case of the Sahrawis of Western Sahara* by **Sidi M. Omar** concentrates on the question of how the people of Western Sahara, the Sahrawis, have been able to build a strong sense of collective national identity given their experiences with separation and dispersion across several exilic and diasporic spaces. The author highlights in his study that this sense of collective national identity has been encouraged, normalized and institutionalized by Sahrawi communities living in refugee camps in southwestern Algeria. The building up of this strong national identity has also been enforced by the transnational experiences of the Sahrawi diaspora and particularly by the Sahrawi State which concentrates on establishing state structures and a feeling of common citizenship. Problematizing the "centrality of territoriality", Omar shows that the Sahrawis have been able to develop and preserve their national identity across differing transnational spaces. The key message of the article *Migration Moves and Shapes Society* by **Marc Hill** and **Erol Yildiz** is that the emergence of diversity due to global opening processes functions as an important urban resource. The authors underline the important role of migration movements for the development of urban spaces. In this regard Hill and Yildiz criticize the continuation of negative discourses on migration and an often claimed resistance of migrants to integration. Focusing on everyday life practices in Cologne, Germany, the paper illustrates the relevance of migration processes for diversity and it gives insights into differing and creative strategies for dealing with social heterogeneity. The authors emphasize that urban spaces function as transnational stages which open up new possibilities, new forms of diversity and foster the development of hybrid life conceptions.

Part III of this collected edition, with the title **Spaces of Tensions: Local – Global** focusses on the fields of global and regional structures, often tense due to power relations and dominant forces, and gives insights into the mutual interdependency of global and local configurations. This section consists of five chapters and reflects on regions including the Irish-speaking region of Ireland, the highlands of Chiapas in Mexico, heterogeneous classrooms in Vienna, northeastern Brazil and virtual 'Third Spaces'.

The first article in Part III, entitled *Private Sentiment and Public Issues – Irish Medium Education and Complex Linguistic and Political Identification* by **Simon Warren** looks at the construction of a non-essentialist politics of place. In his paper, the author critically focuses on cultural politics of language around the Irish education policy for secondary schools in an Irish-speaking region of Ireland. In his article, Warren offers a theoretical framework for a nonessential policy perspective. He presents three theoretical threads which focus on issues of space/place, social/political and public/private. Warren argues that "local identity is formed from the 'throwntogetherness' of place or the collision of 'micro-worlds'" (172) which function as a basis for a politics of place. The author suggests a nonessential approach to a politics of place which disclaims binaries such as the modern and the traditional and opens up possibilities for overcoming oppositions. In his theoretical work *Propuesta Teórica en la Reconstrucción de las Cosmovisiones, Lenguas y Conocimientos de los Pueblos Originarios ante la Globalización,* **Miguel Sánchez Álvarez** concentrates on indigenous people living in a southern region of Mexico, the highlands of Chiapas. The author argues that despite the influence of globalization processes, diverse cultures still exist in this region. The paper aims to make visible the precarious situation of indigenous people in Chiapas. Sánchez Álvarez concentrates in his analysis on impacts of globalization processes, related hegemonic forces and negative consequences for indigenous communities. He argues that globalization processes continue to dominate and somehow "destroy" the basic understanding of sustainable ways of living. He describes the social practices of local people such as their collective orientation, social community life and relationship with nature which often differ from Western concepts of social cohabitation. Being part of the indigenous community in Chiapas himself, the author offers a theoretical framework of an intercultural dialog which addresses indigenous knowledge and social practices in a respectful manner. For Sánchez Álvarez, transnational spaces function as platforms which offer opportunities for exchange about hegemonic influences and support solidarity between different communities on a local, regional, national and transnational level. In their article *Teaching in Heterogeneous Classrooms: The Play of Reason and Unreason,* **Neda Forghani-Arani** and **Anne M. Phelan** explore classroom situations in a secondary school in Vienna which are characterized by a considerable number of transnational students. The authors show in their example of transcultural and transnational urban classrooms how the experiences of teachers are challenged by this diversity in terms of "practical wisdom, judgment and tact" (201). In their essay, the authors present a case study of a teacher in this "culturally, ethnically, nationally and linguistically heterogeneous" (201) setting, arguing that teachers need more than knowledge of diversity and commitment to social justice. The authors point to the fact that to be able to practice culturally responsive teaching, the language of phronesis and tact should be implemented in transcultural and transnational school settings. In his analysis about *The Conflu-*

*ence of Global and Local Currents in Brazil's Municipal Schooling*, **Steven Hales** offers a description of the public school reform in Brazil since the 1990s; more specifically, he introduces an ethnographic study of municipal elementary school curricula in northeastern Brazil in 2008. The author illustrates how the public school reform has been shaped by transnational neoliberal and national non-neoliberal flows. The aim of this reform was to enhance Brazil's economic competitiveness in the global marketplace as well as to decrease societal problems. Hales notes that to accomplish these ambitions, a number of educational policies which promote curricular and pedagogical autonomy of municipal school systems and which reflect the tensions between global forces and local needs have been implemented. In his systematic discourse, he critically addresses the issue that public schooling in Brazil is consistent with neoliberal quantitative conceptions of quality. Hales assumption is that the alignment of public primary education in Brazil is not a replication of a global model but rather a locally forged variation. The piece of writing about *The Development of Transcultural Third Spaces by International and Transnational Students* by **Dave Burnapp, Yan Feng** and **Wei Zhao** discusses the creation of virtual 'third spaces' which support a way of mobilizing and strengthening local identity. The authors argue that the formation of virtual social spaces help to better negotiate transnational spaces. Their theoretical and practical investigation is based on the assumption that if students from different cultures use their own local networks to create online spaces, they more easily overcome social and academic challenges in these new transnational spaces. In their empirical investigation, the scientists describe and argue for the necessity of implementing and supporting the use of such 'virtual third spaces' at the university level. The research data presented by the authors indicates the need for enabling students to be connected with other students through transnational learning activities.

# (Re)Contextualization of Global and Local Place

## Emergent Transnationalism and the Role of Cultural Diversity

*Barbara Schröttner*


### Abstract

*Despite great distances and the reality of international borders many types of social, cultural, economic and political relationships that span the globe have been growing in intensity. As a result, there is increased interconnectivity, new spatial interdependency and heightened mobility between places, and there are also new forms of political engagement which have major implications for global economic, political, cultural and social systems. Because of these developments people are transforming their relations to space and their sense of identity. Transnationalism can be described as a condition in which a strictly confined sense of community becomes outdated and multiple identities and changing representations become the norm. In the discourse of transnationalism place is therefore thought of as a relational structure which includes various social bonds, interactions and formations. It is possible to assert that the above described transformations demand alternative ways of approaching issues surround the social phenomenon of cultural diversity which is a condition of an emergent transnationalism.*


### Conceptualizations: Globalization and Transnationalism

Increasing levels of mobility, interconnectivity and interdependency across national borders can be ascribed to both globalization and transnationalism; this not only has a significant effect on individual relationships, international networks and transnational networks but also on nation-states. Particularly through ongoing de-nationalization processes, nation-states are being reshaped and restructured. In light of this discussion, it is important to understand that the role of place once again gains significance, in particular in transnationalism discourse, because global circuits intersect and create new places of power and centrality.

Regarding these new global spatial relations, this article shows that while former conceptualizations in globalization theory focused on the following two concepts of space, "the subdivided, territorially fixed and hermetically-sealed container that was the national living-room" and the unbound "'space of flows' of the global here and now", the transnationalism debate points to a lack in both approaches to globalization theory in terms of new spatial relations (Bittner/Hackenbroich/Vöckler, 2007: 23). In the discourse of transnationalism, place cannot be perceived of as a container but instead as a relational structure which is composed of diverse social relationships with diverse scope (ibid.: 21f.). Through these relationships and interactions, social formations and ties cut across national borders, and many types of social, cultural, economic and political relationships are transformed (Rizvi, 2011: 184f.). Through these often very dense and highly complex transnational networks, transnationalism can be defined as "a condition in which certain kind of relationships have been globally intensified and now take place paradoxically in a planet-spanning (...) arena of activity" (Vertovec, 2009 in Rizvi, 2011: 184).

## (Re)Conceptualization of the Global and the Local

The challenge today is to recover place in the context of dominant forces such as globalization, new information technologies and the expansion of transnational and translocal dynamics which suggest that place no longer matters (Sassen, 2010b: 5). On the contrary, the role of place in a global world is central. To focus on place helps one to analyze globalization and transnationalization processes because different types of places – such as global cities – are located on "multiple specialized cross-border circuits". Numerous global circuits intersect and position cities with distinct scopes, practices and actors on different "structured cross-border geographies" (Sassen, 2010a: 6). Because of these multiple highly specialized cross-border circuits, the city has to be considered to be a multiscalar system instead of a container or a bounded closed unit (Sassen, 2010c: 7). Through this continuing (re-)contextualization of global space, territoriality linking places to different degrees and corresponding to their respective scope concerning certain issues or motives takes on a very different face for each specific biography, family, company, non-governmental organization, etc. What this analysis of place then suggests is that it is not only necessary to deal with the technological possibilities for overcoming physical distance; it is likewise necessary to practically rearranging the various places, people and things in a concrete way and connect them with one another in meaningful narrative terms (Dürrschmidt/Bittner, 2007: 27).

While the globalization discourse defines the 'local and global' and the 'nation-state and globalization' as being contradictory, the transnationalism debate criticizes this approach and the idea of space that this definition indicates; as a consequence, it specifies how 'the local' is newly constructed at a time of very complex international spatial interdependencies (Bittner/Hackenbroich/Vöckler, 2007: 23). One might note that while one conceptualization of the 'local' has assumed geographic proximity in the form of a strictly defined territorial boundedness and enclosure, another conceptualization has considered the 'local' to be part of a hierarchy of nested scales, especially between political states. These conceptualizations of the local are, to a high degree, adequate for most of the actual practices and formations which constitute the local all over the world. However, these practices and formations are now more and more being questioned in the discourse of transnationalism which is leading to a critical reconceptualizing of the local (Sassen, 2007: 198). As the discussion shows, this discerning reconceptualization is necessary because today the local is being repositioned through various developments, among them new information technologies. Through new information technology, financial service providers, resource-poor (non-governmental) organizations and also households become part of global activist networks (Sassen, 2010a: 6). What is experienced and represented as being the local level can then be described as a "micro environment with global span" (Sassen, 2007: 195) which includes practices that create multiple lateral and horizontal communications, collaborations, solidarities and supports (ibid.: 199). It can be argued that the multiscalar politics of the local is today not limited to moving through a set of nested scales from "the local to the national to the international" but directly accesses other local actors inside or across borders (ibid.: 207f.). To draw a brief conclusion from these facts, it is possible to emphasize that the notion of context which is typically associated with locality and physical proximity begins to be destabilized (Sassen, 2010a: 6).

## (Re)Shaping National Space

Through the greater globalization of production and trade as well as finance and culture, the boundaries of the state have become porous; this increasingly leads to states losing control of their own fortunes. However, while globalization removes power in the national context and undermines the institutions which civil society and the democratic public have until now used for communication, it simultaneously establishes new possibilities for democratic influence on essential common issues such as the notion of the nation-state. This is important considering the fact that the sovereignty of states has been compromised through shifting patterns of regional political groupings and alliances. At the subnational level, the state is challenged by the revitalization of solidarity groups which may be based on region, language, religion, ethnicity or gender and by transnational actions that generate their own solidarity (Torres, 2009: 115f.).

The study emphasizes that the global can be structured inside the national. There are different types of realities with distinct social entities and diverse origins which capture the national as a terrain for the global. Such instances are the localizing of global dynamics in the national and the de-nationalizing of what historically is contained within national frames and still continues to be experienced, represented and coded as such (Sassen, 2010a: 6f.). Alan Harding and Patrick Le Gales (1997: 189) claim in this context that globalization opens up national spaces. Saskia Sassen (2010a: 2) states that globalization should be conceived of "not just in terms of interdependence and global institutions, but also as inhabiting and reshaping the national". As Carlos Alberto Torres asserts, globalization blurs national boundaries and therefore changes alliances within and between countries (Torres, 2009: 114). Considering these approaches to globalization and its relations to the national, it is possible to assume that globalization does not inevitably lead to the general decline of the state but to adaptations to new conditions (Sassen, 2010a: 4).

The debate on transnationalism shows that while transnational processes are "anchored in nation-states" they "transcend one or more nation-states" at the same time (Bittner/Hackenbroich/Vöckler, 2007: 21). In other words: even though the nation-state increasingly loses its political and economic functions, it gains significance if looked at in the framework of transnationalism (Dürrschmidt/Bittner, 2007: 27). However, in the social sciences there exist explicit or implicit assumptions that "the nation-state is the container of social processes", that there is an implied correspondence between national territory and the national and that many components of the national and the non-national are mutually exclusive. That said, one might argue that through transnationalism this key duality is undermined because of the localization of the global, the non-national in national territories and the localization of the national outside national territories. To better understand this, it is important to note that there is an unbundling of national space as well as of traditional hierarchies of scale centered on the national (Sassen, 2010b: 4). To concentrate only on the state system as local, national and international therefore misses much that is essential in explaining alternative responses to globalization, contemporary politics and new styles of governance (Smith, 2000: 143).

The view that a process or condition which is located in a national institution or in national territory is national has held, though never fully, throughout much of the history of the modern state and to some extent until today. Nevertheless, these processes and conditions are today partly, though actively, being dismantled as mentioned above. From this perspective it appears that a process which is located within the territory of a sovereign state is not necessarily a national process; instead it might be a localization of the global. Thus there is "a growing range of localizations of the global" and "what we continue to code as national today may in fact be such a localization". From this viewpoint, "the national can be one of the sites for the global" and the 'nation as container' is therefore unreasonable if taking into account the increase in transnational dynamics and formations. The category of the nation-state as 'container' is moreover challenged by the manifold structurations of the global inside the national which de-nationalizes the historically constructed national. However, because of the fact that the national is highly institutionalized, it is often difficult to identify partial or highly specialized denationalization (Sassen, 2010a: 3).

It is possible to suggest here the "partial unbundling or at least weakening of the national as container of social process due to the variety of dynamics encompassed by globalization and digitization" (Sassen, 2010b: 9f.) and the "re-scaling of what are the strategic territories that articulate the new politico-economic system"; these are two significant conditions for cities as strategic sites (ibid.: 9). Both conditions entail major transformations and therefore destabilize older systems which organize territory and politics. These transformations lead to numerous consequences, for instance new forms of citizenship practices. Through these practices new arrangements of political subjectivity (citizenship) are being constituted as the civic system is being developed (ibid.: 10). A range of local political actors have entered into international arenas that were previously exclusive to formal states. Even those who are geographically immobile such as indigenous peoples and many others are increasingly becoming actors in global politics and gain visibility in international forums. This development leads to a disentanglement of the exclusive authority over territory and people which can be linked to the national state (Sassen, 2007: 190). To briefly make a conclusion, the national as container of social process and power has dissolved in globalized times (ibid.: 194) which has led to the loss of power at the national level and to new forms of power and politics that link sub-national spaces such as cities, which are at the fore in this new geography, across borders (Sassen, 2010b: 5).

## (Re)Configuring Relationships

While globalization theories suggest "deterritorialization", or in other words, the "disappearance and disaggregation of place" and the "space of flows", theories of transnationalism, on the contrary, have the objective of retaining place and therefore reconfiguring relationships between territorial, societal and social circumstances. One of the specific objectives of this paper is to prove that there is a relative emancipation of all types of social actors and milieus from the constraints of geographical space. Through the process of a "latent despacialization" of social relationships and cultural identities, there is a need for social actors who are able to handle the task of reappropriating global space. In order to better understand this challenge, it is important to note that a latent despacialization requires a continuous territorialization at the everyday level. The so called "disappearance of space" or "disaggregation of place" are then replaced by a "reflexive bonding with a place" and an "active creation of links between different spaces" in an enlarged global reference framework. Theories of transnationalization concretize the dialectic of "despacialization and (re-)territorialization" through processes of "disembedding and re-embedding". Looking at this dialectic from a transnationalist perspective, it can be argued that instead of "despacialization" there is nowadays a trend towards "bi-territorialization" or "multi-territorialization" (Dürrschmidt/Bittner, 2007: 27). A closer look reveals the fact that the relationships between 'space' (the physical setting of a place) and 'territoriality' (the social and cultural fabric of a place) are being reconfigured. However to generate the "dynamics of transnational place-making", it is necessary to not only to refer to the differentiation between 'space' and 'territoriality' but also to other differentiations such as between 'locale' and 'place' (see also Anthony Giddens) and between 'locality' and 'neighborhood' (see also Arjun Appadurai) (ibid.: 29).

This chapter concludes by pointing out that the growing mobility of individuals has transformed their relations to space (Rizvi, 2011: 185). Hence, transnationalization is not only characterized by a mobility between places but also by a struggle for the right to be present in one place (Dürrschmidt/Bittner, 2007: 33). The consequence of the "emergence of transnational spaces" is then that social spaces can no longer be defined by a "definite exclusive" but instead by a "multi-polar spatial bond" (Bittner/Hackenbroich/Vöckler, 2007: 21). It is fitting here to refer to the argument of Saskia Sassen (2010b: 5): "Recovering place means recovering the multiplicity of presences in this landscape".

## Identity, Translocational Positionality and Cosmopolitanization

Even though individuals select and negotiate their identities on their own, the available discourses often limit their choices because identity construction processes happen within networks of power and unequal access to economic, social and cultural resources. Identity construction processes strategically position individuals as comparatively powerful or powerless in relation to others and in relation to hierarchies. Processes of identification thus include the construction of boundaries and exclusions because, in the process of defining one's identity, individuals are inevitably differentiating themselves from what and who they are not – a process which is called "dis-identification" (Gewirtz/Cribb, 2008: 40). Transcultural and translocational conceptions are an important counterposition to the more static notions of identity and ethnicity that are mainly used in academic writing and in political action. The emphasis on notions of identity and ethnicity which have been criticized for being too fixed, too stable, monolithic and exclusionary has in turn led to new concepts such as cosmopolitanism and hybridity (Anthias, 2011: 209f.).

This following short aside is intended to draw attention to the idea of hybridity which is often used alongside the term diaspora and which approaches identity not from a mono-culturalist, static and essentialized view but as syncretic and changeable (see also Homi Bhabha). Hybridity means challenging existing paradigms of identity. The term is applied in differing ways: hybridity has been characterized as the "modern condition" in postmodern discourse, it has been a central term in poststructuralist cultural theory and in some variations in globalization theory. The concept of hybridity is also linked to the idea of "new ethnicities" (see also Stuart Hall) which can be understood to be a non-static and non-essentialized view of ethnic culture. Another approach uses the notion of "double consciousness" (see also W. E. B. Du Bois and Paul Gilroy) to represent the hybrid and diasporic condition (Anthias, 2011: 209). The renowned postcolonial theorist Homi Bhabha (1994) argues that the transgression of national or ethnic borders is crucial for the condition of hybridity, through which a double perspective of a voice that speaks from two different places at once but inhabits neither becomes possible. Bhabha describes this origin of space which is never complete and full of discontinuities and gaps as the "space of liminality", as "no place" or as the buffer zone of "no man's land". The hybrids, the people who live in this space, act then as "cultural brokers" (Bhabha, 1994 in ibid.: 209). Floya Anthias (2011: 209) concludes: "Hybridity [...] references cultural syncretism or interpenetration and its transformative as well as transgressive potential."

To understand issues of difference and division it is necessary, as mentioned previously, to not only focus on the notion of identity and ethnicity but to also look at processes of social location and positionality. In other words it is essential to look at where people are placed within relations of social hierarchy within a framework of time and space and how people position themselves as well as "their narrations of their social position". Anthias argues that social locations are not fixed or given, and thus the 'location' is always characterized by "being within, and embedded in, relations of hierarchy within a multiplicity of specific situational and conjunctural spheres". People therefore simultaneously experience "being and becoming, fixity and change". Consequently, positions and positionality are linked to one another in a non-mechanistic way. People take up positionings in relation to their locations "depending on context and meaning as well as 'interest', and in terms of values, goals and projects". The concept of "translocational positionality" demands that attention be paid to spatial and contextual dimensions (Anthias, 2011: 213).

In transnationalization discourse, the term translocality "is used to connote transnational networks, fields and spaces that can ultimately be traced back to concrete translocal social relationships, that is, to relationships between various places 'here and there'"

(Smith in Dürrschmidt/Bittner, 2007: 27). It is for this reason that the term translocality can be compared with the notion of "transnational social spaces" because both describe localities which transcend the territory of a nation-state (ibid.: 27ff.). Jörg Dürrschmidt acknowledges in this context that "the term translocality is used to imply that a location is molded by diverse supra-local influences at the same time as its apparently stable local everyday life is directed in various ways towards people and objects located elsewhere". Dürrschmidt, referring to the well-known social-cultural anthropologist Arjun Appadurai, shows that this has always been the situation and that it applies more or less to any place (Dürrschmidt in Dürrschmidt/Bittner, 2007: 29).

An example of translocality could be an airport or an international hotel, even though these kinds of places are already described as "non-place". Moreover, there are different types of translocal cities such as booming global cities or shrinking local border towns; both examples are forms of a "real existent cosmopolitanism" (see also Bruce Robbins) which goes against a hermetic nation-state society and also against a universally encompassing "placeless cosmopolitanism". One example of a translocal booming city would be the global city of London because it is a part of England, a part of the living Commonwealth as well as a prime example of micro-globalization. It must be kept in mind that in urban settings it is difficult to establish criteria for who is an 'insider/outsider' and who is a 'native/foreigner' because they have such extensive social-cultural mixes and high incidences of mobility; this leads unavoidably to the "cosmopolitanization" of everyday practice (Dürrschmidt/Bittner, 2007: 29). Such a perception of "this as well as that" is for the sociologist and risk analyst Ulrich Beck (in ibid.: 29) intrinsic to the logic of identity construction within real cosmopolitanization.

For Dürrschmidt, real cosmopolitanization is not only about geographic mobility but also about the "mobility of images and ideologies". For him, the core problem exists in the divide between daily inclusionary practices and macro-loyalities (Dürrschmidt, 2007 in Dürrschmidt/Bittner, 2007: 31). Transnationalization supports tolerant coexistence but "everyday embedding and macro-loyalties are increasingly out of kilter in the transnational milieu". As a consequence, "real and virtual neighbourhoods" are drifting more and more apart and therefore transnationalization is not automatically promoting cosmopolitanization but rather "re-ethnicized nationalism" (ibid.: 31). Beck (in ibid.: 31) asserts in this context that "every real existent cosmopolitanization also carries the seeds of a "deformed cosmopolitanism"". Concluding, the concept of cosmopolitanism is not fixed in terms of national exclusivity; it tends to be a wider cultural and justice-related framework and yields a more liberal understanding of difference and cultural values on a global scale (Anthias, 2011: 209).

## Questioning Multiculturalism

Many countries deal with the issue of cultural diversity through the notion of multiculturalism which suggests that citizens with diverse cultural backgrounds should be able to contribute to a nation's cultural and economic development. Based on this policy discourse, which developed during the 1970s, the responsibility of the state and its institutions was to form an environment which allows citizens to express themselves and contribute to national development. This section deals with the fact that multiculturalism was designed to pacify increasingly volatile ethnic communities as well as to reduce the fears of the dominant cultural groups which have been terrified by the changing demography of their cities. Furthermore, multiculturalism became a strategy for managing intergroup relations. It provided ethnic communities with several symbolic resources which supported them in organizing themselves politically. It is in this context that the notion of multiculturalism has been confined within a set of nation-centric assumptions and therefore addresses issues of cultural diversity within a national framework (Rizvi, 2011: 186). Discourses and practices of multiculturalism have mainly focused on cultural difference, promoting policies to make clear the cultural differences of groups, to acknowledge their claims, to counter the social and economic disadvantages experienced by ethnic minority groups and to fight against racism and exclusion. However multiculturalism presupposes the rights of difference of culture and the cultural needs of groups (minority cultures). To define the limits of difference in a multiculturalist vision (in which cultures or elements of cultures are legitimate) is a political question which is decided by the dominant group in the state. While the dominant group culture (i.e. the 'white' or European culture) is mostly perceived of as being universal and not ethnic, minority group culture is defined by cultural contents such as specific kinds of symbolic practices, language, religion and lifestyle. For this discussion, the degrees of tolerance towards social practices are a critical question and related to, as Western thinkers often state, universalistic rules (which also have a social and cultural base). The limits of multiculturalism are further destined to involve battles over the allocation of resources and the prioritization of different cultural needs (Anthias, 2011: 206f.).

The problem of the notion of multiculturalism is the belief that all members of a specific cultural group have the same commitment to that culture. Culture, articulated in terms of a people's ethnicity or identity, leads to the problematic fact that members of minority cultures are homogenized and therefore space for 'diversity within' is not available. It can be argued that multiculturalism assumes that unities of cultures are "definite, static, ahistorical and essentialist" with fixed boundaries and with little space for progress and transformation (Anthias, 2011: 207). This assumption leads to unintended consequences such as excluding communities based on cultural needs and cultural commonalities (ibid.: 208). The view of multiculturalism in intercultural relations is that it sees "difference in terms of negotiations among culturally diverse groups against a backdrop of presumed homogeneity". The problem is that it does not recognize that diversity is forged in histories based on differently constituted relations of power; that knowledge, subjectivities and social practices such as practices of cultural negotiation are often established within asymmetrical and disproportionate cultural spaces. A more liberal multiculturalism similarly promotes "the desirability of a social cohesive society with shared values, albeit in the context in which some cultural differences are tolerated". A policy construct such as multiculturalism which is composed of closed cultural boundaries expressed in language, arts and cultural traditions and the view of culture as a homogenized entity which is located within particular national spaces and which exists outside history and contemporary interactive cultural relations is therefore no longer plausible or viable (Rizvi, 2011: 187).

Concluding, it can be argued that the underpinning of the policy of multiculturalism is not able to adequately react to the challenges of an emergent transnationalism which affects people's identities, their sense of belonging and the cultural spaces in which they live. As a consequence, the notion of multiculturalism cannot solely concentrate on managing interethnic relations within the nation-state. Instead it has to interpret the local and the national within a wider transnational context and it has to deal with the diversity in transnational and transcultural spaces in order to be relevant in the understanding of cosmopolitan futures. Only then is it able to deal with diasporic spaces in which many people at the same time belong to more than one country and to understand their sense of identity with respect to economic, social and political relations that transcend national boundaries (Rizvi, 2011: 186f.).

## Cultural Diversity in a Time of an Emergent Transnationalism

In the transnational context, the interaction between the cultural identities of individuals and their originating cultures is increasingly complex and cannot be captured by a desire for singular attachment, collective memory or nostalgia. The context of an emergent transnationalism therefore demands 'deterritorialized' ways of thinking about cultural diversity. An emergent transnationalism can be characterized by growing levels of mobility and interconnectivity, and thus contemporary transnational processes have transformed the ways in which cultural diversity is experienced. The traditional approach to diversity has presumed diversity to be an exception to the norms of cultural homogeneity which is understood as a natural condition; cultural homogeneity is then disrupted by the arrival of people who are expected to be culturally different and hence break down the presumed homogeneity. As a consequence, a policy of assimilation has been implemented to ensure the continuation of the cultural homogeneity of a nation through the transformation of the immigrants into 'one of us'. Nonetheless diversity has to not be thought of as a homogeneity which is unworkable but of cultural heterogeneity as the norm (Rizvi, 2011: 187).

Specific historical and political conditions and complex personal engagement with changing conditions form the basis of cultural diversity. Cultural diversity has always characterized human societies; however, in a time of increasing levels of global interconnectedness and interdependences, issues of diversity need to be reconsidered. A closer look reveals that due to increasing transnational connections in recent years, experiences with diversity have become more complicated. Diversity has to be thought of not only in a singular national frame but also in its scaled down dimensions. Moreover, cultural diversity has to be viewed in relational terms because of the connections between macroeconomic and geopolitical transformations and the various paths which are part of the politics of identification. In this context it appears that cultural diversity, experienced, interpreted and negotiated in a multiplicity of diverse ways in communities and in different circumstances, can be found at both the personal and social level. However there is a difference in how individuals or groups of people experience cultural diversity and how diversity is portrayed by popular, official and powerful representations. While some groups of people may experience diversity in terms of religion and common representations such as exists in the common popular culture, the state can give greater meaning to race, ethnicity and language. The state creates the framework within which groups of people are able to name and negotiate cultural diversity. The context in which cultural diversity is discussed, the ways in which it is experienced, interpreted, negotiated and represented and the ways in which it is contested and resisted is clearly important. The central questions are then what counts as a significant marker of difference, how this choice matters and who decides which indicators of difference are relevant and significant (Rizvi, 2011: 181-185).

The politics of difference is no longer only located within local and national contexts, and therefore it is highly influenced by cultural shifts produced by the global mobility of people, capital, ideologies, information and images. It is increasingly embedded in spaces that transcend national borders. This understanding provides both new challenges as well as new opportunities for the field of education and for the highly contested political spaces in which claims of inclusion and justice are currently being negotiated (Rizvi, 2011: 187f.). Debates about diversity, linked to issues of cultural recognition and to demands for distribution and redistribution of resources, have been intense and extensive over the past two decades. These debates are also addressed and broadly contested in the field of education (ibid.: 180). Diversity in education is an inevitable consequence of globalization and therefore a dynamic relational conception of cultural diversity which responds to changing social and economic conditions is needed (ibid.: 187). As a consequence, educational systems are required to develop new policies that acknowledge the importance of cultural diversity (ibid.: 185) and to rethink existing policies in order to be able to represent the communities in which they are located (ibid.: 180). Greater educational access and opportunity as well as work towards social inclusion and cohesion is thus of increasing importance. However, the reality shows that cultural diversity as well as interethnic relations still remain trapped within a national framework, and thus the goal is to approach cultural diversity not as a problem but as a productive resource (ibid.: 180).

Diversity is best represented as an expression of transnationality because experiences of cultural diversity increasingly take place in a transnational context which require new conceptual resources to be able to comprehend them within the era of globalization (Rizvi, 2011: 183f.). To draw a conclusion from these facts, it is essential to find a "balance between validating difference, cherishing different traditions of people and finding a common space for civic participation and mutual agreement on core social aims". Hence there is a necessity to move away from the idea of one dominant culture that defines the frame of reference (Anthias, 2011: 208).

## Concluding and Continuative Thoughts

In Europe, many countries struggled with their attempts to construct an imagined homogeneity despite significant internal diversity so solutions were always problematic and temporary. Because of the colonial past of several countries within Europe, there have been many presumptions about non-European 'others'. However within the European project, the protection of people, citizens or not, from being treated differently or poorly because of their physical appearance or aspects of their culture became increasingly important. The challenge of the European Union in making this a reality is that there are extremely different starting points as well as unique national characteristics concerning race, ethnicity and difference. At present, many countries within the European Union struggle with the realities of historically divisive diversities: the tension between constructing a national identity on the one hand and the appearance of a so-called 'new' diversity on the other hand (Gaine, 2008: 35). The problem is that discussions of diversity are mainly used as a code to introduce compensatory mechanisms to decrease inequality and not as radical transformations which point to the ways in which these realities are produced and sustained. There is however a concern in policy debates about the balance of the maintenance of difference and the pursuit of a harmonious society having core values. Social conflict itself is not only a question of difference in beliefs and values; questions of rights, representation and redistribution as well as conflicts and struggles over interests or resources (economic, educational, etc.) are other reasons that can be found to be behind the differences concerning culture (Anthias, 2011: 205f.). This is important to consider because although at one level communities desire diversity, many of them defend their traditions and their cultural distinctiveness against the invading forces of globalization and transnationalism. It is inevitable that people approach the world from a particular normative position and that they hope to remain attached to cultural norms which are familiar and comfortable to them. However, in a globally interconnected world, many cultural practices are without doubt being greatly contested and thus a new understanding of cultural diversity is needed which addresses the increasing intensity and range of sweeping flows of goods, information, persons and symbols (Rizvi, 2011: 185).

As a result of complex combinations of social location, people are living in multiple and differing ways within systems of power and hierarchical relations which are linked to social distinctions, social divisions and inequality. In contemporary societies, inequality, exclusion and forms of discrimination are systemic and multidimensional. Dealing with the issues is first a political concern; second, a strategic issue; and third, a conceptual issue. In light of this discussion, it is important to understand the link between various types of inequality and discrimination because only addressing one of them can increase the other. The dialogical articulation of the boundaries and hierarchies of social relations can be, for example, mutually reinforcing or they can be relational/contradictory. It is then necessary to note that subordination and hierarchy are manifold and develop out of different arrangements of power in various time-space frameworks; likewise it is required to examine the specific combinations that produce systemic inequalities along with their transformational potential. Hence enabling measures have to be implemented in more nuanced ways which do more than focus on the diverse, the migrant or ethnic other and instead also address place and context (Anthias, 2011: 210-214).

It is possible to conclude that the many cross-national, cross-cultural flows and networks, which include the mobility of peoples, objects, images and information and which lead to complex interdependencies of various forms, define and moreover transform the global world of the 21$^{st}$ century. Certainly these transformations require alternative ways of thinking about dealing with cultural diversity (Rizvi, 2011: 184) and its role in contemporary transnational processes wherein new spatial interdependences appear and place can be thought of as a relational structure which includes various social relationships.

## References


Anthias, Floya (2011): Intersections and Translocations: new paradigms for thinking about cultural diversity and social identities. In: European Educational Research Journal. Vol. 10, No. 2, pp. 204-217. http://www.wwwords.eu/EERJ [04.08.2011].

Bittner, Regina/ Hackenbroich, Wilfried/ Vöckler, Kai (2007): Transnational Spaces. An Introduction. In: Bittner, Regina/Hackenbroich, Wilfried/ Vöckler, Kai (eds.): Transnational Spaces. Transnationale Räume. Berlin: Edition Bauhaus. pp. 21-25.

Dürrschmidt, Jörg/ Bittner, Regina (2007): The Effects of Place. An Email Interview between Jörg Dürrschmidt (JD) and Regina Bittner (RB). In: Bittner, Regina/ Hackenbroich, Wilfried/ Vöckler, Kai (eds.): Transnational Spaces. Transnationale Räume. Berlin: Edition Bauhaus. pp. 27-33.

Gaine, Chris (2008): Race, Ethnicity and Difference versus Imagined Homogeneity within the European Union. In: European Educational Research Journal. Vol. 7. No. 1. pp. 23-38.

Gewirtz, Sharon/ Cribb, Alan (2008): Taking Identity Seriously: dilemmas for education policy and practice. In: European Educational Research Journal. Vol. 7. No. 1. pp. 39-49.

Harding, Alan/ Le Gales, Patrick (1997): Globalization, Urban Change and Urban Policies in Britain and France. In: Scott, Alan (ed.): The Limits of Globalization. Cases and Arguments. London and New York: Routledge. pp. 181-201.

Rizvi, Fazal (2011): Experiences of Cultural Diversity in the Context of an Emergent Transnationalism. In: European Educational Research Journal. Vol. 10. No. 2. pp. 180-188. http://www.wwwords.eu/EERJ [04.08.2011].

Sassen, Saskia (2007): A Sociology of Globalization. New York and London: W. W. Norten & Company.

Sassen, Saskia (2010a): The Global Inside the National: A Research Agenda for Sociology. Sociopedia.isa. pp. 1-10. http://www.columbia.edu/~sjs2/PDFs/National.pdf [09.10.2011].

Sassen, Saskia (2010b): The city: Its return as a lens for social theory. City, Culture and Society, 1. pp. 3-11. http://www.columbia.edu/~sjs2/PDFs/Lens.pdf [09.10.2011].

Sassen, Saskia (2010c): Cities are at the center of our environmental future. S.A.P.I.EN.S., Vol. 2. Issue 3. pp. 1-8. http://www.columbia.edu/~sjs2/PDFs/thecenter.pdf [09.10.2011].

Smith, Patrick J. (2000): 'Globalist' versus 'Globalized' Cities: Redefining Urban Responses to Globalization. In: Cohn, Theodore H./ Mc Bride, Stephen/ Wiseman, John (eds.): Power in the Global Era. Grounding Globalization. Basingstoke a.o.: Macmillan Press. pp. 141-154.

Torres, Carlos Alberto (2009): Globalizations and Education. Collected Essays on Class, Race, Gender, and the State. New York and London: Teachers College, Columbia University.

# I

# Transnational Space and Social Networks

# Transnational Social Relations – A Challenge of Everyday Life?

*Angela Pilch Ortega*

## Abstract

*The transnationalisation of social structures can be seen as a growing phenomenon resulting from global and cross-border activities in which not only migrants but a broad segment of the population is involved. This paper focuses on the social relations of people acting transnationally and also on some challenging aspects which come up in daily life when people with different knowledge, diverging perspectives and varying reference systems interact. The overlapping social areas which emerge require biographical reflection. First the transnationalisation from the bottom-up as a research perspective will be discussed briefly. Next the special conditions of migrants (and their family networks) who maintain social connections despite a physical divide will be described. Biographies of transnationally acting peoples can be seen as transnational spaces; thereby the narrative articulations which document such spaces are of particular interest. Finally, this article will give some examples of challenging aspects of transnational interactions and related learning processes.*

## Introduction

Due to the globalisation of economy, worldwide migration movements, the internationalisation of the media and the facilitation of communication processes across national borders, current societies are confronted with social spaces which are increasingly pluricultural, heterogeneous, inconsistent, fragmented and less regionally bounded. Even though globalisation can in no way be considered to be a new social phenomenon, it can be argued that the facilitation of means of crossing boundaries has led to the increasing frequency in transnational movements which have fundamentally transformed the structures of social interaction and communication. The national space as a reference system becomes more and more fragile; political, economical and social spheres of action are being reconfigured (Mau 2007: 19).

The concept of transnationalism focuses in particular on structural transformation processes which are initiated and carried out by social actors. In contrast to globalisation discourses, within which on the macro level, the interaction of anonymous market forces such as financial markets, transnational companies and global players are mainly analysed, the transnationalism approach pays special attention to the transnational social activities and practices which are initiated and developed by people. Migrants and global acting persons establish such transnational structures and networks in their daily lives. Due to the fact that their family and friends live in other countries, they are confronted with the challenge of maintaining their social relations despite the geographical distance. On the one hand new technologies and the decreasing costs of cross-frontier movements and communication support the social interaction beyond borders; on the other hand the convergence of divergent structures of sense and orientation as well as the emergence of new overlapping social areas challenge the life paths of social actors. Experiences with cross-border acting and the social practices for dealing with transnational spaces are being biographically gathered and reflected on. Biographies reference transnational spaces and make clear creative strategies used to deal with complexity, heterogeneity and inconsistency. The social practices which are developed are characterised by individual logic or ways of making sense of things. This leads to a question: How do humans create their own transcultural references in their everyday lives and how do these support the transformation of regionally embedded structures and practices? By taking this question into consideration, it can be concluded that the "irritating potential" which occurs through the confrontation within and among transnational spaces can be analysed and dealt with in learning processes. The aim of this paper is to focus on transnational social relationships and the related challenges such as proximity and distance, the translation of meanings and relevance within diverse and contradictory spaces of sense and the conditions of transnational social contacts. Firstly transnationalisation from the bottom-up as a theoretical approach will be described briefly, then the special conditions surrounding migrant biographies and family networks will be focused on. Finally, challenging aspects of transnational social relations and related learning processes will be discussed.

## Transnationalisation from the Bottom-up

As an effect of increasing transnationalisation, it can be said that social relations are less embedded in physical structures; the presence in a local place is losing its function as a precondition of social interaction. Furthermore the concept of nation-state as a reference system is becoming more and more porous and loses its main function as a political and social regulator (Mau 2007: 8). Global theorists argue in this context that social actors are relatively emancipated "from the constraints of geographical space" (Dürrschmidt/Bittner 2007: 27; cf. Schroer 2006); they allude to the deterritorialisation of space (Appadurai 1996) and the "disappearance and disaggregation of place in a space of flow" (Dürrschmidt/Bittner 2007: 27). In contrast, transnationalisation theorists emphasise that the emancipation of place doesn't mean that place is losing its relevance for structuring and organising processes (Mau 2007: 8). In particular it should be pointed out that the transnationalism approach focuses to a greater extent on transnationalisation from the bottom-up with a subject and action oriented perspective. Social actors and their life world, involvement in transnational activities and the development of transnational practices are at the centre of research interest. In this way transnational activities should not only be thought of as being spontaneous or sporadic but instead are characterised by a certain level of frequency and continuity. Ludger Pries for example describes transnational social spaces as hybrid products of social-structural elements of source regions and destination regions which are distributed pluri-locally and permanently (2000: 416). As noted above, in contrast to global theories, place does not lose its relevance as a structural force; this aspect also came under criticism. Bommes (2002: 93ff.) argues in this context that transnationalism theories continue to follow a container conception of space; furthermore from his point of view social problems of integration, the dynamics of social inequality and hegemonic power are not sufficiently considered. Also Lutz (2004: 210) suggests that the reproduction of social inequality, the pressure of assimilation within nation states and the social conditions of the participants cannot be disregarded in the conceptualisation of transnational spaces.

As was already mentioned, new communication and transportation technologies open up possibilities for cross-border interaction and this "has given rise to new patterns of mobility" (Dürrschmidt/Bittner 2007: 31). Bittner emphasises that the tourism and migration movements are not only a physical reality but also that the images produced have the function of becoming normative standards which leads into the division of globally moving actors and people who are staying at home, regionally bounded due to a lack of financial, cultural and/or social resources which do not allow them to participate in transnational interactions (ibid.: 31). Baumann (1998: 9 cited in Castles 2007: 39) argues in this context as well that "mobility has become the most powerful and most coveted stratifying factor". While the politically and economically well-off are able to move beyond borders at will, the poor have to stay at home: "the riches are global, the misery are local" (ibid.: 74 cited in Castles 2007: 39). Generally it can be said that "in recent years, the disparities in income, social conditions, human rights and security have increased" (Castles 2007: 39). Therefore Castles claims that because of unequal development and the high level of inequality between North and South, "Migration control is essentially about regulating North-South relations. Because northern countries are doing their best to stop migration – with the exception of the highly skilled – movement can often only take place through means classified as illegal by receiving countries" (ibid: 39).

Over the past decades legal regulations concerning cross-border movement has fundamentally changed. On the one hand the free movement of tourists, goods, provision of services and the movement of financial capital was deregulated (primarily benefiting "Western" countries); on the other hand new barriers were erected, mainly for goods and people coming from "poor" countries. Furthermore residence permission and labour permit requirements were tightened. It is not only in Europe that the new regulations and the establishment of intensified border controls (Fortress Europe) seek to repel migration flows of misery; also within the United States, as a traditional immigration destination, the situation for non-citizens is becoming more and more precarious. In this context, research should take into account that re-nationalisation processes structure cross-border movements as well and result in diverging possibilities for participation in transnational activities. In addition Held, McGrew, Goldblatt and Perraton (1999: 9 cited in Vertovec 2007: 162f.) suggest that "the power of national governments is not necessarily diminished by globalization but on the contrary is being reconstituted and reconstructured in response to the growing complexity of processes of governance in a more interconnected world".

Against this background transnationalisation cannot be considered as a homogeneous phenomenon. Transnational structures and spaces are characterised by social tensions, inequality and conflicts. Economic, cultural and social capitals play an important role in defining the possibilities of participation and the acquisition of special competencies for transnational acting. Apitzsch emphasises as well that transnational spaces cannot be seen as congruent. She argues that migration flows do develop paradoxically to political and economical relations. Because of political persecution or precarious economical situations, migrants often have to leave their countries, and they mainly choose destination countries which are different to their country of origin (2003: 68).

The transnational space as a highly competitive arena also becomes visible by means of the development of new social movements which also act beyond national borders. Against the backdrop of the dominance of the financial market, the impacts of neoliberal deregulation, increasing unemployment and social inequality and the exploitation of natural resources, people are organising themselves to a greater extent into social movements around the world in order to counter hegemonic power. Even though these "new" forms of civil resistance are quite heterogeneous, the communication and social interaction through transnational structures allows them to widen their influence to regional and global structures. Tyson Darling argues for instance that "While a minority elite push for further regressive neoliberal and monetarist policies, now is the time to summon the collective will to restore global rules for transparency and accountability that promote human security for the many, protect biodiversity and the survival of natural evolution, and promote sustainable development and an environmentally sound economic growth" (2006: 45f.). These social protest platforms can be seen as collective strategies to (re)gain the power of performative action with regard to social and natural circumstances. Transnational structures support the exchange of information, the discussion and reflection on social situations and the formation of solidarity alliances. On the one hand globalisation and neoliberal policy partially reenforce the powerlessness of people and on the other hand transnational spaces and structures open up opportunities for global formations which question the hegemonic power of the elite and allows for the bolstering of human needs and alternative solutions to current problems and changes.

A nonuniform and temporal facet of transnationalisation can be seen as well on the basis of current developments of cities which are increasingly confronted with fundamental transformation processes due to global opening processes and cross-border movements to a greater extent than rural areas. Increasing complexity, diversity and inconsistency have become a normal reality of everyday life for urban residents. Not only migrants are involved in transnational spaces; also a broader range of people appear as global actors. Yildiz and Ottersbach emphasise as well that on the one hand states lose their force of social inclusion and their central relevance as a frame of reference for the orientation of city dweller. On the other hand re-nationalisation processes and the appearance of new forms of nationalism and fundamentalism show that the national space as an imaginary force is regaining its social and political relevance in the perception of people (Yildiz/Ottersbach 2004: 11f.).

Summing up, it can be said that the focus on transnationalisation from the bottom-up offers a research perspective which considers not only social transformations on a macro level but also pays particular attention to social actors, their involvement in cross-border activities and the developed transnational practises of social actors. For the following part I want to point out that in this article transnational spaces are understood to be relational social areas which are created by social actors in their daily lives.

In particular this article focuses on biographies of migrants and family networks as an example of transnational articulations. In this context I will follow the proposition of Apitzsch (2003) who suggests that biographies reference such transnational spaces and Lutz (2004) who talks in this regard about transnational articulations. As already described, the transnational space is understood to be a highly competitive arena where power relations and hegemonic forces structure the circumstances of social actors.

## Biographies and Family Networks as a Transnational Space

Processes of the transnationalisation of migrants, their biographies and cross-border activities are becoming a central point of research interest. Transnational theories in particular argue in this context that the form and quality of migration movements has changed over the last decades. Migration as a one-time movement from one country to another loses its importance. Glick Schiller, Basch and Blanc-Szeanton (1992: 1) suggest for example that the

> earlier conceptions of immigrant and migrant no longer suffice. The word immigrant evokes images of permanent rupture, of the uprooted, the abandonment of old patterns and the painful learning of a new language and culture. Now, a new kind of migrating population is emerging, composed of those whose networks, activities and patterns of life encompass both their host and home societies. Their lives cut across national boundaries and bring two societies into a single field.

Transmigration processes nowadays can entail various changes in geographical place and location. Migrants establish social relations between different countries due to physical distance from their family and friends. The social relations which migrants maintain through the uses of new technologies and possibilities for low priced transportation are pluri-local, characterised by permanence and more intensive than ever before. Family networks also play a crucial role as Castles (2007: 36), referring to Hugo (1994), mentions: "Research on Asian migration has shown that migration decisions are usually made not by individuals but by families (…) in order to maximize income and survival chances" (Castles 2007: 36). Generally it can be said that contemporary family networks are less tied to the locality; they are more and more pluricultural. Compared to other types of social relations, they are characterised by the fact that they are only partially terminable and partially optional. Members of such networks become involved in transnational spaces and develop strategies for dealing with the geographical distance. In contrast to earlier times, migration movements have changed and are now more and more to an option which can be cancelled; it does not inevitably result in being a biographical break. This aspect does of course depend on the availability of financial and other resources. Mutual emotional, economic and social support remains an important part of the social interaction.

In contrast to the conception of transnational spaces as a primarily geographically local phenomenon where social spheres are accumulated or stacked – for instance Pries

(1997) describes it in terms of ethnicised colonies within global cities – Apitzsch emphasises that transnational spaces are constituted in the biographies of migrants (2003: 65ff.). Thus transnational spaces should not be understood as locations on a map but as relational social areas which are constructed and configured as social actors live their everyday lives. Additionally she points out that overlapping social areas can be seen as people and groups interact with differing biographical knowledge which has been gathered and reflected over the course of participants' lives (ibid.: 68f.). These invisible structures of governmental, legal and cultural transitions are part of the biographical orientation in which they are mired in as a collective of experiences (Apitzsch 2003: 69). Relatedly she notes: "Biographie als Ort transnationaler und transkultureller Räume ist ein Schnittpunkt kollektiver Konstitution und individueller Konstruktion" (Apitzsch 2003: 72)[1]. Lutz seizes on this suggestion of transnational space as invisible structures within biographies. In contrast to Apitzsch she argues for perceiving transnational spaces within biographies as narrative articulations and not as a place (2004: 211f.) due to the fact that the process-dependent character of biography has to be considered. In this context she refers to Stuart Hall's conception of articulation as a relation between subject and discourse which contains, according to the theories of power of Laclau and Mouffee, processes of de-articulation and re-articulation.

Focusing on the biographies of migrants and global acting people, fundamental learning processes for dealing with transnational spaces, their complexity, heterogeneity and inconsistency become apparent. Social actors create their social connections through diverging cultural references. Beside economic resources, the participation in transnational spaces requires particular competencies for managing and reflecting on transnational experiences. Also the capacities to learn a foreign language and to successfully adapt to a new social context are crucial for participation in cross-border activities (Mau 2007: 55). It can be said that due to the transnationalisation of life-worlds, the impetus toward learning and developing strategies is enormous. Transnationalisation also supports the transformation of regionally embedded structures. Focusing on long-term changes, Guarnizo – according to Bourdieu's conception of habitus – claims the emergence of a transnational habitus which entails

> a particular set of dualistic dispositions that inclines migrants to act and react to specific situations in a manner that can be, but is not always, calculated, and that is not simply a question of conscious acceptance of specific behavioral or socio-cultural rules. (…) The transnational habitus incorporates the social position of the migrant and the context in which transmigration occurs. This accounts for the similarity in the transnationals habitus of migrants from the same social grouping (class, gender, generation) and the generation of transnational practices adjusted to specific situations (Guarnizo, 1997: 311).

Stephen Castles mentions that: "It is possible that transnational affiliations and consciousness will become the predominant form of migrant belonging in the future. This would have far-reaching consequences" (Castles 2002: 1158 cited in Vertovec 2007:

---

1 "Biography as a place of transnational and transcultural spaces is an interface of collective constitution and individual construction" (Translation by Pilch Ortega).

155f.). In addition to migrants and their family networks, a wide segment of peoples are confronted with the transnationalisation of their life-worlds, with rivalling conceptions of acting, diverging orientations and understandings. Transnationalisation in general transforms the everyday orientations of social actors and enocourages the hybridisation of life-worlds. Within biographical narratives, strategies for dealing with overlapping transnational social areas which are complex, heterogeneous, fragmented and partially incompatible can be reconstructed. Social actors gain competencies in translating and adapting to new social situations. These changes and challenges in everyday life can also lead into an excessive demand on people. Especially when people are drawn into transnational spaces, the experiences can be dominated by emotions of unease and angst. In the following section some of the challenging aspects of transnational relations in everyday life will be addressed.

## Challenging Aspects of Transnational Social Relationships

As was noted, transnational spaces cannot be thought of as a homogeneous phenomenon. How people create their transnational relations and under what conditions varies widely. The comprehensive transformation of regional structures, social circumstances and biographical orientations due to transnationalisation processes confronts social actors with challenges which have to be mastered and incorporated biographically. The following comments on some challenging aspects of transnational spaces are based on a sort of personal reflection on my daily life with my husband. This contribution offers me the opportunity for personal reflection on a period of life which fundamentally changed my way of living. The description of some challenging aspects cannot be claimed to always be complete. Firstly I will give some context information about the transnational activities within my family network, secondly I will focus on three selected challenging aspects – dealing with proximity and distance, translating meanings and the relevance and circumstances of social contacts – which will be discussed using examples.

My husband was born in Chiapas in Mexico and we have lived together in Austria for eight years. His family network includes people who live in various locations in Mexico and the United States. Contact with several members of his family is frequent – when geographically distant my husband uses new technologies two or three times a week, for instance mobile phone, Skype, e-mail and messenger. About once a year we travel to visit his more immediate family. As his wife I am of course pulled into these transnational social relationships.

Regarding the question of dealing with **proximity and distance**, as a first example I would like to focus on the phenomenon of "a virtual mother-in-law or father-in-law in the living space" which occurred in my daily life because of the frequent contact between my husband and his family, mainly with his mother and father. His parents were often present during my usually relaxing time after work. Even though they were not physically present, because of the camera attached to computer everything I did in the background when my husband was online with them was somehow visible. There was also a sort of invisible pressure to communicate with them as well. This type of social interaction and virtual proximity was something totally new for me; early on in our relationship the "irritation potential" was enormous. These kinds of contacts disturbed my privacy and limited my space for autonomy – for example decisions about with whom and when I had social contact. I was involved in a substantial learning process in order to deal with social proximity in general. For instance there was also a high level of social proximity and collective orientation during a trip to visit my husband's family in Mexico. In the very beginning of our relationship it was very hard for me to live in a house – even if only for a limited time – where social proximity is a standard practice of everyday life. As a person who grew up in a family atmosphere which focuses on being independent, the adaption to this new social context was not an easy task. Moreover I realised that the way in which my husband deals with his social relationships influenced the way I maintained contact with my family and other people I was close to. Looking back, I can say that it gave me the motivation to include my Austrian family more in my life. Additionally I want to add that transnationalisation is often discussed as an individualising phenomenon. This personal experience regarding collective and individual orientation can be taken as an example which documents the mutual influence of diverging orientations. Although individualised perspectives are dominant, it can be said that diverging social reference systems are negotiated in everyday life, even if in an unconscious manner.

Another aspect I want to point out refers to the **translation of meanings and relevance**. The example here are the difficult situations which migration processes often imply when one is in a relationship in terms of working with clients or co-workers or if there are health problems. In situations like this my husband also asks his parents for advice. Observing this kind of communication, I realised that a big part of the conversation is the translation of meanings, relevance, social codes and habits. Even if the social habits, for instance having to do with a problematic situation at work, are based on ascribed constructions, the translation of social situations – highly important inside transnational spaces – requires a high level of awareness of the differences between and similarities of social interactions in different contexts. Furthermore ideas about local places (even if never physically visited) are created and transformed. Communication partners thus also create a specific form of knowledge, for instance communicating implies the development of specific language codes which might only be understandable to those involved. The phenomenon of multi-lingual spaces makes the hybridisation of language as well as the practice of code-switching as a feature of this type of communication more visible. In addition, knowledge concerning how to compare meanings and references with their contradictions and inconsistencies is part of this process. The relations between different meanings and reference systems cannot be described as neutral; it refers to hierarchical structured relationships in which the communicating partners are involved. The translation of meaning is based on interpretations, hence intersubjective traceability plays an important role.

The last example I chose has to do with some of the **conditions of social contacts** among family members of a transnational network. Social contacts during a period of geographical distance are often dominated by the fact that one has to make an appointment to meet in virtual space or even simply to talk to someone on the phone (for example if the person doesn't have a mobile phone). The structure of daily routines must be taken in account as well as the differing time zones. While you're preparing dinner, your niece who lives in another part of the world might be just returning home from school. These circumstances of social contacts beyond national borders sometimes give them the character of being artificial or "overly organised". But additionally spontaneous or unplanned social contacts take place as well. I have observed, for example, that my husband sometimes meets his niece by chance in the virtual space and helps her with her homework. New technologies and media facilitate social contacts and also give transnational relationships the chance to be spontaneous. Another example is related to opportunities for biographical reflection on family relations which might be broken off, not only due to geographical distance. Another niece of my husband who is living in the US with her mother and her brother contacted him after several years without contact. The intensive social relationship which has developed between them has also included biographical reflection on the past as well as some conflicts between members of the family. Virtual spaces occur in this example as a medium which offers opportunities for virtual proximity without being necessarily located in the same place. This form of communication also allows biographical reflection and includes learning processes concerning family relations regardless the geographical distance involved.

## Concluding Remarks

The transnationalisation of social spaces in general is on the increase. Due to global opening processes people are confronted with social contexts and relationships that are pluri-local, more complex, heterogeneous and less regionally bounded. The participation in transnational spaces requires particular capacities, competencies and resources. Relatedly the social resources of people are not equal distributed and the general conditions for participation in transnational networks and cross-border movements differ. As was mentioned, transnational spaces are unequally configured and are characterised by social conflict and tension. The highly competitive arena is structured by power relations and hegemonic forces. The confrontation with transnational spaces with overlapping social references initiates learning processes in everyday life but can also lead into excessive demands on participants.

Transnationalisation from the bottom-up as a research approach offers a perspective which makes social actors, their transnational activities and strategies for coping visible. Subjects interact while having differing biographical knowledge and references; the overlapping social areas which are biographically collected and reflected on bring new challenges which have to be mastered as part of the everyday organisation of life. The complexity, contradictoriness and inconsistency within transnational spaces need to be acquired by the social actors. Accordingly new "coordinates of orientation" are created and diverging systems of references are related or integrated. These processes increase the transformation of regionally embedded structures and practices. The examples of challenging aspects of transnationalisation in everyday life help in describing some aspects of such learning processes.

Transnationalisation brings forward the transformation of everyday orientations and life-worlds by which not only migrants are affected but rather a wide sector of the population. As Guarnizo (1997) argues, these current changes can lead into the habitualisation of transnational experiences. Finally I want to add that transnational spaces remain hegemonic, racist and gender structured spaces. Transnational spaces offer new possibilities for interaction despite geographical distance but also entail the risk of widening social disparity.

## References


Apitzsch, Ursula (2003): Migrationsbiographien als Orte transnationaler Räume. In: Apitzsch, Ursula/ Jansen, Mechthild (eds.): Migration, Biographie und Geschlechterverhältnisse. Münster: Westfälisches Dampfboot. Auflage 1. pp. 65-81.

Appadurai, Arjun (1996): Modernity at Large: Cultural Dimensions of Globalization. Minneapolis: MN University of Minnesota Press.

Bommes, Michael (2002): Migration, Raum und Netzwerke. Über den Bedarf einer gesellschaftstheoretischen Einbettung der transnationalen Migrationsforschung. In: Oltmeer, Jochen (ed.): Migrationsforschung und Interkulturelle Studien. IMIS Schriften 11. Osnabrück. pp. 91-108.

Castles, Stephen (2002): Migration and Community Formation under Conditions of Globalization. In: International Migration Review, 36 (4). pp. 1143-1168.

Castles, Stephen (2007): The Factors that Make and Unmake Migration Policies. In: Portes, Alejandro/ DeWind, Josh (eds.): Rethinking Migration. New Theoretical and Empirical Perspectives. New York: Berghahn Books Inc. pp. 29-61.

Dürrschmidt, Jörg/ Bittner, Regina (2007): Ortseffekte. Ein E-Mail Interview zwischen Jörg Dürrschmidt (JD) und Regina Bittner (RB). In: Bittner, Regina/ Hackenbroich, Wilfried und Vöckler, Kai (eds.): Transnational Spaces. Transnationale Räume. Dessau: Edition Bauhaus. pp. 26-33.

Glick Schiller, Nina/ Basch, Linda/ Blanc-Szanton, Christina (1992): Transnationalism: a new analytic framework for understanding migration. In: Glick Schiller, Nina/ Basch, Linda/ Blanc-Szanton, Christina (eds.): Towards a Transnational Perspective on Migration. Class, race, ethnicity, and nationalism reconsidered. New York: New York Academy of Science. pp. 1-24.

Guarnizo, Luis Eduardo (1997): The Emergence of a Transnational Social Formation and The Mirage of Return Migration Among Dominican Transmigrants. In: Identities, 4 (2). http://www.tandfonline.com/doi/abs/10.1080/1070289X.1997.9962591 [08-09-2011]. pp. 281-322.

Lutz, Helma (2004): Transnationale Biographien in globalisierten Gesellschaften. In: Ottersbach, Martin/ Yildiz, Erol (eds.): Migration in der metropolitanen Gesellschaft. Zwischen Ethnisierung und globaler Neuorientierung. Münster: Lit Verlag. pp. 207-216.

Mau, Steffen (2007): Transnationale Gesellschaft. Die Entgrenzung sozialer Lebenswelten. Frankfurt/ New York: Campus Verlag.

Pries, Ludger (1997): Transnationale Migration. Soziale Welt. Sonderband 12. Baden-Baden.

Pries, Ludger (2000): "Transmigranten" als ein Typ von Arbeitswanderern in pluri-lokalen sozialen Räumen. In: Gogolin, Ingrid/ Nauck, Bernhard (eds.): Migration, gesellschaftliche Differenzierung und Bildung. Opladen: Leske + Budrich. pp. 415-438.

Schroer, Markus (2006): Räume, Orte, Grenzen. Auf dem Weg zu einer Soziologie des Raumes. Frankfurt a. M.: Suhrkamp.

Tyson Darling, Marsha J. (2006): Who Really Rules the World? In: Batliwala, Srilatha/ Brown, David L. (eds.): Transnational Civil Society. Bloomfield: Kumarian Press. pp. 30-50.

Vertovec, Steven (2007): Migrant Transnationalism and Modes of Transformation. In: Portes, Alejandro/ DeWind, Josh (eds.): Rethinking Migration. New Theoretical and Empirical Perspectives. New York: Berghahn Books Inc. pp. 149-180.

Yildiz, Erol/ Ottersbach, Martin (2004): Einleitung: Mobilität zwischen Ethnisierung und globaler Neuorientierung. In: Ottersbach, Martin/ Yildiz, Erol (eds.): Migration in der metropolitanen Gesellschaft. Zwischen Ethnisierung und globaler Neuorientierung. Münster: Lit Verlag. pp. 11-18.

# Transnational Spaces, Hybrid Identities and New Media

*Alexander Unger*


## Abstract

*While there have been forms of transnationalism before, it is quite obvious that the postindustrial formation of society is strongly connected with the increasing emergence of transnational spaces and identities. The globalization of markets and their new logic seems to have a deep impact on former national boards, regional everyday life and seamless identities. Based on this background, the article tries to clarify the role of new technologies within this parlous transformation, by discussing the term "new media" and its characteristics and relevance for the emergence of transnationality and transnational spaces. This discussion will show that we have to distinguish between two interdependent levels of mediatization – first, the one concerning structures of society as a whole and second, the mediatization of the social and communicative everyday practice. The paper will also show that the role of new media in the context of transnationalism is far from being clear-cut: While it seems obvious that new media fosters de-nationalization and de-regionalization, the "net" also offers the possibility to stay in contact with regional social networks. To classify and appraise these contradictory medial influences the paper will take a look at some research concerning the usage of the World Wide Web by migrants, which use it as a space to deal with their transnational and hybrid identities.*


## Introduction

The connection between globalization and the rapid spread of new technologies has been pointed out in the scientific discussion for quite some time. Closely related to globalization, the discussion about transnationalism centers on a variety of references to the relevancy of communication and information technologies, e.g. global expansion of communications in terms of transcultural communication (Hepp, 2008). Next to this common correlation, which seems to reach general consensus, the question of a more specific entwinement of new media, globalization and transnationalism is posed, also regarding their relevance to everyday life. Associated with this is a much discussed grading question: Do new media contribute to a cultural de-traditionalization and the expansion of a capitalistic world system or do they even counteract these tendencies by supporting cultural diversity? This article's goal is to describe more accurately the importance of new media in context of processes of globalization and transnationalization. To do justice to the complexity of this relation, it is important to address the relevancy of new media on the societal macro level, as well as on the micro level of concrete everyday actions. It will be shown that particularly the ways of utilization on the level of everyday action are very differentiated and can display correspondingly different directions of effect: From access to an alleged culturally neutral communication space to consolidation of local and monocultural social networks. In this dispute, special attention is given to virtual communication spaces, such as chat rooms, forums and social networks. Due to their virtual character, they mark a territory beyond national borders and seem to play an important role in forming and processing transnational or "hybrid" identities. The starting point for this project is the attempt to conceptualize the phenomenon of transnationalism and the often-cited transnational spaces.

## Transnationalism and Transnational Spaces

As Ludger Pries notices (2002: 263), transnationalism portrays a research paradigm which has found a use in political and social sciences for decades, but which has nevertheless been linked to very different phenomena and associations. Therefore, transnationalism cannot be considered self-explanatory and as a paradigm exhibits rather blurred outlines. It stands to reason that transnationalism is not a completely new phenomenon, historically speaking. Transnational connections are certainly not only found in modern or even postmodern societies. Nevertheless, this phenomenon seems to take on greater significance in postmodern society. This is due to the fact that these societal developments are linked to boundary dissolution, which concern, beside the economic sector and national borders, the cultural and social space as well.

This transition from national to social and cultural spaces is significant insofar as two different spatial concepts take effect, as Mau (2007) emphasizes. A national state is often associated with a clearly defined space containing a pure and consistent culture, in which social life is taking place. However, with regard to cultural and social spaces it is important to understand this space as relational (Löw, 2001: 224). This refers to the fact that societal space has always been lived space, in which the societal framework bonds with people's everyday practices (Unger, 2010: 99, 105). Interaction and communication between individuals can be interpreted as an absolute condition of social spaces. In the end, social spaces can be described as "lived" environments taking on an increasingly transnational or hybrid character due to globalization[1].

These spaces are not "pure", as opposed to the perception of the national space, but exhibit different hybrid links, transitions and blendings. Such blendings arise when, among others, transnational communities are mentioned, meaning communities and their environmental space, in which cultural practices and social networks of the old and new home merge and thereby transcend the consistent nationalistic or cultural space (Pries, 2002: 264). Furthermore, for more and more people in a global world the human environment is no longer limited to spatial surroundings and regional, social networks. Global living conditions force more and more people to expand their exis-

1 There is, however, a counter movement, namely the attempt of withdrawal and inclusion in to regional and monovalent environments.

tence to faraway "space islands" located in different cultural contexts and thereby create transcultural networks to, for example, stay in touch with their native home[2].

This development is not entirely new, as said above, but seems to generate a dynamic which increasingly challenges the explanatory value of the nationalistic paradigm. In view of this fact, one could make the assumption that globalization describes a process on the macro level, whereas transnationalization describes certain ramifications of this process affecting the meso and micro level of social and cultural life. With this in mind, Ludger Pries defines transnationalism as „Zugehörigkeitsgefühle, kulturelle Gemeinsamkeiten, Kommunikationsverflechtungen, Arbeitszusammenhänge und alltägliche Lebenspraxis sowie die darauf bezogenen gesellschaftlichen Ordnungen und Regulierungen, die die Grenzen von Nationalstaaten überschreiten" (Pries, 2002: 265)[3]. Therefore, transnationalism is a process which is closely connected with the movement of people and has to be seen in the respective local context and generates highly fluid and hybrid social spaces.

But such an understanding also demonstrates that the question of transnational spaces cannot be disconnected from the individuals involved in or creating these spaces: Whoever discusses transnational spaces has to mention the identities of their inhabitants sooner or later. Just as the national and cultural spaces, the individual identities seem to be involved in a process of blending and boundary dissolution indicating new hybrid forms and transitions. Thereby, a line from global processes to individual identity constitution on globalized conditions is drawn. This connection is emphasized by Kai Hugger in his research work on the utilization of so called ethno portals in the WWW by young migrants. Similar to Pries he considers transnational spaces as „qualitativ neue soziale und subjektive Lebenszusammenhänge jenseits der traditionellen nationalen Einheiten von Herkunfts- und Ankunftsregion"[4] (Hugger, 2010: 287). In doing so he stresses the connection between transnational spaces and a parlous form of identity constitution. The experience of transnationalism through migration often entails a hybrid identity structure characterized by multiplicity in the sense of relevant cultural context rather than by cultural unity.

As Hugger shows, this concerns the question of acceptance, since the cultural multiplicity is often precieved as a deficit by the affected people because of the lack of acceptance or sense of belonging to the old or still new cultural context. Transnational identities as hybrid forms therefore challenge essential ideas of unity which are fundamental to the modern comprehension of identity and allow for multiplicity and disparate connections. But contrary to the postmodern opinion, these connections can be

2 As much as critical sociologists like Sennett or critiques of modern technology like Günther Anders assume that the dissolution of the close environment eventually leads to the end of the modern subject, it seems to be about time to develop a concept of "sociability, which does not require compulsory attendance of social partners in a common social and geographical space." (Mau 2007: 8)

3 A sense of belonging, cultural similarities, communication interlacing, work correlations and everyday life practices, as well as related societal ordinances and regulations crossing the borders of national states (translation by A.U.).

4 Qualitatively new social and subjective life contexts beyond the traditional national unities of origin and arrival (translation by A.U.).

distressing too, when, for example, migrants deal with their multiple belonging without ever reaching unambiguousness.

Together, the meaning contexts of transnational spaces mentioned in this chapter can be used to deduce highly varying forms on different levels. Persons with a hybrid identity structure develop a correlative sense of perception, affecting the acquirement of their environment as well as their actions therein. Communicative spaces can assume a transnational character too, for example, when migrants discuss their experiences and problems with their hybrid identities. Even forums, chat rooms and social networks can be used as such transnational communication spaces. Transnational spaces also can be understood as "structural", for example in the form of certain areas and neighborhoods affected by a "transnational" or „foreign" culture and partially existing disconnectedly from the "actual" cultural environment. Furthermore, the social environment can altogether be considered transnational, since the thesis of a culturally "pure" environment is not supportable anymore. Even more abstract would be the idea of an increasing transnationalization in the sense of a global detraditionalization that is less the blending of cultural spaces than their disintegration within a mainstream culture. This is an addition for the comprehension of transnationalism as forms of political relations crossing national borders or as types of international enterprises.

## The Role of „New Media"

After going into transnationalism and transnational spaces and roughly outlining the range of these concepts, the correlation of New Media and transnationalism shall be focused on further. As hinted at before, in this correlation it is important to consider the macro level of encompassing societal transformation as well as the micro level of everyday social practices right up to individual identity constitution. On the macro level, the correlation between new information and communication technologies and topical transformation processes comes initially to the fore, which has intensively been discussed under the designation of the information and knowledge society in the last few years. The information society thereby exposes a very specific "media connection" or connection to new information technologies: The information society is a society whose growth is closely connected to the technical possibilities of generating and distributing information. In this respect, its continued existence is dependent on digitally interconnected technologies and their development. The bottom line is: New Media and their infrastructure are an absolute condition of postindustrial societies. Prime example would be our globalized economy which would be impossible without new information technologies. At that, this technical infrastructure gains more and more in importance in our everyday interaction and communication processes, as will be shown later.

The situation with the knowledge society is somewhat more complicated in regard to the fundamental importance of New Media. Hereby, especially knowledge is considered the new (nationalistic) resource which is gaining importance as compared to material resources. This orientation towards knowledge is accompanied by an increasing growth of the service sector and a closer alliance of science (as in production of knowledge) and economy (as in utilization of knowledge). At first glance, the impression is given that it is not the information technology which is in the centre of attention (like in the information society) but the subject acquiring new knowledge. But in the end, the focus on knowledge and the knowledge worker are the result of a globalized world and economy, which again is based on an encompassing mediatization. The "flexible" handling of knowledge and the accompanying working conditions are also closely connected to technical information and communication systems[5].

Technology, especially in form of digitally interconnected computer technology, seems to effectively stimulate the current societal transition and therefore provide a corresponding relation to transnationalism. Additionally, a development occurs in the globalized world which has been foretold by Adorno and Horkheimer (1998) in their criticism of cultural industry. Ultimately, all areas of society will become dependent on technological infrastructures, from which neither production and employment structures, "education", "recreation" nor social interaction can be excluded. (Media) technology is becoming the irreplaceable "background" of advanced societal formations and all their communicative processes (Gamm, 2000: 284; Unger, 2007: 214).

Next to this infrastructural or global dimension, two further aspects are to be discussed with regard to transnationalism and transnational spaces. On the one hand it is virtual space as new cultural sphere and on the other hand it is the role of New Media and especially the WWW in context of hybrid everyday worlds and identities. Among others, it shall be resolved in what way people with "transnational identities" make use of the offers of New Media and which role is assigned to this technology. But first, the virtual space as a new cultural sphere.

In the search for differences between old mass media and New Media, terms such as interactivity, interconnection and digitalization seem to appear again and again (Unger, 2009: 254). A significance for the process of transnationalism can even be attributed to old "Mass Media". As communication and information media they possess the distinctive ability to communicate even across national borders and therefore contribute to a relativization of space and time. It is not for nothing that the idea of the global village is closely connected with New Media. Such an exchange of information certainly contributes to the blurring of national borders, the opening of cultural spaces and allows for staying in touch with native culture.

However New Media add a new qualitative dimension to this "communicative" dissolution process. As communication media offering most different communication options (Chat, E-Mail, forums, IM, VoIP, etc.), they allow for a further relativization of time and space boundaries and a formation of a global information and communication network. Due to interactivity of media, this communication is certainly not one-sided anymore, but makes different forms of interaction possible right up to the possibility for appearing as producer and sender (YouTube, MySpace, Flickr, etc.). In terms of transnational spaces, New Media also exhibit a new quality by opening up the virtual cyberspace. In a way, cyberspace is a "potential" space which is opened up by digital interconnection and generated by specific programming and utilization. In this respect, applications such as Facebook, YouTube, etc. can be considered as specific locations in

5 Nowadays it's a popular procedure to recruit work force not only from the local setting, but to establish contacts via the WWW and corresponding portals such as Xing. The entire cooperation and communication is done purely online, without any kind of physical presence.

the cyberspace. They achieve concretization of this initially empty space which only receives a meaningful or cultural context by social acquisition and utilization.

In this sense, cyberspace in its potential form is the actual transnational or transcultural space, since it is in its virtual form devoid of culture, exists largely detached from national borders and therefore transcends everything cultural or national. But it is crucial how this space is configured, acquired and integrated into everyday practices. A view on the diverse offers of the WWW in terms of concretization of cyberspace reveals a strong, western dominated mono culture, which is dominated, for example, by global providers such as Microsoft, Apple, and "consumer places" like amazon or the Apple App Store with their globally distributed products and applications. This dedifferentiation can be applied to a multitude of offers, which are seemingly culturally neutral or create a sphere of cultural neutrality. For example, the game world "Azaaroth" of MMORPGS "World of Warcraft" is set in a fictitious cultural setting, where millions of players with different cultural backgrounds participate and cooperate with each other.

Social networks like Facebook support transnationalism in a different sense by allowing cultivation of social networks beyond cultural borders. They not only eliminate spatial distance, but create the possibility of contacting all friends or specific groups, providing a certain participation in someone's everyday life. Especially the sharing of seemingly mundane activities can create a sense of closeness, even if the reader is located hundreds of miles away. The structure of self-portrayal on social networks like Facebook in turn is devoid of a specific cultural frame and creates a supposed "neutral" sphere of presentation. Insofar, the accusation of "McDonaldization" in the sense of overriding cultural characteristics with a capitalist-western mono culture can be warranted. On the other hand, the WWW can in no way be considered a unified "cultural space", its divergence certainly rivals that of the "real" world. This understanding leads to another relevant point, namely if a line can or should be drawn between virtual and real spaces altogether. Surely, there might be analytical reasons for this. But several examinations show virtual locations and communicational relationships becoming more and more an integral part of everyday practices (Wagner/Theunert, 2006; Süss, 2004) and influencing our identity formation (Turkle, 1997). Often, the transitions between real and virtual modes of communication are not even recognized in everyday practices. It rather seems to be that real social relationships and networks are enriched by virtual elements and thereby transitioned into a hybrid form.

As shown before, virtual spaces open up very different possible uses, from participation in a transnational or cosmopolitan communication space to the utilization of virtual spaces for participation in and passing on regional social networks and cultures. Thereby, cyberspace emphasizes a crucial aspect mentioned before in the course of the discussion about transnational spaces: New Media contribute in great measure to the fact, that social and cultural spaces, connections and identities can no longer be easily defined by the immediate environment and physical presence. Steffen Mau suggests the development of an understanding of sociability without the need for geographical presence (Mau, 2007: 8). This coincides with the credo of online research, which has demanded for quite some time to detach the understanding of social communities from the immediate environment and the presence of a geographical place (Marotzki, 2002). This also favors a relativization of national borders and closely confined social environments in regard to the development of social communities right up to individual identity formation.

Virtual spaces and associated social networks can by all means be understood in regard to new forms of reflexivity and literacy, for example in context of involvement with hybrid identity structures against the backdrop of migration experiences. They function more and more as surroundings, in which processes of socialization, learning and education takes place and which therefore influence intersubjective processes by functioning as a frame for interaction and communication. Thereby, the gap between the influence of New Media as informational infrastructure on the global world, its transformation of general "communication configuration" up to everyday use is bridged. To illuminate the importance of these virtual social spaces and set a counterpoint to the thesis of a forced unified culture via the WWW, one has to glance at the different uses of virtual spaces and networks by the way of people with "hybrid" or "transnational" identity patterns.

## Transnational Media Spaces and Cultural Identity

As mentioned before, New Media do not only serve communication in the traditional sense, but offer virtual environments able to assume different forms with which the user can interact. Digital games and office applications represent two possible forms of environment performing wholly different functions, namely "entertainment" and "work". Such software environments are considered interactive, since they react to the user's input with a more or less meaningful output. The actual new part of New Media goes beyond this interactive form. Global interconnection allows for communication between two or more persons within a computer mediated environment, through which technology fades into the background. It serves "only" as mediator and creates a seemingly "natural" communication surrounding.

Still, this communication mode differs from conversation in person, since many aspects of face-to-face communication are relativized. These virtual spaces have a double relevance for the discussion of transnationalism, as shown before. On the one hand on the ontological level, since virtual spaces are freely configurable and therefore "without culture". But due to concrete utilization and acquirement they are ultimately charged with cultural content. On the ontic level, meaning everyday practices, virtual spaces in form of social networks open up new possibilities of expanding existing social networks, creating new ones or keeping in touch with regional communities. Thereby, these offers can also be employed to re-regionalize and pass on cultural practices and behavioral patterns, although New Media decisively contribute to globalization and detraditionalization.

This becomes evident, for example, with so called ethno portals usually used by people with migration experience. Kai-Uwe Hugger did empirical examinations of such portals as transnational educational space. As shown before, he connects migration with a hybrid identity structure due to the diverging cultural context (old and new home), which characterizes the individual experience and identity and therefore prevent locating oneself within a cultural context (Hugger, 2010: 285)[6]. Against this backdrop, ethno portals not only offer the possibility to swap ideas with like-minded people or people with similar experiences, but create a place for negotiation, where different ideas can be discussed about how to handle double or multiple cultural "references"[7]. To this belongs the question of how the relation to one's own national cultural roots, the diaspora and new cultural "space" can be defined. The answers to these questions aren't only action-oriented, meaning rather opening oneself to new culture or identifying with native culture. They are also extremely relevant to the often burdening and pressing questions connected to one's own self-image against the background of multiple cultural belonging. Hugger considers this involvement with cultural roots a decisive aspect of transnational identity work oriented towards affiliation and recognition, for which New Media offers a framework in form of ethno portals. They cannot possibly replace recognition and integration in the offline world. But on the other hand they should not be underestimated in their importance and orientation for the individual, because they make it partially possible: „die (…) kulturelle Ortlosigkeit der Migranten zu verorten, d.h. deren prekäre Zugehörigkeit (…) zu verarbeiten" (Hugger, 2010: 288)[8]. In a sense, these portals offer a place for people, whose identity structure is dominated by a lack of belonging. Cyberspace cannot replace a genuine or natural home, but is a place where they can swap ideas with people with similar backgrounds, work on their self-image or develop action strategies.

The examination reveals several strategies of action and utilization, which come to use for dealing with the precarious identity structure (Hugger, 2010: 289). These strategies can be located between "decisive" and "ambiguous". Ethno-portals and their communities are used, among others, to approach possibly buried primary cultural-national roots, to reduce fear of contact or preserve certain cultural traditions. While this approach can indeed be seen within a frame of expanding or balancing the hybrid identity, the assurance of one's own roots can be undertaken with the goal of dissolving the multiple affiliations by means of a distinct cultural identification. A third strategy appears in the attempt of adapting to the precarious affiliation and supporting others in this difficult task. This can be considered as a specific form of dealing with ambiguity in a tolerant way. To shape this, it is necessary to examine, which relation one's own self-conception has to the allegedly default standards of old and new cultural context and if a biographical continuity can be established. This small glimpse into the usage of ethno-portals, as worked out by Kai-Uwe Hugger, shows that these spaces can neither offer a home, nor ensure the sought-after recognition. But they provide a transnational or transcultural space of communication and reflection, which expands the environmental space of action and can indeed help to counteract or process globalization tendencies.

---

6 Twenty qualitative interviews with young Turks of the second migrant generation were the basis for this study. (Hugger 2010: 289)

7 Therefore, these portals exhibit a rather homogenic user group, foremost persons with migration experience, who create a new "transnational" territory after experiencing territorial loss or territorial dissolution.

8 To locate the lack of cultural belonging, that is to say to process their parlous affiliation (translation by A.U.).

## Conclusion

In the discussion about the transformation of modern societies due to globalization New Media are rather marginalized or associated with a distinctive impact. Often, this is due to the support of a capitalistic mono culture at the expense of cultural diversity. As the article tries to show, there is no point in denying that New Media are very closely linked to the globalization process, in fact, their infrastructure can be seen as a requirement. Therefore, they are part of the multiple processes associated with the term transnationalism. But this poses the question, if transnationalism can be interpreted as cultural dedifferentiation or as a new, transformed form of cultural multiplicity. Without being able to answer this question concludingly, a lot seems to speak for a cultural transformation, which can especially be associated with the term "hybrid". With the relativization of clean lines, transitions, blends and conglomerates emerge, which "did not exist before", but what can't serve as an argument of ignoring them. This hybridity becomes obvious, when no longer the national space as a container, but the social space of the environment and its cultural condition is focused on. Similar to the credo of the Cultural Studies, the focus lies on the individuals, who certainly cannot influence the global framework itself, but are not only determined victims, because they create their own forms of processing. Especially in their everyday practices they characterize the mentioned hybrid connections and demonstrate *what people do* with the impact of globalization. As shown in the article, it is crucial to come back to the New Media, but this time not in the sense of an encompassing framework, but in a manner of how they are incorporated into everyday practices and the above-mentioned hybridization process. On the action level, there is a very sustainable and differentiated application of New Media and especially of the offers of the WWW. As the involvement with ethno portals has shown, their utilization can have very diverse effects, for example, with regard to individual cultural self-understanding and identity. Therefore, the by now common thesis can be invoked again: it does not make sense to speak of New Media or the WWW in general. The multitude of offers and utilization possibilities are so numerous, that a concretization is in order, if substantial statements are to be given. Ultimately, the article raises two further questions in terms of transnationalism and transnational spaces. On the one hand, there is the question about the state of cyberspace as social space: can it be regarded as a transnational space and if, how does it differ from other forms of transnational spaces? This leads to the second question about the general state of transnationalism: Is an increasing de-culturization in terms of dissolution of cultural differences part of this or is it about the connection of giving entities generating a new quality? The concept of hybridization as developed by Donna Haraway (1991), seems to be especially relevant to the second position.

## References


Adorno, Theodor/ Horkheimer, Max (1998): Dialektik der Aufklärung. Frankfurt a. M.: Fischer.

Gamm, Gerhard (ed.) (2000): Nicht Nichts. Studien zu einer Semantik des Unbestimmten. Frankfurt a. M.: Suhrkamp.

Haraway, Donna (1991): Simians, Cyborgs, and Women: The Reinvention of Nature. London: Routledge.

Hepp, Andreas (2008): Globalisierung der Medien und transkulturelle Kommunikation. In: Aus Politik und Zeitgeschichte. No. 39. pp. 9-16.

Hugger, Kai (2010): Bildungsräume junger Migranten im Internet. In: Bachmair, Ben (ed.): Medienbildung in neuen Kulturräumen. Die deutschsprachige und britische Diskussion. Wiesbaden: VS Verlag. pp. 285-296.

Löw, Martina (2001): Raumsoziologie. Frankfurt a. M.: Suhrkamp.

Marotzki, Winfried (2002): Zur Konstitution von Subjektivität im Kontext neuer Informationstechnologien. In: Bauer, Walter/ Lippitz, Wilfried and Marotzki, Winfried (eds.): Weltzugänge: Virtualität - Realität - Sozialität. Jahrbuch für Bildungs- und Erziehungsphilosophie. Hohengehren: Schneider-Verlag. pp. 45-62.

Mau, Steffen (2007): Transnationale Vergesellschaftung. Frankfurt a. M.: Campus.

Pries, Ludger (2002): Transnationalisierung der sozialen Welt? In: Berliner Journal für Soziologie. No. 2. pp. 263-272.

Süss, Daniel (2004): Mediensozialisation von Heranwachsenden. Wiesbaden: VS Verlag.

Turkle, Sherry (1997): Life on the screen. London: Orion Publishing.

Unger, Alexander (2007): Technological Transformation of Education. In: Heil, Reinhard/ Kaminski, Andreas/ Stippak, Marcus/ Unger, Alexander and Ziegler, Marc (eds.): Tensions – Technological and Aesthetic (Trans)Formations of Society. Bielefeld: Transcript. pp. 213-223.

Unger, Alexander (2009): „Vernetze Produktion und Kooperation. Neue mediale Praxen und die (Gegen-) Kultur der Informationsgesellschaft", In: Banse, Gerhard/ Wieser, Mathias und Winter, Rainer (eds.): Neue Medien und kulturelle Vielfalt. Konzepte und Praktiken. Berlin: Wissenschaftsverlag. pp. 251-270.

Unger, Alexander (2010): Virtuelle Räume und die Hybridisierung der Alltagswelt. In: Grell, Petra/ Marotzki, Winfried and Schelhowe, Heidi (eds.): Neue digitale Kultur- und Bildungsräume. Wiesbaden: VS Verlag. pp. 99-118.

Wagner, Ulrike/ Theunert, Helga (2006): Neue Wege durch die konvergente Medienwelt. München: Fischer.

# Social Networks and Identity Building Processes through Transnational/Cross Regional Experiences of Experts in Southern Europe

*Estrella Gualda, António Fragoso, Emilio Lucio-Villegas, Teresa González Gómez and Vània Martins*

## Abstract

*The frontier between the south of Spain and Portugal is established by the river Guadiana. Next to the sea, the cities of Ayamonte (Spain) and Vila Real de Santo António (Portugal) are facing each other on opposite banks of the river. The research on which this chapter is based focuses on these two cities. We study specifically personal and social relationships and processes of the identity building of experts on cross-border cooperation in the southern European cross-border area of Spain and Portugal. Are the experts who are frequently involved in cross-border experiences, as a result of their personal and professional lives, experiencing or having transnational lives and transnational flows? To answer this question we analysed the biographies of a wide range of people with different life experiences regarding cross-border cooperation in both countries. The interviews were open-ended and included a structured module for analysing the social networks of the respondents. The results suggest that there are no traces of a significant transnational character in the relationships established in this particular cross-border area.*

## Introduction

Space and time have always been present in social life. Throughout history, peoples' lives have developed within socio-temporal frameworks, and this has been demonstrated as a crucial regulator of social life by classical authors in the social sciences (Mauss/Beuchat, 1904-5) and will persist into the future. However, there has been a shift: what is potentially novel about socio-temporal frameworks presently is that 'space' has incorporated new nuances of 'virtual spaces' (e.g. the Internet), and 'virtual social relationships'. A considerable number of people today spend a large amount of time maintaining personal and social relationships without necessarily being in the same physical place, which differs greatly from previous times. The possibility of 'living together' in real time, even when separated by significant distance, in addition to being able to carry on social lives (not only one-to-one conversations), has a large impact in society and personal lives. The emergence of the new Information and Communication Technologies (ICTs) (and their consequences in social practices) has precipitated the necessity to revise some traditional concepts in the social sciences, and this has much to do with the psychic mobility characteristics of a globalised world. How do we envisage terms such as 'space' and 'spatial mobility'? How can we recognise the beginning of the global and the end of the local? What does the concept of *glocalisation* add to these quandaries (Guilianotti/Robertson, 2006)? How should we interpret social movements and social mobilisation processes? Are they locally or globally based? Are the new technological methods of mobilisation potentially the cause of the wider impact of some recent socio-political movements (Gualda, 2010)? In this sphere, important paradoxes have surfaced that can be applied to areas such as the cross-border of Andalucía-Algarve-Alentejo. Information about what is occurring in other countries can generally be accessed through various media outlets (websites, television, etc.), which makes the world much smaller. Despite the constant access to information, however, it is possible to be unaware of what is happening in one's immediate surroundings. It could be said that through technology, the world becomes smaller regarding international issues; yet at the same time local events could go unnoticed.

Globalisation has a large impact on the boundaries of territories, which changes the nature of social relationships. In the global context, a common argument is that the 'space of flows' overcomes the 'space of places' (Castells/Henderson, 1987; Castells, 1989, 1997). In this argument, the dynamic features of a territory would consist mainly of the connections within the territory, with activities and decisions produced beyond the natural limits of locality. From the point of view of organisations and dominant social interests, the logics and dynamics of territorial development will be increasingly deterritorialised. However, Castells and Henderson also argue that we should consider a second territorial process: even if dominant interests are losing their sense of place with regard to development, community social relationships still act according to local logic, meaning towards the place itself (Bauman, 1998) or, in the terms of Castells, towards the space of places. The more the dominant logic is based on flows, the more the defence mechanisms of specific interests integrate themselves into an anchored local experience. Regional and local movements, community organisations, and others function to oppose the organisations and interests that operate with the logic of flows.

This reasoning is fundamental when considering current cross-border cooperation dynamics. Cooperation can presumably be achieved if cross-border areas exist as zones characterised by *spaces of flows*, meaning flows that pass across intermixed and fluid social networks that include both Spanish and Portuguese citizens. In the southern Spanish-Portuguese cross-border area, for example, spaces of flows would be more important than spaces of places. Cross-border cooperation would maintain its instrumental function of reinforcing the tendency of flows, promoting new development dynamics or strengthening existing ones. However, the opposite trend can also occur; cross-border zones are still *spaces of places* with a lesser tendency towards flows (Gualda/Fragoso/Lucio-Villegas, 2009).

Perkmann, who has closely examined cross-border cooperation in the European Union, posits that cross-border cooperation is a process based on cooperation that is more or less institutionalised between sub-national authorities with the aim of overcoming the diverse barriers created by national frontiers (2003). Illustrative of Perkmann's definition of cross-border cooperation is the current construction of an Andalucía-Algarve and Alentejo Euroregion in southern Europe. This newly institutionalised and joint body for cross-border cooperation aims to create flows of exchange in the institutional setting. At the same time, Medeiros (2011) argues that the ideal type cross-border cooperation model takes place in a mature phase where cross-border flows are strong, social equipment is shared by the population, there is solid cooperation between the technological and economic fields and participation by civil society and local actors is high. In other words, cross-border cooperation, when characterised as a space of flows, is possible at those borders that have a significant tradition in cross-border cooperation.

Based on this framework, this chapter focuses on the personal and social relationships and processes of the identity building of experts on cross-border cooperation in the southern European cross-border area of Spain and Portugal. Are the experts who are frequently involved in cross-border experiences, as a result of their personal and professional lives, experiencing or having transnational lives and transnational flows? Further, how does the space of flows and space of places influence the views of cross-border agents?

## Objectives

Cross-border areas are potentially situated between local and global flows. Even the territory is not only univocally socially constructed except in comparison with neighbours. The political implementation of a Euroregion[1] may even bring about the reformulation of social representations, identities and social relationships. Social actors or experts in both areas who are in charge of building such a Euroregion, or even those who were working on Interreg projects[2] or previously developed formal and informal cross-border activities, may have experienced a shift in their personal networks and identifications. This comes as a reflex of the transition from the spaces to the flows, translated here into personal biographies. With this focus on micro changes, we attempt to observe social and personal networks in addition to the self-identifications of people who were involved in cross-border activities in the Andalucía-Algarve-Alentejo area during the last decade, when the Interreg projects began. How does the tension between the global and local appear to be solved in personal lives?

Knowing that identities, identifications and social and personal networks change over the course of a person's life, we are interested in whether experts working in an area of cross-border cooperation express signs of having cross-border lives. Sassenberg and Matschke (2010) and Bodenhausen (2010) argue that exchange and social relationships appear to mediate the construction of identity. Does this mediation effect also happen in the border area, or are people maintaining local identities?

---

1 Euroregion here as "a transnational co-operation structure between two (or more) contiguous territories located in different European countries. Euroregions represent a specific type of cross-border region" (http://dictionary.sensagent.com/EUROREGION/en-fr/). See also in Council of Europe, 2011.

2 Interreg is an EU-funded programme that helps Europe's regions form partnerships to work together on common *projects.*

## Methodology

This research has been designed with a multi-method approach (Brewer/Hunter, 1989), and with the criteria of triangulation between methods, techniques and results (Bryman, 1995; Pourtois/Desmet, 1992). Likewise, we also incorporated our experience in the more extensive area of Andalucía, Algarve and Alentejo, from a previous research carried out in the area (Gualda et al., 2008; Gualda/Fragoso/Lucio-Villegas, 2009).

As the project progressed, we focused on the cross-border region, in particular the towns near the border, along the southern part of Guadiana River and/or those areas with a significant role in the implementation of cross-border initiatives over the border region. The data come from parallel life histories from both sides of the border, which were recorded using a single methodological design. Additionally, a series of focus groups were run in the most relevant towns, Vila Real do Santo Antonio and Ayamonte. In fact, some of the details in our first investigation (Gualda et al., 2008) suggested that there were interesting issues in Vila Real de Santo António and Ayamonte, which should be subject to an exploration in greater depth, particularly in regards to social networks and border cooperation. The initial investigation results also showed that these two populations were centres in an area that we defined as periphery (southern Spain-Portugal).

We analysed the biographies of a wide range of people with different life experiences regarding cross-border cooperation in both countries. The respondents were from a variety of professional fields such as fishing, sailing, minor trade, public administration and services. This sample included both men and women of varied ages and levels of education. They were residents of municipalities and the participants included both local and non-local natives who had lived in the Portuguese-Spanish cross-border area for an extended period of time. While some had formal or institutionalised cross-border experiences through their participation in border projects, others had informal experiences or simply personal or family reasons for contact with the other side.

The interviews were open-ended and included a structured module for analysing the social networks of the respondents. We asked each of them to name up to 25 people with whom they regularly maintained relationships. Throughout the following text, quoting what they said in interviews and focus groups, names have been changed to preserve anonymity.

## Personal and Social Networks: Predominance of Endogamic Profiles

In addition to the personal biographies of the respondents, quantitative data concerning the personal networks of those interviewed was also collected. By applying social network analysis techniques, we were able to examine the social networks of the experts interviewed. Although all of them have professional contacts and functional relationships with people on the other side of the border (such as carrying on cross-border projects), this does not necessarily mean these personal relationships are important or that they continue in touch outside of work or after promoting other cross-border activities. We analysed the networks of those in our sample, from which we developed a typology of the three types of networks. To summarise, we will present one case as a representative of each type.

*Type 1. Mixed or hybrid network*

A mixed or hybrid network was an exceptional case amongst the interviewed. When asked to cite people who were in their personal network, only one expert demonstrated a hybrid profile based on Spanish and Portuguese contacts (such as family, friends or colleagues). Approximately half the network was Portuguese, with Spanish comprising the other half, which is represented in Chart 1. Interesting to note was the reason for belonging to both; in this case, he was member of a Sport Club that had both Spanish and Portuguese participants. Thus, his network included people from Spain (specifically Ayamonte, the municipality directly on the border, and Huelva) and Portugal (in particular Vila Real do Santo António, which is directly on the border, and from other places in the Algarve region). He was the only respondent who explicitly stated that having a specific cross-border identity was linked to his daily relationships with people from the two countries. In the Chart 1, the majority of people on the left were Spanish, while those on the right side were Portuguese. Some Spanish-Portuguese people play important roles as bridges between the two subgroups. The network is densely interconnected, however, which means that if a person leaves, the group will most likely remain.

Chart 1: Mixed or hybrid network (type 1)

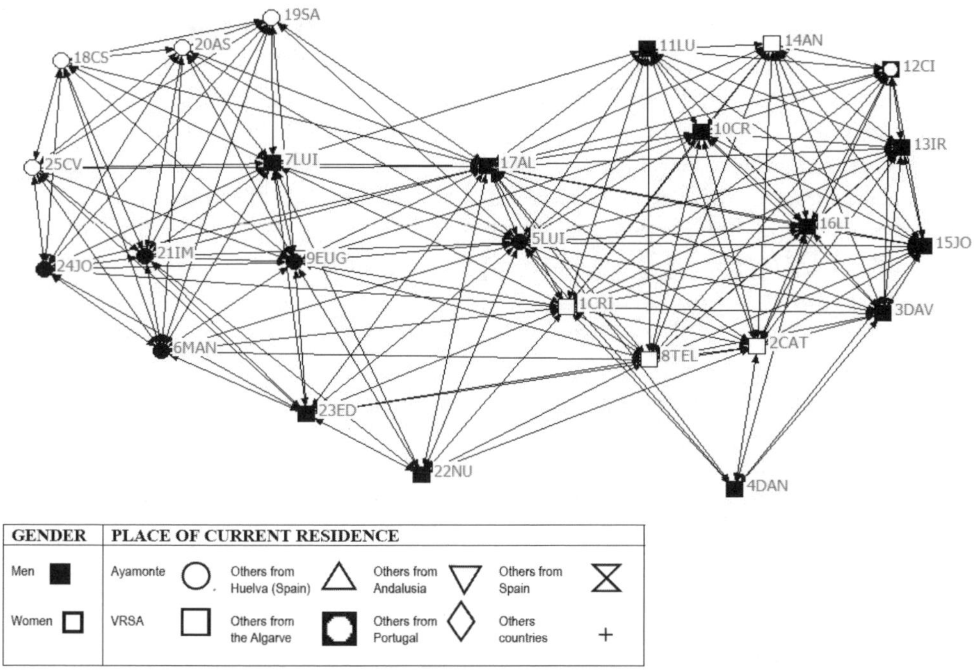


Source: Portuguese men from VRSA, 43 years old (personal interview, 2010).

*Type 2. Local/regional profile, with contacts on the other side*

In this case, we highlight the network of a Portuguese woman; however, it also represents the situation for other Spanish and Portuguese networks. Once again we found a very dense network, where the majority of the respondents' contacts were from the same municipality (Vila Real do Santo António in this example), although there were some members in his network that were from other locations in Portugal. The second type mainly shows people with relationships focused on the local-regional area with some exceptional contacts from the neighbouring country. In this case, only one contact was from Spain (out of twenty-five), and the majority were from the same municipality.

Chart 2: Local/regional profile, with contacts on the other side (type 2)

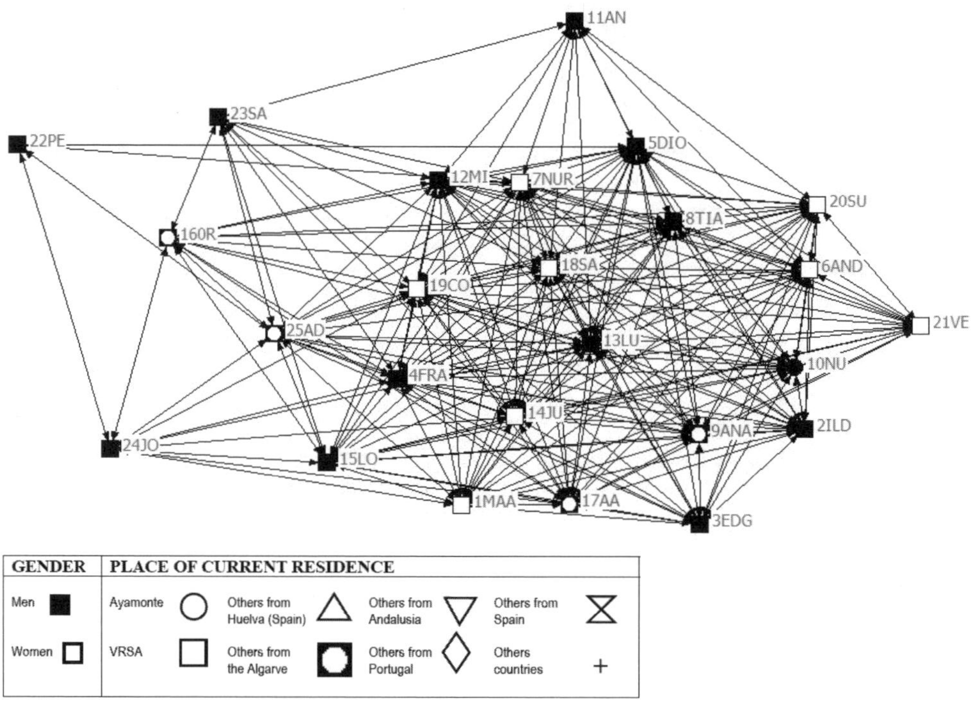


Source: Portuguese women from VRSA, 25 years old (personal interview, 2010).

*Type 3. Local profile*

In the third type of profile, which was common both in Spain and Portugal, the majority (if not all) of the people in their personal networks were from the same country. Despite having contacts on the other side of the border due to employment, such contacts were not integrated in their personal networks in daily life. Following Barrera (1980), personal networks can be defined as comprising people who provide support or assistance. In our questionnaire, we defined personal networks as people with whom one maintains frequent or habitual contact, and provide support or assistance. The typical networks we found were similar to those in Chart 2; i.e., the majority of people in the network were from the same municipality, while those who were not were from different locations in the same country. Endogamic relationships (regarding territory) were especially found here.

Chart 3: Local profile (type 3)

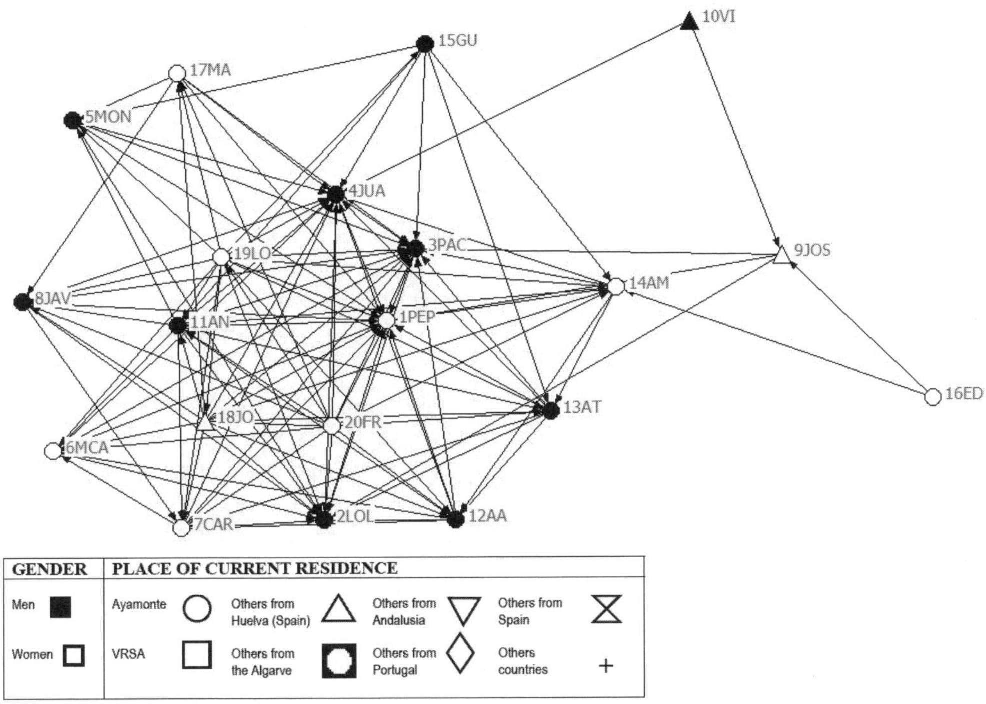


Source: Women fron Ayamonte, 41 years old (personal interview, 2010).

Regarding feelings of belonging, many experts of the "local profile" type regarding personal networks have reported dual identities for both regional and local belongings to the same country.

## Identity and sense of belonging in cross-border areas

When examining the networks of experts from neighbouring areas along a border, questions arose concerning whether these identities and senses of belonging are shared among the citizens of each area. Similarly, to what extent do the roots of identity relate to history, politics, culture, geography and social networks (e.g. family, friends, neighbours, and workmates)? Identities and identifications are rooted in many factors that are present in everyday life, which makes examining them particularly complex (Esser, 2009; Jackson, 2009; Ueno, 2009). We also wonder if identities and belongings are rooted in the same factors along the border.

Another possible factor for identity construction could be interventions such as those involving the Interreg or other measures carried out at the Spanish-Portuguese border (Epson, 2007; The Parliament Magazine, 2007). These interventions could have an impact on identity construction and act as a new factor in the formation of identities, in addition to the influence of social networks, family socialisation (Umaña-Taylor/Bhanot/Shin, 2006) or others.

The adaptability of identities has also been observed in individuals who, though not residing in a physical border region, were socialised with the symbolic border that separated their immigrant parents from the native population (origin vs. destination country). Adaptability was also observed at the physical borders where numerous political changes were experienced. This environment provoked a complex map of intensive social relations among *temporary* or current citizens and ethnic minorities, such as Russian minorities living in the former Soviet Republics.

Residing on the edge of the southern border separating Spain and Portugal can be understood, in terms of the reconstruction of identities, as existing between two sociocultural worlds, which may contribute to make individual meanings and multiple or hybrid identities (Brettell/Nibbs, 2009; Cara, 2010; Tsolidis/Pollard, 2009; Vermeij/Van Duijn/Baerveldt, 2009).

Identity construction based on social relations is not particularly grounded in the building of cross-border regions between neighbouring but separated countries under European Union cross-border policies. However, several factors may affect how identities are constructed at the Spanish-Portuguese border. The construction of identities and identifications is a subjective process in which context and daily life play an important role. As mentioned previously, space and time (more precisely, border space and a continuum in the time span) are the basic parameters for social life and, in this case, for identity construction. In this regard, sustaining programs during a time of cross-border cooperation demands attention. Identities and identifications are mutable and vary over time, so it is possible to design programs to be applied in the border area that affect the construction and reconstruction of identity to the extent that these programs could provide facilities, amenities, and opportunities for people of different areas to interact with each other and, therefore, to influence the identification process. Nevertheless, it must be kept in mind that identity construction does not occur through sporadic or punctual projects or initiatives and that the physical or territorial space can be projected onto an imagined border-space.

At the same time, one person may feel a sense of belonging and identify in more than one way. The idea of a shared sense of belonging or identity, then, seems to be a complementary construction to other types of identities, including local, regional, national or European identities. The feeling of belonging to an "imagined communities" or "political communities" (Anderson, 2006; Schnapper, 1994) can be fostered by institutions such as the European Union's Erasmus Programmes (which admittedly could also be the result of cross-border cooperation in the southern Europe area). Additionally, in a global context, the sources that affect the construction of identity could extend beyond specific local areas, and individuals could be influenced by multiple contexts. It is therefore crucial to assess whether local or global parameters are more important for the construction of identity in the border region separately from observing the influence of region, border and other elements that may impact the construction of identity.

## Discussion and Conclusions

The biographical interviews conducted with experts in cross-border cooperation issues confirmed local/regional dominance. Most respondents exhibited a local identity, and only two people showed an international one. In cases of national identity, people identified with their country of origin and were open to working and living anywhere in that country. In cases of international identity, however, people did not feel a sense of belonging to one country or locality, but rather were open to working or living in any part of the world. Our results indicate that territory and people's view of it is still important in identity construction and social relationships while the political process of building the Euroregion is taking place.

If globalisation suggests transgression of borders, does something similar occur when the top-down process of building a Euroregion is occurring? Will it produce long-term in-depth changes to the cross-border regions? Or will space of place continue to predominate as was demonstrated by this research?

Is it possible to construct a border identity without developing strong social relationships? Does the border connect or divide? The border is a symbolic space that allows people to situate, identify and differentiate themselves from others. Is a border a way of building identities, and will the disappearance of some borders result in the end of particular cultural identities?

Now we will shift focus to the discussions included in this book. Diverse international situations emerge from our data. In fact, we found professionals carrying on local or regional personal lives, while at the same time engaging in cross-border (or international) works or participatory actions. This occurred in a context where some immigrants were settled and in the process of developing transnational lives. Living in a globalised world has complex results and leaves the doors open to further discussions about the impacts of globalisation, global-local issues and global-local interplay at the border.

It seems undeniable that we live in an era where globalisation, due especially to the Internet, has conveyed the progressive annihilation of space over time. However, our interviews showed that most people build a local identity. In the cases where national identities were important, people opened up to the idea of working and living elsewhere in that country. Only two respondents, however, showed an international identity. This suggests that there are no traces of a significant transnational character in the relationships established in this particular cross-border area. If we return to the framework of Castells, it is possible that we are witnessing a movement of implicit or explicit resistance that, based on local and regional communities and organisations, is opposed to those who want to connect outside their original territory. This zone, then, appears to remain a space of places.

It should be stressed, however, that cross-border areas by nature have a higher degree of complexity. Despite the fact that people and goods can move freely throughout 'the ancient border', borders are symbolic constructions that have the ability of creating difference and constructing the identities of 'us' and 'the other' (Boman/Berg, 2007). In this perspective, social networks in the southern territory are not sufficiently intertwined, so identities of 'us' are more important than the identities 'of the other'.

Finally, the results appear more relevant when the political process of building the Euroregion is taking place, and in a context where, as Beck (2009: 287, 289) explains, national and international spheres are now dissolving as a result of an Europeanisation process, in a new meta-power game of multi-governance that is not yet well understood. Finally, we question if this is going to produce significant changes in the long run in cross-border regions. Is it possible that spaces of places are going to predominate as a way of opposing this clear tendency of building space of flows?

## Acknowledgements

We thank the Consejería de Presidencia (Secretaría de Acción Exterior) for supporting and trusting in our team for this research (Expte. SEGAEX/ SRICI/ CR 08.44103.82A.015). This text was also made possible by the support of different institutions that benefited the authors: the Portuguese Foundation for Science and Technology (FCT), the Junta de Andalusia, Programme for PhD Students, the Spanish Ministry of Education through the Salvador Madariaga's Programme (PR2010-0524) and the hospitality of the Center for Migration and Development at Princeton University that benefited one of the authors. We are also very grateful to the Spanish and Portuguese people, citizens, experts, politicians, and everybody who made the research possible.

## References

Anderson, Benedict (2006): Imagined Communities: Reflections on the Origin and Spread of Nationalism. London: Verso.

Barrera, Manuel (1980): A method of assessment of social support networks in community survey research. In: Connection. 3. pp. 8-13.

Bauman, Zygmunt (1998): Globalisation. The human consequences. Cambridge: Polity Press.

Beck, Ulrick (2009): The Cosmopolitan Condition. Why Methodological Nationalism Fails. In: Theory, Culture and Society. 24 (7-8). pp. 286-290.

Bodenhausen, Galen V. (2010): Diversity in the person, diversity in the group: Challenges of identity complexity for social perception and social interaction. In: European Journal of Social Psychology. vol. 40. (1). pp. 1-16.

Boman, Julia/ Berg, Eiki (2007): Identity and institutions shaping cross-border Co-operation at the margins of the European Union. In: Regional & Federal Studies. 17. pp. 195-215.

Brettell, Caroline B./ Nibbs, Faith (2009): Lived hybridity: Second-generation identity construction through college festival. In: Identities: Global Studies in Culture and Power. vol. 16 (6). pp. 678-699.

Brewer, John/ Hunter, Albert (1989): Multimethod research. A synthesis of styles. California: Sage.

Bryman, Alan (1995): Quantity and quality in social research. New York: Routledge.

Cara, Olga (2010): Lives on the border: Language and culture in the lives of ethnic Russian women in Baltinava, Latvia. In: Nationalities Papers. vol. 38 (1). pp. 123-142.

Castells, Manuel (1989): The Informational City. Oxford: Blackwell.

Castells, Manuel (1997): The Power of Identity. Oxford: Blackwell.

Castells, Manuel/ Henderson, Jeffrey (1987): Techno-economic Restructuring, Socio-political Processes and Spatial Transformation: a Global Perspective. In: Henderson, Jeffrey/ Cas-

tells, Manuel (eds.): Global Restructuring and Territorial Development. London: Sage. pp. 1-17.
Council of Europe (2011): What is a Euroregion? http://www.coe.int/t/dgap/localdemocracy/Areas_of_Work/Transfrontier_Cooperation/Euroregions/What_is_en.asp [17-03-2011].
Epson (2007): Cross-border cooperation – Cross-Thematic Study of INTERREG and ESPON activities. Luxembourg: European Union.
Esser, Hartmut (2009): Pluralisierung oder Assimilation? Effekte der multiplen Inklusion auf die Integration von Migranten. In: Zeitschrift für Soziologie. vol. 38 (5). pp. 358-378.
Giulianotti, Richard/ Robertson, Roland (2006): Glocalization, Globalization and Migration. The Case of Scottish Football Supporters in North America. In: International Sociology. vol. 21 (2). pp. 171-198.
Gualda, Estrella (2010): Social Movements, New Technologies and New Strategies for the Mobilization. In: Evans, Rob (ed.): Local Development, Community and Adult Learning: Learning Landscapes between the Mainstream and the Margins. Vol. II. Magdeburg: Nisaba Verlag, pp. 175-180.
Gualda, Estrella/ Fragoso, António/ Lucio-Villegas, Emilio (2009): Cross-Border Co-operation: margin-margin relationships to improve development and social integration. In: Evans, Rob (ed.): Local development, community and adult learning: learning landscapes between the mainstream and the margins. Vol. I. Magdeburg: Nisaba Verlag.
Gualda, Estrella/ Lucio-Villegas, Emilio/ Fragoso, António/ Figueira, Eduardo/ Gualda, Juan Manuel/ Barrera, Nashira/ Almeida, Maria Luisa/ Ramalho, Vania/ Maya, Isidro (2008): Realidad Social en Andalucía, Algarve y Alentejo. Huelva: Universidad de Huelva.
Jackson, Kelly F. (2009): Building cultural competence: A systematic evaluation of the effectiveness of culturally sensitive interventions with ethnic minority youth. In: Children and Youth Services Review, 31(11), pp. 1192-1198.
Mauss, Marcel/ Beuchat, Henri (1904-5): Essai sur les variations saisonnières des sociétés Eskimos. Étude de morphologie sociale. In: Année Sociologique. vol. 9. pp. 39-132.
Medeiros, Eduardo (2011): (Re)defining the Euroregion concept. In: European Planning Studies. vol. 19 (1). pp. 141-158.
Perkmann, Markus (2003): Cross-border regions in Europe: significance and drivers of regional cross-border cooperation. In: European Urban and Regional Studies. 10. 2. pp. 153-171.
Pourtois, Jean Pierre/ Desmet, Huguette (1992): Epistemología e instrumentación en ciencias humanas. Barcelona: Herder.
Sassenberg, Kai/ Matschke, Christina (2010): The impact of exchange programs on the integration of the hostgroup into the self-concept. In: European Journal of Social Psychology. vol. 40 (1). pp. 148-159.
Schnapper, Dominique (1994): La communauté des citoyens: sur l'idée moderne de Nation. París: Gallimard.
The Parliament Magazine (2007): Portugal-Spain Cross-Border Cooperation. In: The Parliament Magazine. 249. 2. http://www.e-pages.dk/dods/50/38 [17-07-2009].
Tsolidis, Georgina/ Pollard, Vikki (2009): Being a "wog" in Melbourne-young people's self-fashioning through discourses of racism. In: Discourse: Studies in the Cultural Politics of Education. 30 (4). pp. 427-442.
Ueno, Koji (2009): Same-race friendships and school attachment: Demonstrating the interaction between personal network and school composition. In: Sociological Forum. vol. 24 (3). pp. 515-537.
Umaña-Taylor, Adriana J./ Bhanot, Ruchi and Shin, Nana (2006): Ethnic Identity Formation during Adolescence: The Critical Role of Families. In: Journal of Family Issues. vol. 27 (3). pp. 390-414.
Vermeij, Lotte/ Van Duijn, Marijtje J./ Baerveldt, Chris (2009): Ethnic segregation in context: Social discrimination among native Dutch pupils and their ethnic minority classmates. In: Social Networks. vol. 31 (4). pp. 230-239.

# The Role of Transnationalism, Personal Networks and Social Networks in the Migratory Projects of a Small Cameroonian Community in Huelva

*Estrella Gualda and Carmen Márquez*

## Abstract[1]

*Although there has been much recent research in the area of transnationalism, social networks, social capital and cultural capital, little has been written about immigration and social networks from a Social Network Analysis (SNA) perspective, and little has been published about immigrants' small communities with this perspective. A great portion of studies on immigration are focused more on majority ethnic groups settled in a country than on minority ones. This text examines the trajectories of Cameroonian immigrants from their place of origin until their arrival and establishment in Huelva (Spain). Through their life stories and the application of a SNA module, this study examines the role of social networks in determining or influencing immigrants' complete migratory project (from their decision to migrate and the origin of the funds to do it, through the decision to stay in Europe and, for some, their planning to return). This chapter's main objective is to assess the role of Cameroonians' personal networks in the migratory project and in their integration. This chapter also attempts to assess how far transnational networks influence and configure the immigrants' lives. We discovered the presence of people from different countries who appeared in all the personal networks. Many people cited as members of support networks were of Cameroonian origin, but they were living in the same area (not in the country of origin or another country), indicating the importance of proximity to daily life in our cases. This was accompanied by the tendency to reproduce and reinvent the homeland in the destination country. Intensive and extensive transnational practices were found in a minority of cases.*

## Small Communities, Social Networks and Migratory Projects

Recent literature has been frequently focused on transnationalism, social networks, social capital and cultural capital, but the number of scientific publications regarding small immigrant communities and social networks is few, and little has been published on these issues from the Social Network Analysis (SNA). This chapter examines the role of social networks in the constitution and development of a very small Cameroonian community and the factors that influence the integration of immigrants who were born in Cameroon into Spain. We are also interested in the transnational nature of the

1 An initial version of this chapter was discussed in Toulouse (Analyse des réseaux sociaux: quoi de neuf ? RT 26 appel à communication. 2ème journée d'études 2010. Toulouse, 16-17 marzo). We gratefully acknowledge the feedback obtained there.

migratory project, especially transnational lives and social practices. Our objectives in this text are to determine the degree of integration of the Cameroonian population settled in Huelva and to examine the role of networks and transnational links in their integration. We believe all these dimensions are significant. Therefore, we will analyse the migratory projects that permeate the personal biographies of immigrants and that are linked to several important events in their lives. A migratory project is the immigrant's personal plan to accomplish a goal in his or her destination country. Such projects are influenced by external factors such as economic necessity or political instability, but they are ultimately shaped by the immigrant himself or herself. While very complex, these processes can be characterised by a few essential moments that drive them (Izquierdo, 2000).

Today, integration into societies that receive immigrants can be especially influenced by the way immigrants maintain connections with their countries of origin. If difficulties in maintaining daily contacts with home once encouraged immigrants to integrate into destination communities, researchers have found that it is now possible for immigrants to simultaneously carry on lives in both origin and destination countries (Portes and Rumbaut, 2006; Portes and Rivas, 2011). Some investigations and debates in the social sciences have focused on the extent to which transnational lives or transnational organisations contribute to the integration of immigrants into destination societies and to the development of home countries (Faist, 2010; Fong and others, 2010; Metykova, 2010; Gowricharn, 2009; Portes and Rivas, 2011; Portes and others, 2008; Guarnizo, 2006, Ostergaard, 2009).

However, it seems clear that the decision to migrate is not monocausal. Although some elements seem to be very decisive in some contexts (poverty, hunger, conflicts, etc.), there are many factors that lead to the initiation and maintenance of the migratory project, such as the existence of personal and social networks that put new immigrants in touch with ethnic communities already established in destination countries. These communities can play a dual role both as groups that attract immigrants and as support networks for new immigrants and other residents (as suggested by works such as Massey, 1999; Espinosa and Massey, 1997; and Portes and Rumbaut, 2006). These communities can then be important for immigrants' integration into destination countries while also promoting the implementation of transnational projects in countries of origin.

Although there is a large body of literature concerning migratory chains and psychological adaptation connected with immigrants' social networks (Maya, 2009: 274), other important issues have theoretical value. One of them is how migratory projects have been conducted when there are no social support networks in destination countries. Is it possible to find differences between the migratory project of people who do and do not have support networks in destination countries? This chapter aims to evaluate the role of social networks at different stages of the migratory project, to study their possible influence and to examine the features that are present in migratory projects that lack these networks at the beginning of the migration. We consider here the idea of "social support networks" as a "subset of the individual's personal network that provides information, instrumental and affective support" (Maya, 2009: 282).

For a long time, social research has been concerned with the study of communities, often following a comparative framework under the influence of the classic theory of *Community and Society* (Tönnies, 1963). There have been many studies of communities and their specific connections to societies, and some have also discussed the positive effects of living in a community on integration (Martinez-Brawley, 2000). Factors such as daily treatment, emotional and instrumental support or the fact that members of a small community used to know each other are elements that can have positive influences on individuals. However, those factors could be counteracted by other characteristics of small communities, such as strong social control, that can lead immigrants to stay 'shut in' in their community (Pascual, Miguel and Solana, 2007). In fact, it is common for immigrants to transfer previously existing social support structures into the destination society. This also happens with the reproduction of sociocultural patterns and values in the destination country (Misawa, 2001; Moldenhawer, 2005). We chose a small Cameroonian community as the focus of this chapter after conducting a research project that examined the personal and social networks of the Cameroonian population in Huelva."[2] This community, whose members do not always reside in the same locality, will be the focus of the remainder of this chapter.

## Objectives, Methods and Techniques

*Objectives*

In this chapter, we will evaluate the role of personal networks of Cameroonians in the migration process and determine whether these networks are transnational or local in character. To this end, we want to determine what kind of social networks they had at each migratory phase (endogamic/exogamic, dense/sparse) as well as these networks' composition in relation to the place of origin of their components. We are also interested in knowing whether the personal networks were near or far (in the same locality, region, country or in a different country), and whether they were the cause of transnational links. It was also important to examine whether the small number of people born in Cameroon and living in Huelva affects their integration. This text tries to answer the above questions, and we explore the idea that belonging to a small community in a province that is not very large could act as facilitator for integration and could affect the way in which the composition of social networks over time is set.

*Methods and techniques*

This text is part of a larger investigation with a multi-method approach. In this chapter, however, we focus on biographical interviews conducted in Spain. Questionnaires for building life stories had two parts. One part was more qualitative, covering the migratory project, their life-courses, location, etc. The other was more quantitative, based on a module for analysing social networks. Our work is particularly focused on quali-

2 Huelva is a province belonging to the Spanish region of Andalusia, which is located in southwestern Europe. The region of the Algarve (Portugal) borders on Huelva to the west and the Andalusian province of Seville borders on Huelva to the east. This province is located in the north of Africa, about 300 miles from Morocco.

tative evaluation. We used the following question to generate names: "Please, tell us a list of 15 people with whom you usually have relationships (...) This includes persons who are or are not in Spain (...)" Various additional questions were asked concerning instrumental support, emotional support and related topics, inspired by Barrera's (1980) idea of social support.

We only interviewed Cameroonians who had lived in Huelva for at least a year in order to study support networks used after the arrival at the destination country. In the fieldwork, we identified at least ten people with this profile (eight of whom were interviewed), settled in two different places in the province (Bonares and Huelva). We gained access to respondents through acquaintances, migration experts and the same interviewed Cameroonians (the snowball method).

## The Small Cameroonian Community in Huelva

First, we want to emphasise that only 0.1 per cent of the total foreign population in Huelva was born in Cameroon, representing a total of 45 people officially registered in 2009 (Instituto Nacional de Estadística, 2010). Nobody was registered in 2002 or before. Most of the population consists of men (84.4 per cent). Most are young people. Bonares, an agricultural municipality, stands out as a place of settlement in the province. In fact, the Cameroonian population was mainly settled in two municipalities of Huelva: the capital and Bonares. While the former is the main urban centre of the province, with a total population of approximately 149,000 inhabitants in 2009 and a specialisation in the chemical industry and related services, Bonares is a highly specialised agricultural town (30 kilometres distance from the capital), and had a population of 6,000 in 2009. The Cameroonians in our sample have resided in the province for more than four years, used to have stable jobs (in the tertiary sector or in agriculture), and tend to have usual relationships among themselves and with the receiving community (two of them are married to Spanish women and one has a Spanish girlfriend). All of them had legal status and legal work permits at the time of the interviews, but none of them are naturalised as Spanish and none want to be naturalised because this would entail the rejection of Cameroonian nationality. Everyone wants to return to Cameroon in the future. When we conducted the interviews, subjects imagined that they would return after a long time, once they achieved their objectives in Spain.

After the completion of the interviews, we organised a focus groups with other Cameroonians, and other small populations of Cameroonian origin were identified within the province. The majority were newcomers and were working in agriculture. The total number identified through various sources[3] was small (less than 50 people in total), and they possessed great mobility (not always reside in Huelva). The number of women was very low, and the people were working in agriculture more so than in other economic sectors. There is also a mixture of documented and undocumented immigrants.

3 Experts on migrations, NGOs and Social Services staff, immigrants interviewed, etc.

## Support Networks of Cameroonians in Huelva

*Country of birth*

We found three types of personal networks: (1) networks composed largely of Spaniards (more than 50 per cent in the network), (2) networks composed of co-ethnics (at least 50 per cent) mixed with a presence of people from other places and (3) networks with a significant majority of co-ethnics (more than 70 per cent of members in the network). By co-ethnics we always refer here to people born in Cameroon, including the individuals interviewed (Gualda and Márquez, 2010). This typology was based on the answers obtained when applying the name generator, taking into account that alters interact often with respondents. Alters here are people referred in the interviews as integrating ego's personal networks, and egos or subjects were those people who were interviewed.

Subjects receive some support (instrumental, affective, etc.) from these alters. It is necessary to note that because we asked for alters with whom subjects interact frequently, our data do not correspond to subjects' entire personal networks. Every subject could have a multitude of other social contacts.

All Cameroonians have in their network of regular contacts at least some relationships with people from two countries (usually Spain and Cameroon). In this sense, one could say that their daily relationships are at a minimum *bi-local*, following De Federico's idea that migrant communities tend to have mixed profiles of integration. However, six of our eight interviewees included in their networks people from a third or fourth country, which may then be included in the type *cosmopolitan* (De Federico, 2004). But we must note here that their cosmopolitanism was oriented in Spain more toward regular relationships with people from the same country who reside in the same towns than toward connections with people who live in other countries. Personal networks described by Cameroonians were international (in terms of *alters'* birthplaces), although, as we shall see, they have a strong local orientation in terms of where alters currently live (see Appendix).

Having incorporated a temporal perspective in our analysis, it was possible to identify the key people who supported Cameroonians and helped them along the migration process at different moments. At the same time, *alters* who are from the same country and who helped them at the beginning of the migration process were anecdotally mentioned, and one-third of Cameroonians who were interviewed did not cite any co-ethnics who helped them in the initial phase of their migration and with whom they maintained a regular relationship. However, co-ethnics were very important during the arrival in Spain and during the settlement phase.

The support of people from Spain during the immigrants' arrival in this country and during the settlement phase was also of some importance (especially in the case of Nicolas[4] and Modeste, who had more than 50 per cent Spaniards in their networks). One interesting aspect of the interviews is that only a small number of people living in Cameroon at the moment were cited as personal networks. Several interpretations could be provided for this phenomenon, depending on the case we analyse.

4 All the names mentioned in the text are pseudonyms.

*Place of residence and transnationalism*

Although the support networks of Cameroonians include people from different countries, in most of the cases the members of the network lived nearby. Still, this finding varies depending on each case and each trajectory. As pointed out by De Federico (2004), "Migrants are just par excellence actors at the same time local and non locals, and their ways of integration in different systems of meso-relations reflect their wider relations to the societies of origin and destination". Therefore, it is important not only to study immigrant communities from the perspective of the local community but also to incorporate the perspective of the transnational community. What we found in our descriptive analysis is, however, that people from different countries appear in all the personal networks, but the people cited as members of support networks mostly lived nearby, in Spain, and above all in the same province and even in the same town, indicating the importance of proximity in our cases.

The fact that subjects predominantly mentioned people who live nearby suggests that personal networks are reconstructed and reinvented once immigrants reach their destination (Avila, 2009). And paradoxically, in our case, personal networks eventually became more "local" than "non-local", albeit with a multi-ethnic character. Nevertheless, two out of eight subjects interviewed work in a transnational organisation that performs activities in both the destination and the origin countries. This organisation executes transnational projects, particularly in Africa and Latin America, using a co-development framework. The leader, one of the Cameroonian interviewees, created this foundation as an instance of political transnationalism (Ostergaard, 2009). He combined two ideas: helping other immigrants with their integration processes in Spain and trying to help development processes in his country of origin and, by extension, in other African and Latin American countries. He explained in more detail:

> Then you start to reflect on it, to look at things very closely, concerns emerge (…): Why this table is here and in my home is set to the left? Why here the water is coming out from a faucet and my compatriots take the water from a well? Why here is asphalted (…) and not in my village? Why here I eat three times and in my house only one? Here, I have thrown rice; do you know that in my house, my brother or my cousin, have not eaten today? From here I try since 2002 to set up an agency for direct cooperation between Cameroon and Andalusia (…) after the international agreement between Cameroon and Spain (Nicolas, personal interview, 2010).

## Integration and Personal Networks at Different Stages of the Migratory Project

In this section, we evaluate the role that personal networks have had in the Cameroonians' migration projects in connection with their integration. In the cases we studied, two paths summarise the role of support networks in the process. A first group of people left their country of origin with planned relational supports in the country of origin and/or destination. In these cases, migration took place to study and/or fulfil a family project. The arrival in Spain is straightforward, they travel by plane and they have a legal status for entry and stay. These elements make integration easier, avoiding other personal costs. This group includes Angèle, Nicolas, Modeste and Thomas. A second group of people left their country of origin without planned support in the country of origin and/or destination and went through various and complicated itineraries. They arrived via boat and had irregular entry in Spain. Successful integration takes longer in contrast to the previous group. Their responses to situations of insecurity or lack of work are more complicated, revealing their vulnerability. This group includes Samuel, Jacques, Antoine and Charley.

The interviewees reported some important actors in the past who are not present today in their networks. We found through the interviews some actors who are a part of the extensive network of contacts of each respondent (*weak ties*, Granovetter, 1973) and who played an important role in the life courses (in the case of Antoine, for example, he met an important football player in Spain whom he knew from his neighbourhood when he was a child and who gave him money in a key moment. Antoine did not name this famous football player as one of the people who are important for him at this moment, but the football player played an important role in the past – a fortuitous or unplanned role, producing a kind of *random* support).

What is relevant here is that, although the interviewees have acceptable living conditions (legal status, work, etc.), the road has been most difficult when personal support was not available. This stresses that the planning of migration could be a significant factor in integration. Moreover, in cases like Charley's, who changed from agricultural work to create his own business without any support, human capital is relevant; indeed, Charley was already a merchant in his country of origin. This human capital pushed him to become an entrepreneur in Spain, but to get there took a great effort. In the case of Angèle, she is still saving money to create her own business, following in her family's footsteps. Charley and Angèle are very different from people such as Modeste. Though Modeste has a job that is not particularly good or safe, he has always had his brother's support in Spain. This support gives him security in insecure times, including during the current economic crisis. For other subjects (Jacques and Antoine), job insecurity compels them to go elsewhere to look for work, as they are more vulnerable. Given all of this, we also want to underline that, though small in number, people belonging to this community are not homogeneous and there exist differences regarding their resources and opportunities for the future. Even so, it seems clear that the existence of support networks, in cases where they exist, has greatly influenced the development of interviewees' migratory projects, allowing them achieve goals in less time.

## Discussion and Conclusion

We have examined the networks of most of the Cameroonian community's members who have been settled in Huelva for at least one year, observing the process of establishing this small community and how the two people who came first (one to the rural and the other to the urban area) played an important role in supporting those who came after them. A community of Cameroonians with other Cameroonians as major providers of support eventually emerged, although it exists in an immigration context where it is feasible to find people from different countries, especially Spaniards, who are sometimes incorporated into their networks. This tendency toward associating with those from the same country of origin is broken in cases like that of Nicolas or Modeste, whose personal networks mainly include Spaniards. Primarily associating with others born in Cameroon is more common among those living in rural areas. In the case of Nicolas, he has not only an important link with other Spaniards, but he is also in charge of a transnational organisation working for the development of African countries. His entire migratory project as well as his organisation was supported by a Spanish man. Curiously, Nicholas' family is divided in more than three countries.

Still, the name generator portion of the interviews, which documented the subjects' basic personal support, revealed a picture of the community. By triangulating names mentioned spontaneously by all respondents, we determined the names of other people in the community and their connections. We also observed that some actors, such as Thomas, play an important role of go-between, connecting people in the two localities and bringing the Foundation closer to other Cameroonians. Subsequent studies will discuss in more detail how a social network emerged from a number of personal networks. At the same time, being a small community allowed most of the subjects to know each other, a process made easier by close proximity. In addition, the combination of life histories (using a qualitative analysis, which was aided by software such as Atlas ti), together with the introduction of social network analysis (supported by Ucinet and Netdraw) and the employment of strategies to triangulate the information, methods and techniques throughout the research process, contributed not only to consistent results but also to the discovery of some contradictions and paradoxes that opened new issues in the course of the investigation. For example, what does it mean when one respondent said the following: "What is your marital status?"/ "Married in Cameroon, and single in Spain" (Nicolas, personal interview, 2010).

Why did he forget to cite key actors in his networks, his two wives living in Cameroon, when the Social Network Analysis module was applied? Why did he omit them in the SNA, but not in the life history, where he reported sending them remittances? Does this mean that he does not have regular contact with them, or is this simply an oversight? Or does he not cite them just because they are not important to him at this moment of his every day life? Has he reinvented his support networks? Or is it that some people were important in the past, but not now? Or does this reveal a dual transnational identity, which is very common in immigrants?

Moreover, having social networks in the countries origin and destination to support the immigration process was not the only factor that influenced the process of integration. Another important factor was that these networks were activated in a planned manner in the country origin (especially as financial support to migrate) and at the destination (minimising inherent problems of the immigrant population such as the search for papers, jobs and housing upon arrival), as has already been highlighted in other investigations. Globalisation and the reduction in the price of communications make the proliferation of transnational networks and migratory chains easier (Capel, 2001).

This chapter has highlighted that the personal networks of Cameroonians fit three types of relationships: mostly Spanish oriented, mostly Cameroonian oriented, and a mixed type with majority presence of Cameroonians, but with a varied international composition. We also found that people from different countries appeared in all the personal networks. Many individuals cited as members of support networks were of Cameroonian origin, but they were living in the same area (not in the country of origin or another country), indicating the importance of proximity to daily life in our cases. This was accompanied by the tendency to reproduce and reinvent the homeland in the destination country. Intensive and extensive transnational practices were found in a minority of cases, as other investigations have found (Fong and others, 2010). As they are first-generation and very recent migrants, it would be a worthwhile challenge to investigate how personal networks and transnational practices vary over time, along with their incorporation into the Spanish society.

## Acknowledgements

This text was made possible by the support of the Spanish Ministry of Education through the Salvador Madariaga's Programme (PR2010-0524) and the hospitality of the Center for Migration and Development at Princeton University that benefitted one of the authors. We are also very grateful to the Fundación para la Cooperación Norte-Sur, the Cameroonian people, and everybody else who made this research possible.

## References

Ávila Molero, Javier (2009): Redes personales de africanos y latinoamericanos en Cataluña, España. Análisis reticular de integración y Cambio. In: Redes. Revista hispana para el análisis de redes sociales. Vol.15. 5. http://revista-redes.rediris.es [15.03.2011].

Barrera, Manuel (1980): A method of assessment of social support networks in community survey research. In: Connection. 3. pp. 8-13.

Capel, Horacio (2001): Inmigrantes extranjeros en España. El derecho a la movilidad y los conflictos de adaptación: grandes expectativas y duras realidades. In: Scripta Nova. 81. http://www.ub.edu/geocrit/sn-81.htm [02.08.2010].

De Federico, Ainhoa (2004): Los espacios sociales de la transnacionalidad. Una tipología de la integración relacional de los migrantes. In: Revista Hispana para el análisis de redes sociales. Vol. 7. 4. http://revista-redes.rediris.es [05.03.2011].

Escobar, Cristina (2010): Exploring Transnational Civil Society: A Comparative Study of Colombian, Dominican and Mexican Immigrant Organizations in the USA. In: Journal of Civil Society. 6. 3. pp. 205-235.

Faist, Thomas (2010): Towards Transnational Studies: World Theories, Transnationalisation and Changing Institutions. In: Journal of Ethnic and Migration Studies. Vol. 36. 10. pp. 1665-1687.

Fong, Eric and others (2010): Out of Sight, Out of Mind? Patterns of Transnational Contact Among Chinese and Indian Immigrants in Toronto. In: Sociological Forum. Vol. 25. pp. 428-449.

Gowricharn, Ruben (2009): Changing forms of transnationalism. In: Ethnic and Racial Studies. Vol. 32. 9. pp. 1619-1638.

Granovetter, Mark S. (1973): The strength of weak ties. In: The American Journal of Sociology. Vol 78. 6. pp. 1360-1380.
Gualda, Estrella/ Márquez, Carmen (2010): The Role of Social Networks in the small Cameroons' Community in Huelva (Spain): In the Way to Inclusion. In: Lucio-Villegas, Emilio (ed.): Transforming/ researching communities. Valencia: Diálogos red. pp. 127-140.
Guarnizo, Luis (2006): Migración, globalización y sociedad: teorías y tendencias en el siglo XX. In: Ardila, Gerardo (ed.): Colombia: migraciones, transnacionalismo y desplazamiento. Bogotá: Universidad Nacional de Colombia. pp. 65-113.
Instituto Nacional De Estadística (2010): Revisión del Padrón municipal de habitantes a 1 de enero de 2009. Madrid. http://www.ine.es [14.10.2010].
Izquierdo Escribano, Antonio (2000): Panorámica de la Inmigración en España en la antesala de 2000. In: Sociedad y Utopía. 16. pp. 57-70.
Martinez-Brawley, Emilia (2000): Close to Home: Human Services and the Small Community. Washington DC: NASW Press.
Massey, Douglas (1999): Why does the Immigration Occur? A theoretical Synthesis. In: Hirschman, Charles/ Kasinitz, Philip and De Wind, Josh (eds.): The Handbook of International Migration: The American Experience. New York: Russell Sage Foundation. pp. 34-52.
Massey, Douglas/ Espinosa, Kristin (1997): What's Driving Mexico-U.S. Migration? A Theoretical, Empirical and Policy Analysis. In: American Journal of Sociology. 102. pp. 939-999.
Maya, Isidro (2009): Mallas de paisanaje: el entramado de relaciones de los inmigrantes. In: Revista Hispana para el análisis de redes sociales. Vol. 17. pp. 273-300.
Metykova, Monika (2010): Only a mouse click away from home: transnational practices of Eastern European migrants in the United Kingdom. In: Social Identities. Vol. 16. 3. pp. 325-338.
Misawa, Takehiro (2001): Reproducción social y cultural de las familias de los inmigrantes japoneses en México: su impacto sobre la conformación de las expectativas de las relaciones intergeneracionales de los Nisei. In: Scripta Nova. Revista Electrónica de Geografía y Ciencias Sociales. No. 94. 52. http://www.ub.edu/geocrit/sn-94-52.htm#volver [12.1.2002].
Moldenhawer, Bolette (2005): Transnational migrant communities and education strategies among Pakistani youngsters in Denmark. In: Journal of Ethnic and Migration Studies. Vol. 31. 1. pp. 51-78.
Ostergaard, Eva (2009): La política a través de las fronteras: reflexiones sobre la dimensión transnacional de la participación política de los migrantes. In: Escrivá, Angeles/ Bermúdez, Anastasia and Moraes, Natalia (eds.): Migración y participación política. Estados, organizaciones y migrantes latinoamericanos en perspectiva local-transnacional. Madrid: Colección Politeya, CSIC. pp. 17-41.
Pascual, Angels/ Miguel, Verónica de/ Solana, Miguel (2007): Redes sociales de apoyo. La inserción de la población extranjera. Bilbao: Fundación BBVA.
Portes, Alejandro/ Escobar, Cristina/ Arana, Renelinda (2008): Bridging the gap: transnational and ethnic organizations in the political incorporation of immigrants in the United States. In: Ethnic and Racial Studies. Vol. 31. 6. pp. 1056-1090.
Portes, Alejandro/ Rivas, Alejandro (2011): The Adaptation of Migrant Children. In: The future of children. Vol. 21. 1. pp. 219-246.
Portes, Alejandro/ Rumbaut, Rubén (2006). Immigrant America: A portrait. Berkeley: University of California Press.
Tönnies, Ferdinnand (1963): Community and Society. New York: Harper & Row.

# Appendix I

Cameroonians' networks in Huelva and their typology by place of current residence

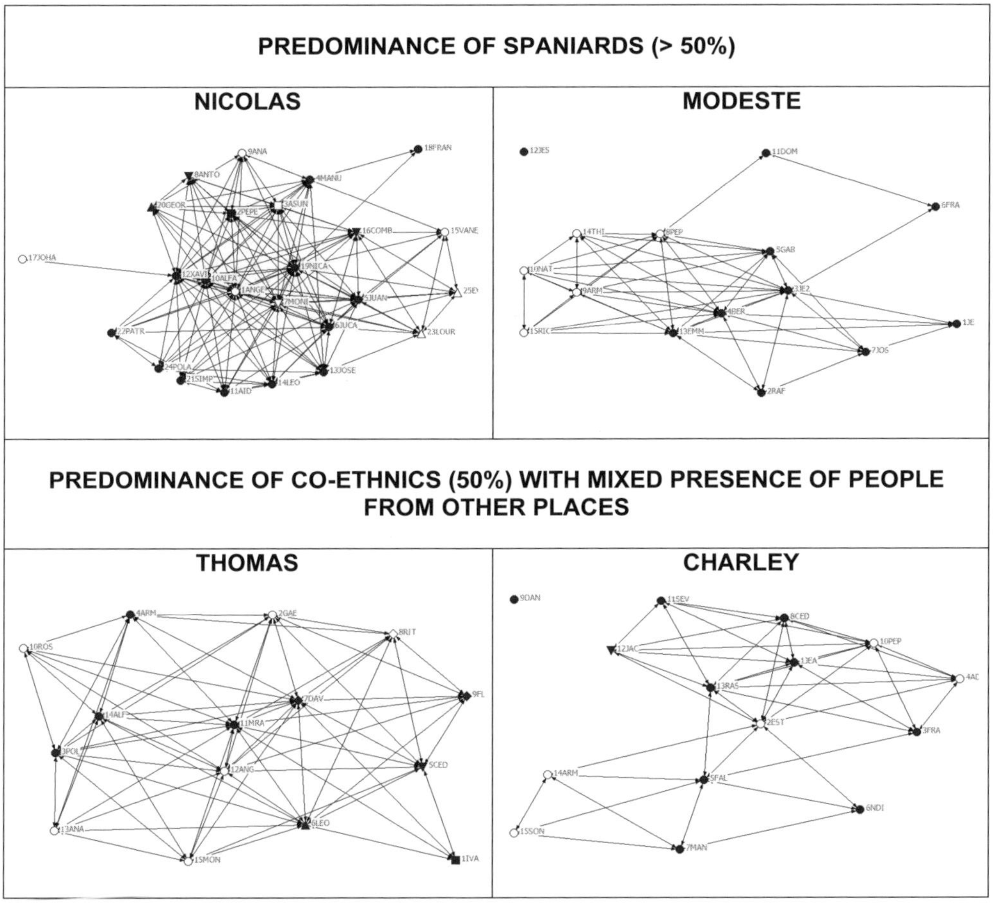


| GENDER | | PLACE OF CURRENT RESIDENCE | | | | | |
|---|---|---|---|---|---|---|---|
| Men | ■ | The same town or city than EGO | ○ | The same province (Huelva) | ▽ | The same region (Andalusia) | □ |
| Women | □ | Other place in Spain, not Andalusia | ◇ | Other European country | △ | Other countries | ⧖ |

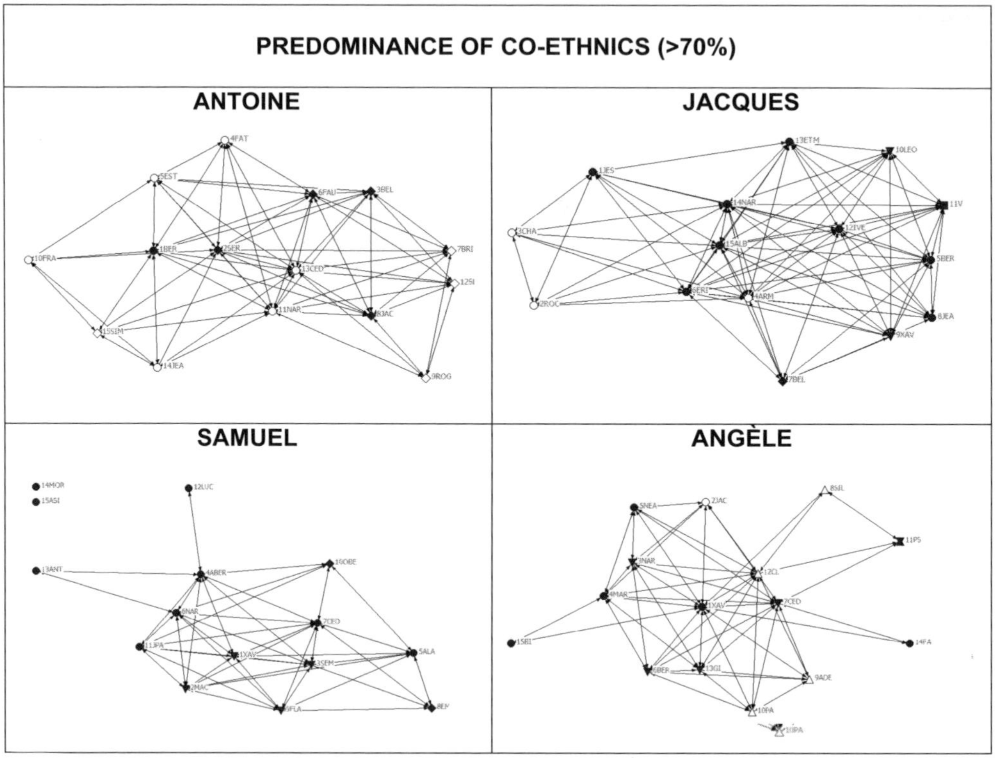


| GENDER | | PLACE OF CURRENT RESIDENCE | | | | | |
|---|---|---|---|---|---|---|---|
| Men | ■ | The same town or city than EGO | ○ | The same province (Huelva) | ▽ | The same region (Andalusia) | □ |
| Women | □ | Other place in Spain, not Andalusia | ◇ | Other European country | △ | Other countries | ⧗ |

Source: Authors, with the help of Ucinet 6 and Netdraw 2 software. All names are pseudonyms.

# Appendix II

Cameroonians' networks in Huelva and their typology by place of current residence

*Predominance of Spaniards (> 50%)*

**NICOLAS**

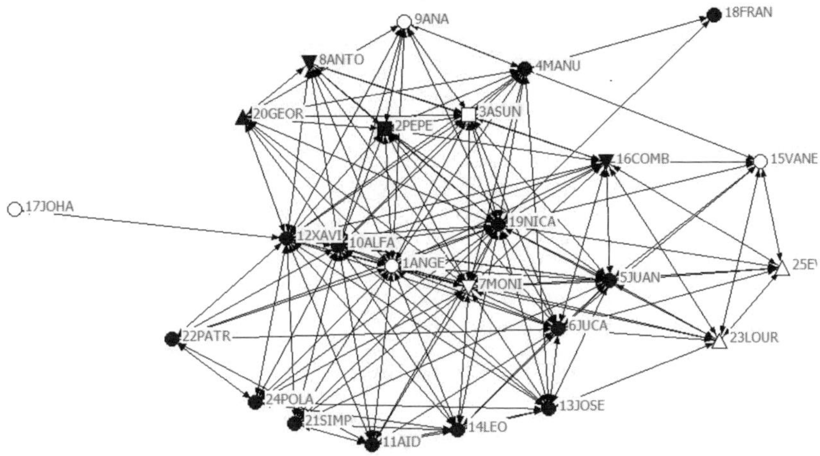


**MODESTE**

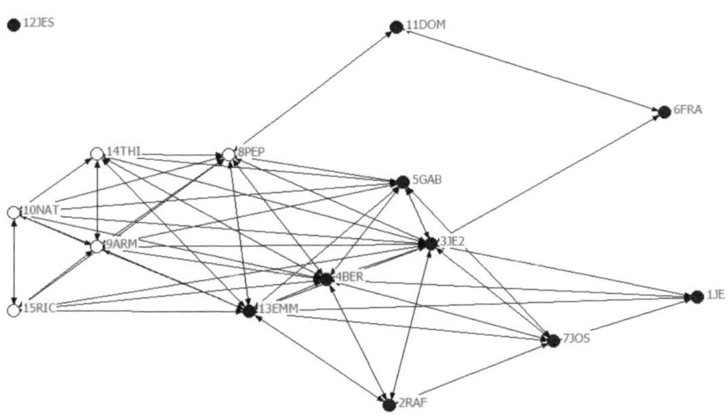


| GENDER | | PLACE OF CURRENT RESIDENCE | | | | | |
|---|---|---|---|---|---|---|---|
| Men | ■ | The same town or city than EGO | ○ | The same province (Huelva) | ▽ | The same region (Andalusia) | □ |
| Women | □ | Other place in Spain, not Andalusia | ◇ | Other European country | △ | Other countries | ⧗ |

*Predominance of co-ethics (50%) with mixed presence of people from other places*

**THOMAS**

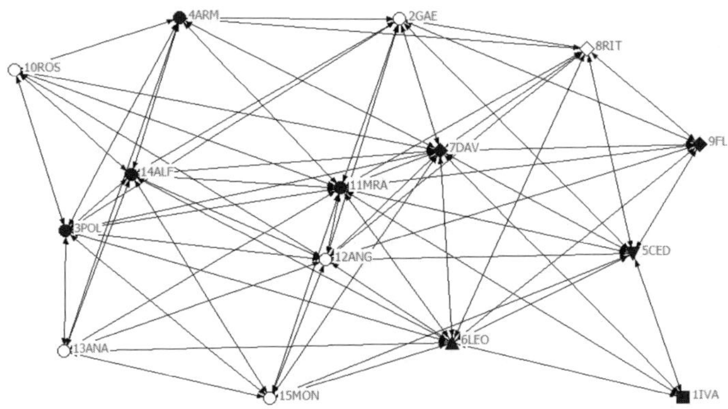


**CHARLEY**

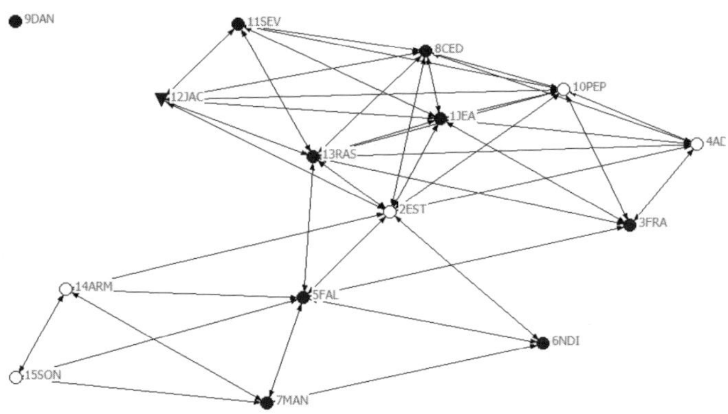


| GENDER | | PLACE OF CURRENT RESIDENCE | | | | | |
|---|---|---|---|---|---|---|---|
| Men | ■ | The same town or city than EGO | ○ | The same province (Huelva) | ▽ | The same region (Andalusia) | □ |
| Women | □ | Other place in Spain, not Andalusia | ◇ | Other European country | △ | Other countries | ⧖ |

*Predominance of co-ethics (>70%)*

**ANTOINE**

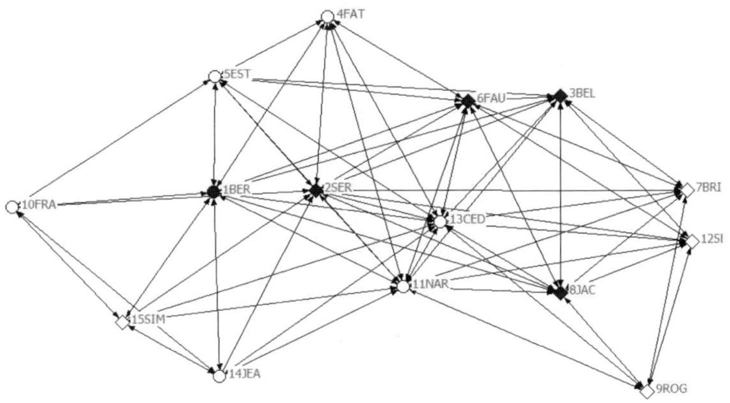


**JACQUES**

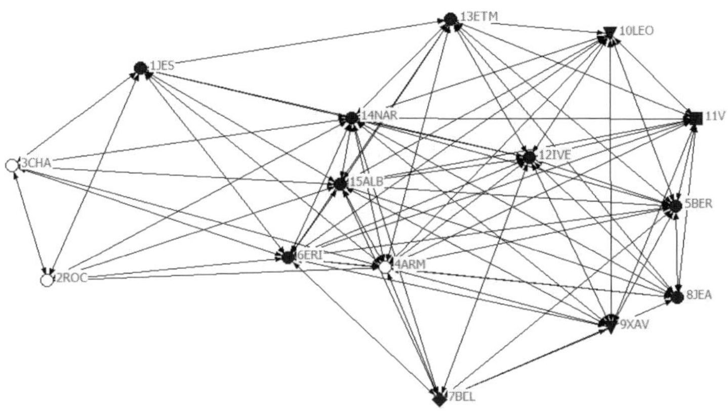


| GENDER | | PLACE OF CURRENT RESIDENCE | | | | | |
|---|---|---|---|---|---|---|---|
| Men | ■ | The same town or city than EGO | ○ | The same province (Huelva) | ▽ | The same region (Andalusia) | □ |
| Women | □ | Other place in Spain, not Andalusia | ◇ | Other European country | △ | Other countries | ⧗ |

## SAMUEL

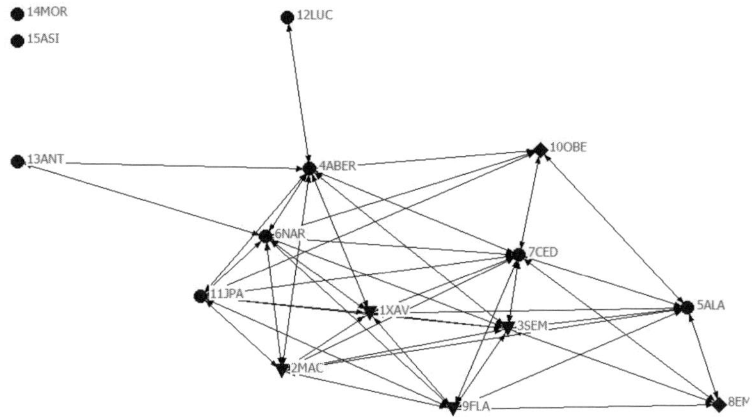


## ANGÈLE

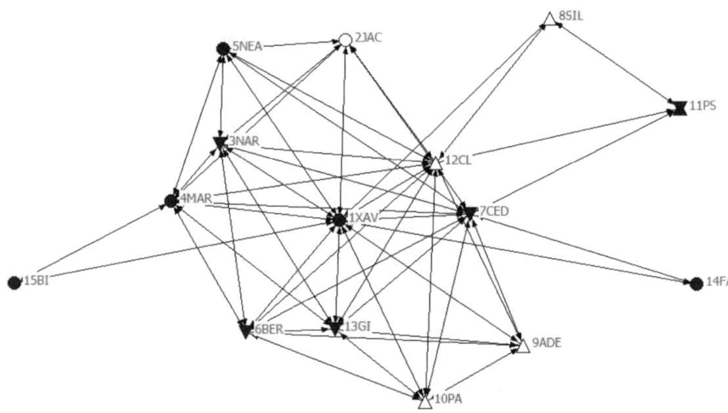


| GENDER | PLACE OF CURRENT RESIDENCE | | |
|---|---|---|---|
| Men ■ | The same town or city than EGO ○ | The same province (Huelva) ▽ | The same region (Andalusia) □ |
| Women □ | Other place in Spain, not Andalusia ◇ | Other European country △ | Other countries ⧗ |

Source: Authors, with the help of Ucinet 6 and Netdraw 2 software. All names are pseudonyms.

# How to Share Space?

## Inside/Outside/Along/Within/Together

*Elke Krasny*

> *What is it that has been given up in the shift from the investigative and the analytical to the performative and the participatory?*
> Irit Rogoff (2011)

## Abstract

*Social relations, cultural politics and identity struggles are organized spatially. In a transnational perspective, spatial definitions like inside, outside, along, within or together take on new social, political, cultural and artistic meanings. Sharing needs spaces. The archaic if idealized idea of sharing becomes highly politicized. Paradigmatic sharings with three individuals, who have never met each other, form the structure of this text as an act of sharing. Their everyday and artistic practices represent differences within transnationality. Different practices and spaces are mobilized to explore ways of sharing transnationally. The three of them consider sharing of political, social, cultural and artistic importance. Therefore they not only happily agreed to become part of the exchange but also wanted to share their names. Consequently, their subjectivities and positionalities constitute this transnational sharing. Acting under their names and not being rendered anonymous leads to a transnational presence of their voices constituting the creation of this text as a space of sharing. All the voices together build and weave this text. Sharing not only needs spaces, but also practices of reflecting the very conditions of their making. The text's structure is based on sharings with Estela Tschernutter, an immigrant whose biography is marked by colonialism, war and love and who works at a Fair Trade World Shop in Vienna, Branka Cvjeticanin, a Zagreb based artist, whose family history is marked by migration and wars ever since the late 19th century which permeates her artistic practice and Dan S. Wang, a writer, printer, artist and activist, based in the Midwest of the US, who explores the trajectory of his family's ancestry in China addressing issues of missing solidarity. The text echoes the structure of the sharings, gradually revealing the altered meanings spatial adverbs such as inside, outside, along, within or together take on in individuals' transnational every day.*

## Introduction: On the Importance of Sharing

What is it that we are gaining in the shift from the investigative and the analytical to the performative and the participatory? Shifting within a question, like the one posed by Irit Rogoff (2011), from loss to gain, is applied to the key question of this chapter, which is, what we gain, rather than what we lose, when we try to produce knowledge on how to share space transnationally. This chapter examines the idea that we are in need of new ways of sharing to understand how space is produced transnationally. Sharing is a profoundly spatial question. I focus on the question of how to share space under transnational conditions. This led to a research process on how to share space transnationally based on paradigmatic encounters with three individuals, Estela Tschernutter, Branka Cvetajevic and Dan S. Wang. Their transnational trajectories form the basis to work out two concepts of transnationality, which I want to call itinerant transnationality and localized transnationality. Whereas the first denotes the traditional notion of transnationality characterized by migration processes and layered senses of belonging, the latter refers to radical changes of any given place, be it through wars, revolutions or profound shifts in political regimes and ideologies, leading to equally layered senses of belongings for the individuals who still carry on in the same place which, after all, is not the same place at all.

In shifting from the analytical and the investigative to the performative and participatory, this chapter not only aims at revealing the two concepts of transnationality, but also at how space can be shared transnationally as a specific way of knowledge production from within together with others. Trans means across, through or beyond. "Going beyond" means that I opened up the text as a platform of sharing. And, above all, the condition of transnationality presses us for other ways of knowledge production. I understand this text as a contribution to sharing counteracting hegemonial conditions dictatorially imposing that we neither have space nor time for sharing, even though it is only through acts of sharing that we could eventually arrive at a transnational practice of writing the history of our present.

## Boundaries and Junctures

Following the work of Henri Lefebvre space is identified as the "production of space" (Lefebvre, 1991), which today has to be understood as a transnational practice of the production of transnational spaces. Space or rather "thirdspace" in the words of Edward William Soja is where "everything comes together (…) subjectivity and objectivity, the abstract and the concrete, the real and the imagined, the knowable and the unimaginable, the repetitive and the differential, structure and agency, mind and body, consciousness and the unconscious, the disciplined and the transdisciplinary, everyday life and unending history" (Soja, 1996: 57). Are we to understand space as everything coming together, then sharing on space with others opens up a complex production of knowledge on how space is produced transnationally. Starting from thirdspace we will have to develop an understanding of what I would like to call trans-space, thirdspace produced as itinerant and temporally layered space running through people's biographies as a connector yet also differentiator. Looking closely at the word trans-space, I will use all the three parts of the words, as a conceptual device of reflection. The word in itself becomes a trans-space composed of trans and space and a hyphen which I understand as a dynamic border, a 'culture of the frontier spatially becoming literal, setting apart what it connects, connecting what it divides. The hyphen acts as the border within, joining the two parts of the word together, yet still stringing along their being separate. They have an influence on each other which is owed to and multiplied by the hyphen, the border within. I am looking at the hyphen as a border and a juncture. The hyphen becomes constitutive for the making of a trans-space establishing a connection as an act of sharing between "trans" and "space", but this sharing is not only to be seen as an easily achieved connection, it can equally be seen as conflictual and agonal. This is what this chapter aims to do, establishing acts of sharing between "trans" and "space" questioning borders and junctures from within together with others. Sharing establishes junctures between the here and the now, the "there" and the "then". The space of sharing needs to be resilient yet adaptable, emerging yet reliable, transforming yet trusted and recognizable. Sharing trans-space becomes a critical act.

## Sharing Transnationality

The first sharing is based on an interview with Estela Tschernutter who works at the Weltladen Lerchenfelder Street Vienna. Estela Tschernutter's narrative of her biographical trajectory connects Lisbon, Luanda, Salzburg and Vienna. Itinerant transnationality joins the spaces of her biographic trajectory. Localized transnationality shaped these spaces, be it the Angolan War of Independence, which the Portuguese called the Portuguese Colonial War, or the Carnation Revolution in Portugal. Estela grew up in Angola during the time of the war. She returned to her homeland Portugal with her parents. Angola ceased to be a Portuguese colony. During her school days, Portugal turned from a dictatorship into a democracy. When Estela Tschernutter left Portugal for Austria, she was a citizen of the EU. Upon entering Austria, she was still a citizen of the EU, but living outside of the EU, as Austria at that point in time had not joined the EU yet. Both, the itinerant transnationality and the localized transnationality come to the fore in Estela's narratives.

The second sharing is based on an exchange with Branka Cvjeticanin, a Zagreb-based, whose family history is marked by migration ever since the late 19th century, when it comes to the male line of the family, and by changing regimes, states and ideologies, ranging from the Habsburg-Monarchy to Yugoslavia and to current Croatia when it comes to the female line of the family. Wars, upheavals, ethnic and religious tensions surround the Krbava field, where the female part of Branka's family resided. This former battlefield is a vast empty space surrounded by small villages. The matrilinear transnationality follows the concept of localized transnationality whereas the patrilinear transnationality follows the concept of itinerant transnationality going from a remote and isolated village near the Krbava field to New York City. Branka grew up in what is now called Ex-Yugoslavia. She has lived in New York City for several years and has now returned to Zagreb. Branka's artistic research leads to a performative exploration of family constellations around the battlefield of Krbava, where she travelled together with me, as her only audience. Again both, the itinerant transnationality and the localized transnationality, played out powerfully in Branka's site-specific and spatially reflective performance.

The third sharing is based on an e-mail exchange with Dan S. Wang, a writer, printer, artist and activist, based in the Midwest of the US, who currently explores the trajectory of his family's ancestry in China, though not so much under a biographical focus, but rather from a critical angle revolving around late capitalism and the overarching theme of missing solidarity, be it in the U.S. or in China. Dan's experience of having lived in Michigan now resonates with his artistic research process in Penglai, China. Itinerant transnationality marks his travelling to Penglai. Localized transnationality marks his observations of the blatant similarities between Detroit and Penglai owed to the dramatic effects of globalization.

## Interview with Estala Tschernutter

The meetings with Estela Tschernutter took place at the Weltladen. Surrounded by the smells of organically cultivated and fairly traded coffee, we settled down for the interview. As Estela hospitably offered me a cup of coffee, we started talking about her biographical trajectory. Born in Lisbon in 1967, Estela spent her childhood in the city of Luanda, Angola. "As a child I spent several years in Angola. That was at the time of the colonial war. My father fought in the war in the bush. My mother had a normal job" (Tschernutter, 2010: 220). Even though she has never returned to Angola, the place is still within her. Estela emphasizes that she feels "close to the sub-Saharan Africa". "The house where I lived in Luanda had a huge advertisement for beer on it. This advertisement was for a brand of beer by the name of Cuca. It was a big neon sign. People, who are familiar with Luanda, know the house I am speaking of, they recognize it immediately" (Tschernutter, 2010: 220). Not only can she identify the house for others, who know Luanda, but she also procured an image of it by describing it to someone at the Angolan embassy in Vienna. Upon returning to Lisbon, Estela went to a Montessori-oriented elementary school. The Carnation Revolution, which changed Portugal from an authoritarian dictatorship to a democracy, shaped Estela's early school experiences. "We were allowed to paint all the walls. During recess we held political meeting. What happened all over the country, also happened at our school. We were given permission to let this happen at our school. (…). The revolution changed the schools, since the revolution girls and boys were given the right to attend the same schools" (Tschernutter, 2010: 220). In 1991 Estela arrived in Austria. She moved from Lisbon to Salzburg: "I arrived in Salzburg in December 1991. I came with my books and my clothes and a shell collection from the sea side" (Tschernutter, 2010: 222). The initial transition was a smooth one. Her sense of being pushed outside arose along with a profound change of the political climate. "At the beginning I really enjoyed it. But then it became very difficult. At that time the rise of Jörg Haider happened" (Tschernutter, 2010: 222). Estela Tschernutter's itinerant transnationality corresponds with spatial layers of memory production and multiple senses of belongings. Each specific place of her trajectory is marked by localized transnationality. Even if she would go back, the Angola of her childhood and the Portugal of her school days does not exist any longer. Estela Tschernutter's biographical trajectory stands for a specifically European transnationality marked by the complex history of colonialism and by political shifts from an authoritarian dictatorship into a democracy in Portugal as well as by political shifts to right-wing everyday racism in Austria. Itinerant and localized transnationality together shape

Estela Tschernutter's biographical trajectory which is part of a transnational European history of the present yet to be written.

## Walking and Talking with Branka Cvjeticanin

The meeting with Branka Cvjeticanin involved a preparatory process via e-mail and a walk across the Krbava field. It was at a walk project on issues of women's history and remembering which I conducted in Zagreb in 2010 when Branka approached me with the idea of being her audience when crossing the Krbava field which in turn led to my invitation to make this text. In February 2011 I travelled to Croatia by train, crossing several boarders within Europe. The next day we travelled to the Krbava field by car. Branka's partner Sandro assumed the role of the driver. He took the car to the other side of the field and awaited us there. Branka and I set out to traverse the Krbava field, leaden with historical implications. The Krbava field is where a battle was fought between the Ottoman Empire and the Kingdom of Hungary in 1493. Nobody ever traverses the field in its entire length. Rumors of wolves and mysterious myths keep people out. Ever since the Balkan wars a group of men from Bosnia herds sheep in the field. They had been prewarned of our coming and had consented to let us cross peacefully. Already after the first few steps into the field, our cheeks and fingers went numb from the cold. The wind chill factor added to the relentless cold. Branka unpacked two black pieces of cloth. They were the same ones her maternal grandmother would have worn to protect her from the cold when she dared to venture into the field. All along the walk, which took a little over four hours, Branka would unpack objects from her backpack and stage the scene for performative encounters with the vast landscape and its connections to her family history and its displaced memories. All the houses, Branka explained, were built around the field. The field was to be watched only, but not to be traversed or used for farming. The field came to represent the complex layers of changing historic constellations. The lives of the females in her family were marked by changes in regimes, ideologies and political constellations. Yet, they stayed, passed traditions on and invested themselves in the localized transnationality. They knew how to orient their houses so the wind could pass through and the smells from within would not bother the neighboring houses. They knew how to tell stories to the little ones to keep them out of the field. They knew how to keep in touch with their husbands who had left them behind for the better life in New York. They knew how to compose family photographs even though the family was never united in one place. Branka used each of these pieces of information to turn them into part of the performance on the field. She created an ephemeral trans-space vulnerably exposed to the strong wind and the bitter cold. With a seemingly endless horizon, the former battle field was turned into a physically challenging trans-space rife with personal and collective memories. It was Branka's intention to evoke these memories, if only for a moment. Her artistic research into the transnational constellations of her complex family history involves a performative approach of mixing storytelling with facts. Branka opened up a radical moment of sharing with only one member of audience, me. She plans on repeating this one-to-one encounter by inviting others to traverse the battle field with her in the future.

Branka Cvjeticanin's story stands for a specifically European transnationality marked by the history of emigration since the late 19th century as well as by the history of wars and upheaval marking the shifts in regimes and ideologies for the ones who stayed in a place which never remained the same. The two concepts of transnationality embodied through Branka's family constellations become even more complex in their genderedness. While males of the family being the ones on the move, the females of the family being the ones staying behind. Branka Cvjeticanin's trajectory brings both of these gendered positions of her family constellation together in her own biography. She grew up in what is now called Ex-Yugoslavia. She went on to live in New York. She returned to live in Zagreb. Transnationality runs through her family constellations and her performative artistic explorations.

## E-mail Conversation with Dan S. Wang

The sharing with Dan S. Wang evolved through an e-mail conversation, which is in part shared in this text. In the fall of 2010, I was part of the conference "space Re:solutions. Intervention and Research in Visual Culture", convened by Christine Hohenbüchler, Peter Mörtenböck and Helge Mooshammer. This is where I first met with Dan S. Wang and heard him speak about his artistic research connecting Detroit, Michigan and Penglai, China. The sharing in our e-mails is organized spatially by means of interspersing, underlining and referring back.

"In using your biographical constellation (...) you established a transnational trajectory leading to a mapping transcending the personal by far. (...) In this context I would like to ask you if your attributions of what you consider inside and outside have changed through the process? Maybe you could extrapolate if there was a preconceived notion of inside before you departed? If there was an outside after your return? If inside and outside played a role in the spatialisation of your thinking" (Elke, e-mail to Dan 2011). In his answer to my e-mail Dan explored the questions of borders and junctures of inside and outside and how these not only constitute space but become embodied as lived spatial practice.

"The question of inside and outside, where does the one end and the other begin, how one is made to exist either inside or outside, and what exactly is the nature of any given space that for whatever reasons is divided into inside and outside – certainly these questions ring loudly throughout all the phases of my research. This is precisely because, to begin with, the methods at a base level are, as you say, irreducible to my embodied self, in space. After all, I am traveling to these different places. So on a profoundly literal bodily level, I am "inside" Detroit when I've crossed into the city and "outside" before and after the visit. I was "inside" Penglai for the five days I was there, and I am "outside" Penglai now. The experience of crossing national boundaries, especially in the post-9/11 era, is a brute reminder that the bodily level matters a great deal when it comes to determining whether where one plants a foot is inside or outside (...)" (Dan, e-mail to Elke 2011).

In responding to Dan's e-mail I shifted the question to the embodiment of spaces and how they are still within when physically left behind.

"What I am wondering is if there is a longing on your part, which might also be a driver which is used methodologically or comes to fruition conceptually, to reconstitute insides and outsides as experiences made distinguishable from each other. There seems to be a disruptive entanglement of insides and outsides which culturally bleed into each other and feed each other, but are disrupted and tormented politically and socially. What I would like to ask as a next step of movements of extrapolations is how much of an inside of Detroit within you and of an inside of Penglai within you filters into the afterwards, the outside again. What is the residue resonating through this and how could a socio-political agenda be formulated exactly through this bodily construct of a cultural struggle taking place within (…)" (Elke, e-mail to Dan 2011).

Dan's answer to my e-mail started a discussion on global citizenship in which he challenges conventional notions of existing juridical regimes limiting the political status as democratic citizens to territorially-defined units. Dan continues to question the very idea of borders. "Perhaps this slippage of identity particularly in regard to place-identification could be the beginnings of some theory of belonging that attacks the borders of, say, nation-states, and lays the foundation for some well-reasoned claim on a global political agency that transcends, circumvents, and/or renders national boundaries irrelevant or peripheral. Obviously, international borders are enforced with the full might of the state's coercive powers. But, even there, as with the details that go into the various rights of return and the crush of undocumented migrants in countries all over the world, ambiguities remain present. Governmental efforts to define, address, or even find, exactly, who is in and who is out, only exposes the reality of this slippage happening all around and within us, all of the time (…)" (Dan, e-mail to Elke 2011).

Based on his artistic practice and the strategies involved, Dan perceives the body as a site of border crossing and transnationality as a deep connectedness between places and regimes albeit marked by distinctly different shapings of history and histories. "Making a link between Detroit and Penglai through the course of an artistic research project offers a far cry from the concreteness of my Illinois-Wisconsin job/life. But nonetheless, the whole point of the project is to ask, if the condition and fate of society in Detroit have something to do with the condition and fate of the people who visit Penglai nowadays as tourists and the economic trends of Penglai in general? If the answer, as I show through all of my research, is a very complicated yes, then the grounds of our political claims must include, for the strength in its irreducibility, the body as a site of border crossing and multiple, shifting belongings. (…) Opening up transnational space in the kind of research I do is exactly about stretching, condensing, perforating, and liquefying one's experience and notions of space, distance, and time, such that the irreducibility of the embodied experience becomes only one of many spatial modes. A more pointed reason for such flexibility would be to dilute as much as is possible the control regimes – mostly administered by security forces, police, and national authorities – that keep bodies inside or outside" (Dan, e-mail to Elke 2011).

Dan S. Wang's artistic research stands for both, itinerant as well as localized transnationality, joining American-Chinese and Chinese-American relations by way of bringing to the fore the most blatantly striking similarities between Detroit, Michigan and Penglai, China. His practice as an artist follows his network of kin relations, which serves as a ready-made basis for cultivating a longer term relationship to the part of the world where his family immigrated from. Yet, this is not to be mistaken with a sentimental nostalgia or a simple seeking for one's roots. Quite on the contrary, Dan is more than critical of reducing artistic practice to biographical conditions or, in other words, to the determinism of origin and ancestry. What he tries to do as an artist, is open up a strategy of transnational research that mobilizes this positionality of a subjectivity marked by a history of immigration, but using it structurally and politically to address issues otherwise not explored. Even though he is very aware of risking a reproduction of certain traditional values of essentialism and determinism of which he is very critical, he acts out what family relationships mandate, in order to transcend these relationships through a transnational artistic practice establishing insights and connectivities between times, spaces and regimes.

## Conclusion: Why Sharing Needs Spaces

Creating ways of how to share space in order to understand how space is produced transnationally orients our thinking "toward a history of the vanishing present" (Spivak, 1999). It is both an individual challenge and a collective task to establish spaces of sharing in order to create narratives of the conditions we live in.

In order to open up a space of sharing which reveals the potentialities but also the inherent problematics of borders which need to be crossed over and over again when it comes to the very creation of sharing transnationally, I invited three individuals whose every day and artistic practices not only result from transnationality but also use these ready-made conditions as a mandate of critical reflection, action and creation. Their knowledge and experience serve as the basis of making manifest that sharing needs spaces that allow for meetings. Different spaces lead to different meetings. Different meetings produce very different potentials of reflexivity and knowledge production on transnationality. Transnational sharing is neither fixed nor preconceived, but rather situational and specific. This article is based on this situationality and specificity in order to emphasize its general importance, which is not to be mistaken with an essentialization or generalization, but rather opens up the potentiality of general demands on the creation of transnational spaces which allow for sharing without the impediment and restrictions of borders. The political is challenged by the personal. By demanding spaces for transnational exchange it then becomes clear that the quest for situationality and specificity posits the requirement for political, social and cultural change. The seemingly minoritarian and humble position of situationality and specificity under transnational conditions aiming for spaces of transnational sharing addresses issues of history (with capital H), wars, migrations, borders, political regimes and economic systems. The knowledge gleaned from transnational sharings like the ones this article is based on leads to the explosive connections and demands between the political and the personal from a transnational perspective in a lived in and acted out trans-space yet to be produced, yet to be produced over and over and over again.

Sharing is both a cultural and a spatial practice intended to unfold the importance of connectivities and resonances between spaces connected through the cartographies and constellations of people's biographies bursting wide open the narrow confines of the traditional writing history still following the shadows and echoes of the nation-state under the altered conditions of transnationality. In a transnational perspective, inside, outside, along, within or together take on altered spatial meanings. Resonance and connectivity can be considered the key words for the writing of a history of the present as a trans-space based on shared experiences of transnationality. Sharing needs spaces for critical differentiation of both, itinerant as well as localized transnationality.

## References


Lefebvre, Henri (1991): The Production of Space. Oxford, Malden: Blackwell Publishers Ltd.

Rogoff, Irit (2011): What is a Theorist? http://www.transformazium.org/log/2011/05/irit-rogoff-what-is-a-theorist/ [31.08.2011].

Soja, Edward William (1996): Third Space. Oxford, Malden: Blackwell Publishers Ltd.

Spivak, Gayatri Chakravorty (1999): A Critique of Postcolonial Reason. Toward a History of the Vanishing Present. Cambridge, London: Harvard University Press.

Tschernutter, Estela (2010): Estela Tschernutter. Weltladen Wien 1080. In: Heide, Angela/ Krasny, Elke (2010): Aufbruch in die Nähe. Wien Lerchenfelder Straße. Mikrogeschichten zwischen Lokalidentitäten und Globalisierung. Other Places. Vienna Lerchenfelder Street. Micro-histories between local identities and globalization. Wien: Turia + Kant Verlag. pp. 220-223.

E-mail Exchange between Elke Krasny and Dan S. Wang, Summer 2011.

# II

# Migration and Border Regions

# A Transnational Politics of Mobility

## Thinking From and Across Borders

*Jennifer M. Murphy*


### Abstract

*This chapter explores the following question: how do we begin to talk about and theorize the distinct movements of peoples across borders and boundaries in a way that critically assesses the uneven geographies of transnational movement constitutive of borders? I contend that it is innocuous to construct a theoretical "transnational politics of mobility" without first probing the uneven transnational movements of peoples and the unequal rules that govern and sanction mobility. Thus, the theoretical concept of "the coloniality of power" must be the starting point of any theoretical discussion on transnational mobility. It is only through understanding the "coloniality of power" that a transformative transnational politics of mobility can be constructed and our territorially fixed notions of the nation challenged. This requires thinking from the borders to reconfigure our epistemologies of the global and the local, unsettle the colonial project, and challenge the hegemonic imaginary and the technologies of power that manage space and movement.*


### By Way of Introduction: Borders and Boundaries

From March to May of 2011, *The New York Times* published multiple articles on "illegal" immigration globally. Examples include "Fleeing North Africa and Landing in an Italian Limbo" (Donadio, 2011), "Smuggling People Is Big Business – X-rays Prove It" (Corcoran, 2011), and "Now Feeling Free, but Still Without Work, Tunisians Look Toward Europe," (Sayare, 2011). These articles address "illegal" movements of people and the problems that arise in categorizing "them" once outside the bounds of commonly accepted national identifiers. Are they "illegal" immigrants, refugees or asylum seekers? The topic of transnational movement (border crossings) and its categorization is an interdisciplinary one that has been taken up vigorously in the last decade by students and practitioners of globalization studies, postcolonial studies, citizenship studies, human geography and critical theory. The discourse has crossed back and forth between the humanities and social sciences, albeit not always in intentional conversation with one another. The main point here is that these types of "forced-choice" cross-border movements are integral to the epistemologies of transnational movement and boundaries and borders – transnational spaces to localized territories. However, it is necessary to transform our immediate perceptions and assumptions with regards to such movements in order to critically examine first how we talk about, label and represent them and second the implications of such discourses and orderings.

In this light, what happens if I pose the issues in a considerably different although parallel manner, setting internationally accepted politico-juridical terms and signifiers against detailed and disturbing *New York Times* descriptions? What analytical perspectives can be gained through the media's captured x-ray images of "ghostly outlines of a clandestine business worth billions a year," people "packed tighter than cattle and transported like consumer goods in tractor trailers" (Corcoran, 2011) or "thousands of bodies" fleeing unrest and economic hardship in North Africa only to be imprisoned indefinitely in Puglia Center, an Italian immigration detention camp (Donadio, 2011)?

Suddenly, the politico-juridical categorizations appear inadequate. In fact, by juxtaposing these two interrogatories, it is possible to see how our sterile and simplified analytic designations not only fail to capture the individual stories of the "movers," but also displace them from critical context, mostly notably, historical colonial dynamics and current neoliberal globalization global-system level structures and processes. This context is essential to real understanding. When it is not included, it is as though the acts of movement across national borders and boundaries somehow exist in a (geo)political, economic and social vacuum, one which spontaneously produces the "illegal" immigrant, the refugee and the asylum seeker.

These dehistoricized and "rootless" constructions do not factor in the weightiness of a Euro-United States colonial history/present or domination and subjugation inherent to global capitalism(s). These peoples moving across borders and boundaries have been uprooted from their "homelands" for reasons as diverse or as inclusively connective as conflict, famine, economic hardships, political discriminations, sexual persecution etc. Their new designations often disregard their histories, personal stories and places in global capitalist economies. Thus, these prescribed identities bury critical details: they fail to consider the situations of these transnational movers or that forced-choice migrations are "historically and geographically contingent," determined and generated by "unequal power relations" (Hyndman, 2000: 60).

Does it necessarily follow that by having multiple identities linked to more than one nation, these movers actually "challenge academic orderings, territorially fixed notions of nation, and assimilationist narratives of immigration" (ibid.: 167)? Does it follow that our understandings of cultural and political identities, now hybrid and dynamic due to such transnational movement, are "more about routes than roots" (Cresswell, 2006: 1)?

Simply put, the answer is no, but as all things human, it is not that simple. When these peoples are subsumed in the territorial master narrative of the nation they are disempowered, and territorially fixed notions of nation remain unchallenged. Even their transitory or prolonged existence in spaces that appear to be supranational, above the nation-state, like the Puglia center, are treated as states of exception, the camp, (Agamben, 2005) and are still very much a part of the territorial and sovereign order of things. In this paradigm, their act of movement, which in and of itself is an autonomous act of agency, cannot unfortunately be separated from the relationship of their individual circumstances and the "coloniality of power" (Quijano, 1997: 2000) that subjugates them to unequal and racialized power relations. Before the act of movement has been set in motion it has already been territorialized. The idea of being uprooted from homes and historical realities discussed above is embedded in the very language we use to describe such movement (Malkki, 1992: 24-28). These categories help reinforce in a politico-juridical way already established orders of domination that are complex and dynamic, interconnected and transnational. In short, these acts of transnational movement do not liberate the actor or the action from the master territorial narrative.

It is not, however, the mobility of peoples and their categories or the causes resulting in such movements that concern me. Rather, my analytical inquiry lies in the tendency to ground transnational globalization (globality/locality) discussions on migration and displacement of peoples on the false premise that they have somehow transcended or are contesting, both figuratively and physically, the bounds of the nation-state simply by crossing them. In this view, movement across borders and boundaries is seen as a liberating force that frees our conceptual understandings of ontological orientation from territory. I began my inquiry by suggesting that neat, tidy and legal terminologies do not adequately reflect the real life messy, entangled and "illegal" movements of peoples. Similarly, these transnational examples do not automatically free us from the confines of the nation-state, thereby creating a "transnational politics of mobility," (Hyndman, 2000) a concept I explore in detail below. I contend that we cannot construct a theoretical transnational politics of mobility without first probing the "coloniality of transnational mobility" that is closely connected to place, geography, history and the nation.

## Transnational Politics of Mobility

In a speech at an IBEW (International Brotherhood of Electrical Workers) labor leadership conference on June 9, 2011, Stanford professor Clay Carson, history professor and executive director of the Martin Luther King Jr., Institute for Research and Education, stated that people "move" in two ways to improve their status in society: via migration to the city and across borders, usually under duress and breaking laws in order to find greater economic opportunity and via political struggle. Therefore, such movements constitute acts of struggle that defy existing structures. This comment forces the following question: how do we begin to talk about and theorize the distinct movement of peoples across borders and boundaries in a way that critically addresses the "uneven geographies of power and status" constitutive of borders (Hyndman, 2000:1) as well as transnational movements?

Hyndman argues that a transnational politics of mobility "aims to theorize unequal power relations in a context that pays attention to identities formed within, beyond, and in spite of nation-states (...) in a transnational context" (ibid.: 30). It involves the "ongoing crossing of borders – political, cultural, economic, and social" (ibid.: 190). In this context, movement across space is both political and active and national borders are "cartographies of struggle," as well as regulators of how mobility is understood and constructed (ibid.: xvi). Such movements belong not only to a discourse of conventional geopolitics, but also to discourses on movement itself (Cresswell, 2006). The ability or "right" to move may be prohibited and stigmatized as in the figure of the "illegal other" or privileged and justified like the "legal traveler/tourist". Mobility is, simply, regulated.

These regulations and our conceptualizations of movement are constructed by our discourses on movement, which are often contradictory. In a "modern" context, mobility has been defined "as progress, as freedom, as opportunity, and as modernity," while also signifying "shiftlessness," "deviance," and "resistance" (Cresswell, 2006: 1f.). Movement – freedom of or barred against – is imbued with meaning. Movement is also a signifier of power and the representations of mobility "capture and make sense of" how we are "allowed" to relate to the world (ibid.: 3). These productions of meanings are many times ideological, a dynamic that Cresswell denominates "ideological codings of mobility" (ibid.: 9). Mobility means "X." Mobility means social surveillance, control, domination and marginalization, while simultaneously meaning progress, freedom and change (ibid.: 43). The questions then arise, for whom and constructed by whom?

Cresswell concludes that this differential of mobility that projects sociopolitical meanings and legitimization onto bodies creates either the "alien" or the "citizen" – the legitimate or the illegitimate – and is state-imposed (ibid.: 193). Furthermore, these meanings are by their nature political and derive from characterizations of health, class, race and gender. Thereby, surveillance, simulation and security mix with a "hybrid space of code, people, and physical structures" (ibid.: 238). However, Cresswell sees these relationships of dominance working within the structure of the state, rather than part and parcel of the state as structure. The power of the state to impose meaning on an individual or group is not a dihistoricized power. Hyndman correctly asserts that borders breed politics and uneven geographies of power and status, but similar to Cresswell, she misses a very important point. Borders do not generate marginalization, racism and other unequal relations of power (Hyndman, 2000: 27). They are in and of themselves marginalizing, racist and unequal. The state is intrinsically classist, racist and gendered.

To bridge the conceptual gap between the important theoretical conversations begun by Cresswell and Hyndman, it is useful to employ the concept of "coloniality of power." This theoretical orientation helps us tease out why (and why not) and how we create meaning around mobility. Mobility cannot challenge territorially fixed notions of the nation until the concept of coloniality of transnational mobility is explicitly incorporated into this challenge. The concept of coloniality of power helps translate our very epistemologies of how people move in the world, how these movements are understood, how they are constructed and the meaning inherent in such constructions.

## Coloniality of Transnational Mobility

In order to construct a theoretical outline for a "coloniality of transnational mobility," I fuse the overlapping and intimately related ideas and critical analyses of Anibal Quijano (1999, 2000), Ramón Grosfoguel (2008) and Walter Mignolo (2000, 2008). As stated above, before the idea of a "transnational politics of mobility" can even be introduced, it is necessary to first sketch out the "coloniality of power" inherent in such movements. In this regard, Quijano argues that the structure of power globally was and continues to be organized around the colonial axis (Quijano, 2000: 568). Fundamental to his argument is the idea that this colonial model of power specifically organizes and structures the world's population around the idea of race and rationalizes this systematic construction of global power around one origin, Eurocentrism.

According to Quijano, this racial axis has a colonial origin and character that has proven to be more durable and stable than the colonial system in which it was engineered (ibid.: 533). Therefore, today's globally hegemonic model of power contains by extension an element of coloniality. Furthermore, the main signifier of this colonial model of power is white, male and European. The colonial model of power functions like a sieve, one all encompassing reference point and origin through which knowledge is created and the production of knowledge(s) filtered, thereby producing, reproducing and legitimizing models of domination. Although race is a mere mental construction, the coloniality of power breathes life into it. The coloniality of power is itself the mediating factor for organizing global power and controlling the world's population.

Quijano's concept of coloniality is very much entwined with and cannot be separated from global capitalism. In fact, the continuity of colonial forms of domination constitutive of "coloniality" is absolutely situated in global capitalist structures. Grosfoguel explains that Quijano's concept of coloniality captures the "mutually constitutive relations between the international division of labor, the global racial/ethnic hierarchy and the hegemonic Eurocentric epistemologies" (Grosfoguel, 2008: 95). This "modern/colonial world," a term coined by Walter Mignolo (2000: 723), no longer consists of direct colonial rule and administrations (with the exception of 16 non-self-governing territories), yet the colonial axis persists and perpetuates relations of exploitation between capital and labor and relations of domination and sanctions and produces particular (Euro-American) subjectivities and knowledges about the "modern" world (Grosfoguel, 2008: 96). Key to coloniality is agency or point of view. "Europeans imagine themselves as the exclusive bearers, creators, and protagonists of that modernity" (Quijano, 2000: 542). The notion of coloniality therefore functions as a complex matrix linking modernity, colonialism, capitalism and racism.

Grosfoguel challenges the assumption that nation-states are independent units as well as the conclusion that global inequalities result from "the natural dynamics of each nation-state" (Grosfoguel, 2008: 96). He utilizes Mignolo's theoretical framework, "modern/colonial world," and the critical analysis of Quijano (1993) to deconstruct this deep-seated mythology and in order to highlight two essential and related ideas. First, he attests that the Euro-American procedures of nation building (citizenship rights and development of parliamentary regimes) were very much created in a global colonial/racist imaginary that established internal and external borders; second, he refutes the fact that we live in a decolonized world (Grosfoguel, 2008: 98f.). The first point challenges dehistoricized and deracialized (end of history and post-racist) narratives around the nation and our "modern" world. The second point is crucial for understanding the political implications of how we "conceive social change, struggles against inequality, scientific descriptives, knowledge productions, utopian thinking, democracy and decolonization" (99). The two are intimately linked and challenge us to reconfigure our epistemologies of space and time and thus any discussion today around the local and the global.

Hence, transnational mobility must be reconceived from the perspective of "coloniality." However, to link transnational mobility to coloniality does not foreclose opportunities to conceive of and analyze projects of transnational mobility beyond these parameters. Along the analytical lines of Mignolo, I advocate a reframing of transnational mobility from the perspective of coloniality and the modern frame of the modern/colonial world (2000: 722f.). However, before a reframing can even be considered, a highlighting of the coloniality of power is necessary. Within this order, control mechanisms like those monitoring and allowing movements across borders are racialized, colonially organized and historically contradictory. Within these colonial structures, as Mignolo is quick to point out, the slave understands both the logic of the master and the slave, whereas the master only understands the logic of the master (ibid.: 733).

If we return to the politico-juridical terms that I introduced at the beginning of this work – the "illegal" immigrant, the refugee and the asylum seeker – we see that they are constructed and easily subsumed in coloniality of power master narratives. Movement across borders does not break the colonial binds that create these forced-choice movements. In fact, in their very naming, they are claimed by the coloniality of power. To pierce this powerful and pervasive mindset requires a dramatic and concrete counteragent, a "from the borders" figure that spotlights the coloniality of mobility and reproductive modes of domination and challenges their conceptual foundations.

## Maternity Tourism

On March 29, 2011, *The New York Times* issued an article entitled "Arriving as Pregnant Tourists, Leaving with American Babies" (Medina, 2011). The article's purpose was to address a relatively new phenomenon in the United States denominated "maternity tourists." A maternity tourist is a foreign woman who pays tens of thousands of dollars to birth her baby on U.S. soil in order to make him/her an automatic U.S. citizen. This particular case study involved women from China. Interestingly, the debate over "birthright citizenship" gained renewed force this past year in the U.S., predominately regarding immigrants entering "illegally" from poor countries from Latin America, but also from other regions of the world to access the "North American market" through the Central American and Mexican "corridor" (Corcoran, 2011).

This relatively new phenomenon with links to distinct places like Mexico, South Korea and Turkey, has received harsh criticism from groups in the U.S. known for being "tough on" immigration controls, surveillance and policies. Some suspect (or fear) that it may have already entered a more institutionalized and "business" phase, advertising packages that arrange doctors, insurance, postpartum care and even baby stays complete with a stroller. When asked specifically about "maternity tourism," Mark Krikorian, Executive Director of the Center for Immigration Studies, expressed grave concern over it:

> These people aren't doing anything in violation of our laws (…). But if anything, it ["maternity tourism"] is worse than illegal immigrants delivering a baby here. Those kids are socialized as Americans. This phenomenon of coming to the U.S. and then leaving with people who have unlimited access to come back is just ridiculous (Medina, 2011).

In response to 'illegal' movements of people and echoing a concurrent French debate, some U.S. political leaders have called for an end to birthright citizenship. This would require an amendment to the 14th Amendment, which guarantees automatic citizenship to any baby born in the United States. This debate has particularly centered on "illegal" and poor immigrants entering the United States from Latin America. In this specific case of "maternity tourism," however, the women were relatively wealthy and "legally" in the United States on tourist visas. Furthermore, most of these women returned to China with their "American" babies – their "insurance policies" (Medina, 2011). This dynamic, evident in Korkorian's remark, is viewed as even more dangerous because it is legally sanctioned and disrupts the normalized and hierarchized flow of people – the coloniality of power's natural order of things.

Ironically the only way to combat such a hacking of the system is to adjust citizenship itself, a building block of modernity and the nation-state.

> Mobility as freedom – as liberty – lies right at the heart of some of the foundational ideologies of the modern world. The claim to the universal that ideas of rights, and the right to mobility in particular makes, disguises the specificity of the conflation of liberty, freedom, citizenship, and mobility within a liberal framework (Creswell, 2006: 166).

Originally, in U.S. law, movement was inscribed in the law as a right of citizenship; it therefore produces meanings of mobility by authorizing or prohibiting it (Creswell, 2006: 150f.). The only response available to the system that protects the "inside" of the nation-state and effectively combats these legal methods of "undoing" surveillance modalities is to delink birth from citizenship, to place conditionality on citizenship, on the very basis of the nation-state. As movement is inscribed and deeply embedded in the law and thus the construction of categories – "illegal" immigrant, refugee and asylum seeker – it is only through the law that these maternity tourist transgressions can be addressed. However, by reformulating the law so as to regulate the coloniality of power of the nation-state, the very protectors of the modern nation-state unhinge what Agamben calls the old trinity of state-nation-territory (in this case, it is not the refugee that does the unhinging) (Agamben, 2003: 8; see also, Agamben, 1998: 127-135).

The modern nation-state equates citizenship and sovereignty. Within this construct birth and nation are indistinguishable. The origin of the modern nation-state relies on the fiction of birth, citizenship, nation, state and sovereignty. In essence, birth or natural life is inscribed in "the juridico-political order of nation-states" (Agamben, 1998: 127; 133). By removing the birthright of citizenship from the law, the regulators of the system attempt to prohibit the maternity tourist from successfully breaking down the system. Instead, they reveal the originary fiction of the equivalence of birth and nation (Agamben, 1998: 131; Spivak, 2003: 85). The very act of protecting the system against the maternity tourist unintentionally reveals the insidious nature of the coloniality of power – economized global racial/ethnic hierarchies and hegemonic Euro-American epistemologies of movement.

The figure of the maternity tourist is a concrete example that illuminates the functioning of the coloniality of power. At the same time, the maternity tourist is such an affront to the logic of the coloniality of power that the only way to rearticulate the coloniality of power in reaction to these acts of insubordination to the system is to break from the logic of the master narrative. If we accept, albeit critically as does Malkki (1992), that we have a tendency to place boundaries and borderlands at the center of our analytical frameworks of the nation thereby territorializing it, then we are simultaneously if not purposefully containing the very idea of mobility across boundaries and borders within these analytical frameworks. We also bind them in metaphysical translations of identity. We condition mobility on some degree of non-movement and marry rootedness to the nation. Indeed, it is important to first acknowledge our "commonsense assumptions linking people to place" and "nations to territory" (Malkki, 1992: 26) before it is possible to unhinge this very naturalized and essentialized territoriality of birth and nation at the core of modernity and citizenship for the purpose of calling out racialized and hierarchized understandings of "nations" and "identity."

Creswell argues that legitimized forms of mobility oppose mobilities that "undo" the "established spatial order" (2006: 159). Although he acknowledges that it is "necessary to disconnect citizenship" from the mobility of the other that threatens the established order and that mobility is racialized in the law (ibid.: 159-161), he never names this established order – the coloniality of power. The maternity tourist functions as the figure that allows us to incorporate Hyndman's transnational politics of mobility into the coloniality of power and thus bridge the conceptual gap left by Cresswell and Hyndman. As meanings are "ascribed to mobility through the construction of categories" (Cresswell, 2006: 150), it follows that it is impossible to talk about transnational spaces of movement without first breaking down the coloniality of mobility, which is directly related to territorial localization, borders and boundaries. By hacking the colonial system, the "maternity tourist" allows us to clearly see these colonial/racist structural relationships. Understanding these relationships must be the starting point for any discussion of transnational mobility that hopes to alter our perceptions and assumptions regarding transnational movement.

## Transnational Politics of Mobility and Border Thinking

When Hyndman talks about "territorialized identities," the "absence of representation" and "fragmented geographies of displacement" (2000: xxii), she parallels Grosfoguel's argument that examines such inequalities as constitutive of "multiple, heterogeneous, entangled, and complex processes within a single historical reality" (Grosfoguel, 2008: 101). When Cresswell states that citizenship is the correct way to practice mobility, citizenship meaning "white, male, wealthy, able bodied" (Cresswell, 2006: 160f.), he too is talking about complex politico-juridical processes within a single historical modern-colonial reality. This single historical reality is coloniality, the "power grid" that fuses modernity, colonialism, capitalism and racism (Krishnaswamy, 2008: 101). It conceptually unites them. Thus, historically specific configurations of geopolitics and cultural and economic relations of power (Hyndman, 2000: 32), the heterogeneous, entangled and complex processes, exist within a single historical reality. It is only when this component of the coloniality of power is added to Hyndman and Cresswell's theoretical evaluations of movement that a transnational politics of mobility becomes a useful tool for analyzing the movements of people.

Furthermore, if we look at Hyndman's geopolitics of mobility and the fact that international borders are more porous to capital than to the "illegal" immigrant, the refugee and the asylum seeker, we are able to see capitalist economies of power that regulate and determine movement (2000: 30; 32). Once again, the interlinking concept that helps understand how money, power and space are mediated and shaped unevenly is the coloniality of power. The naturalized discourses on movement taking place within the historical configuration of the coloniality of power serve to produce and reproduce the institutional global frameworks for right or denied right to transnational movement and create the standards and controls by which these movements are legitimized and accepted. Opportunities to cross borders and to move within a country depend on, as Hyndman explains, prevailing politics, economic resources, gendered access to jobs and other key positionings (2000: 33); however, these determinants cannot be understood outside of or separated from the coloniality of power.

What consequences does such an analytical starting point have for our sociopolitical constructions of space, place and movement between transnational spaces (of rooted place)? Can we create a transnational politics of movement that may not undo the coloniality of power, but at least takes it into consideration? The figure of the maternity tourist vividly demonstrates the functioning of the coloniality of power; it is a creative way to contest clear Euro-American knowledge(s) production on transnational movement. Border thinking as conceptualized by Mignolo involves similar creative strategies for transforming hegemonic imaginaries from the perspective of people in subaltern positions (2000: 736f.). These subaltern knowledges are critical of global coloniality, imperial global designs, and of internal coloniality, anticolonial nationalist strategies (Grosfoguel, 2008: 97). Grosfoguel states that colonialist discourses (which I interpret as ideas, policies and action) reproduce the North-South colonial divide and that nationalist discourses reproduce an internal colonial divide within nationalist constructions (ibid.: 97). The "colonial difference" that emerges from such critical analysis from the borders overcomes the limitations of global and internal coloniality.

If the dominant imaginary is still colonial, then a transnational politics of movement must take into account that complex and entangled hierarchies of gender, race, sex and class are deeply embedded in geopolitical, economic, cultural and social processes. Here Hyndman's analysis of difference and Cresswell's cultural concept of "hybrid" and "dynamic" routes complement Mignolo and Grosfoguel's theorization of border thinking. Hyndman argues for a more transnational approach to broaching difference, such that difference is not a question of accommodation or harmonized "us" and "thems," but of connection, a series of unequal and uneven links between different subjects (Hyndman, 2000: 67). If it is understood that these unequal and uneven links stem from the coloniality of power and result from structural relations within the capitalist world system, this conceptualization of difference can be applied to a transnational politics of movement. Equally applicable is Creswell's cultural concept of movement as hybrid and dynamic. Both are capable of breaking through coloniality of power presuppositions and assumptions and undermining continued Euro-American exploitation of "developing" regions. In this theoretical understanding of a transnational politics of mobility, the subject, the transnational mover is capable of breaking the essentialist connections that frame our understandings of "nation and "citizenship."

A transnational politics of mobility must concomitantly break down the naturalized and hierarchized order of nation-states and racialized "belonging" and the technologies of power of the modern-colonial world-system managing space and movement. "The borders that have been erected to keep us separate" (Ahluwalia, 2008: 168) are forms of geopolitical and socioeconomic segregation. They maintain the slave order and the "post"-slave world of "separate, but equal." Modernity's normative values of individualism, democracy, reason, citizenship and nation continue to construct a geopolitics of mobility. As stated above, Hyndman contends that a transnational politics of mobility aims to theorize unequal power relations in such a way that identity formation is viewed in a transnational context (within, beyond and in spite of nation-states). She illustrates two kinds of spatially coded border crossings, financial (Euro-American) and corporeal (African) (Hyndman, 2000: 31). In this global context, transnationalism and by extension hybrid cultural forms have the potential to respond to the local and remake global and international forces, thereby presenting possibilities for transformative politics (Canclini, 1995; cited in Hyndman, 2000: 165). Furthermore, the local and the global are negotiable and transnational connections across borders open up the transnational space to contest easy binaries like North and South, East and West, modern and traditional. Viewed this way, the very act of excluded bodies moving across borders challenges the coloniality of power, the normalized discourses of the modern.

I am not merely talking about thinking from the borders, but actually moving from the borders in order to create a transnational politics of mobility that generates "potentially strategic constellations of power" (Hyndman, 2000: 60) that unsettle the colonial project and hegemonic imaginary. By "belonging" or rather breaking the binds of belonging, these bodies challenge the nation-state-territory trinity and the very rules by which we distinguish the inside and the outside. When so acknowledged, these analytically designated "bodies" can be recognized as empowered peoples, potential agents of challenge and change. By understanding unequal relations of power as contingent of the coloniality of power, a transnational politics of mobility (the continual crossing of borders both figurative and real) opens up local and global possibilities for crashing the colonial system.

As Hyndman declares, borders are cartographies of struggle and crossing them is a political act full of meaning. While recognizing that the coloniality of power still entraps postcolonial and diasporic subjects in "a web of citizenships, passports, and ascribed identities (Ahluwalia, 2008: 175), it is through these struggles that the relationship between the local and global are forged and defined. In this context, our epistemologies of political practice are "global through the knowing multiplication of local practices" (Sassen, 2008: 91).

## By Way of Conclusion

The figure of the maternity tourist clearly brings to light the functioning of the coloniality of power with regards to transnational movement. She forces us to question and rethink the naturalized logic of citizenship and the trinity of nation (birth), state and territory. Ironically, it is the politico-juridical response to this figure and not the figure *per se* that punctures the essentialized understandings of the nation-state and the citizen and of the very logic of the modern colonial system. What figure then best represents the coloniality of power – the economized global racial/ethnic hierarchies and hegemonic Euro-American epistemologies of movement? The answer is the outsourced surrogate Indian mother and her "Google Baby," the "final product" of the transnational baby production industry facilitated online by outsourcing the surrogacy element (the bodies of Indian women) (Frank, 2009).

Juxtaposing these two figures opens the conversation to the paradoxical processes of "de-naturalization", the taking away of the immediate birthright of citizenship from the children of undocumented people, and "de-territorialization," the outsourced surrogate mother. Both figures stretch our spatial conceptualizations of the nation and of movement, the first through using the very rules of the sovereign to beat the system and the second through a biopolitical transgression of national borders. Yet, the maternity tourist is an expression of resistance within the coloniality of power while the outsourced surrogate mother is the epitome of the coloniality of power *par excellence*. The question is not just whether or not such baby outsourcing is ethical. The point is that such a relationship only makes sense, only exists in the realm of the coloniality of power. Only in the coloniality of power would someone have the "right" to a better life (economically) by "choosing" to birth the master's baby. To analyze a transnational politics of movement within the context of the coloniality of power is to perceive the local, global and transnational spaces differently and from and across borders and boundaries. From this power grid imaginary it is possible to contest and unhinge uneven geographies of power, status and transnational movement.

## References


Agamben, Giorgio (1998): Homo Sacer: Sovereign Power and Bare Life. Stanford/California. Stanford University Press.

Agamben, Giorgio (2003): Beyond Human Rights. In: Cadava, Eduardo/ Levy, Aaron (eds.): Cities Without Citizens. Philadelphia. Slought Books. pp. 3-12.

Agamben, Giorgio (2005): State of Exception. Chicago. University of Chicago Press.

Ahluwalia, Pal (2008): Death and Politics: Empire and the 'New' Politics of Resistance. In: Krishnaswamy, Revathi/ Hawley, John C. (eds.): The Postcolonial and the Global. Minneapolis. University of Minnesota Press. pp. 166-177.

Buchanan, Ruth/ Pahuja, Sundhya (2008): Law, Nation, and (Imagined) International Communities, In: Krishnaswamy, Revathi/ Hawley, John C. (eds.): The Postcolonial and the Global. Minneapolis. University of Minnesota Press. pp. 261-274.

Canclini, Néstor García (1995): Hybrid Cultures: Strategies for Entering and Leaving Modernity. Minneapolis. University of Minnesota Press.

Corcoran, Katherine (2011): Smuggling people is big business – X-rays prove it. In: The New York Times. Friday, May 20th. p. A4.

Cresswell, Tim (2006): On the Move, Mobility in the Modern Western World. Routledge Taylor & Francis Group. New York.

Donadio, Rachel (2011): Fleeing North Africa and Landing in an Italian Limbo. In: The New York Times. Tuesday, March 31. pp. A4, A6.
Frank, Zippi Brand (2009): Google Baby. VPRO.
Grosfoguel, Ramón (2008): World-System Analysis and Postcolonial Studies: A Call for a Dialogue from the 'Coloniality of Power' Approach. In: Krishnaswamy, Revathi/ Hawley, John C. (eds.): The Postcolonial and the Global. Minneapolis. University of Minnesota Press. pp. 94-104.
Hyndman, Jennifer (2000): Managing Displacement, Refugees and the Politics of Humanitarianism. University of Minnesota Press. London.
Krishnaswamy, Revathi (2008): Postcolonial and Globalization Studies: Connections, Conflicts, Complicities, In: Krishnaswamy, Revathi/ Hawley, John C. (eds.): The Postcolonial and the Global. Minneapolis. University of Minnesota Press. pp. 2-21.
Malkki, Liisa (1992): National Geographic: The Rooting of Peoples and the Territorialization of National Identity Among Scholars and Refugees. In: Cultural Anthropology 7. No. 1 (3). pp. 22-24.
Medina, Jennifer (2011): Arriving as Pregnant Tourists, Leaving with American Babies. In: The New York Times. Tuesday, March 29. pp. A1, A23.
Mignolo, Walter D. (2000): The Many Faces of Cosmo-polis: Border Thinking and Critical Cosmopolitanism. In: Public Culture. No. 12 (3). pp. 721-748.
Mignolo, Walter D. (2008): The Logic of Coloniality and the Limits of Postcoloniality. In: Krishnaswamy, Revathi/ Hawley, John C. (eds.): The Postcolonial and the Global. Minneapolis. University of Minnesota Press. pp. 109-123.
Quijano, Aníbal (1993): "Raza", "Etnia", y "Nación", en Mariátegui: Cuestiones Abiertas. In: Forgues, Roland (ed.): El Otro Aspecto del Descubrimiento. Lima, Perú. Empresa Editora Amauta S.A. pp. 167-187.
Quijano, Aníbal (1999): Coloniality and Modernity/Rationality. In: Therborn, Goran (ed.): Globalizations and Modernites, European and Latin American Experiences and Perspectives. Stockholm. Furksningradnamnden.
Quijano, Aníbal (2000): Coloniality of Power, Eurocentrism, and Latin America. In: Nepantla: Views from South. Volume 1. Issue 3. pp. 533-580.
Sassen, Saskia (2008): The Many Scales of the Global: Implications for Theory and for Politics. In: Krishnaswamy, Revathi/ Hawley, John C. (eds.): The Postcolonial and the Global. Minneapolis. University of Minnesota Press. pp. 82-93.
Sayare, Scott (2011): Now Feeling Free, but Still Without Work, Tunisians Look Toward Europe. In: The New York Times. Thursday, March 24. p. A17.
Spivak, Gayatri Chakravorty (2003): Harlem. In: Cadava, Eduardo/ Levy, Aaron (eds.): Cities Without Citizens. Philadelphia. Slought Books. pp. 55-86.

# Borders are Narratives
## Habitual Involvement in Ethnic and Social Spaces

*Rudolf Egger*

*In the minds of all the Balkan nations there are two maps with two different borders. One is the contemporary map, usually called the political map of one's state. The other is the historical map, a map sometimes secretly and often openly cherished.*
(Former Macedonian foreign minister Denko Maleski In: Maleski 2008, o. S.)

## Abstract
*Many years following the end of the several wars in southeastern Europe, the area of the world formerly known as Yugoslavia remains a potentially unstable region of Europe. The selective memory characteristic of the nationalist rhetoric primarily serves domestic policy purposes; it can be located somewhere between a tragedy and a myth in the stories of the people. In this article I show, using Kosovo and the Greek part of Cyprus as empirical examples, how life stories are linked to ethnically fixed memory spaces. The paper explores the idea of borders as narratives and as metaphors in terms of 'Balkan' and 'Cypriote' identities in the context of contemporary European culture.*

## Introduction

Over the last few years I've spent a good deal of time analysing the relationships between the "inner and outer borders" in Kosovo and in Cyprus. The political demarcations of the "inner and outer logic" of these two states have changed fundamentally since the project to unite Europe and moreover since "1989", and opened up a new space of social and subjective experiences. As if out of the blue, there was no longer "East and West" in the traditional sense; the borders changed but the interpretation of history didn't. Aside from these changes many historical symbols haven't lost their gravity – the cultural consequences of these (t)old stories should not be underestimated. Powerful (especially economic) forces are working to overcome the old borders; the maps that are emerging do not fit the varying ethnic and socioeconomic situations. The new maps are also linked to different stories of the modern which my work in Kosovo showed. There I found an ethnically fixed memory space, a web of historical, cultural, social, mythological and social-psychological structures which have a tremendous impact on the development of the civil society. The stories in the entire Balkan regions are based on a never-ending narrative of conflicts and wars which have caused people to fear each other. My project in Cyprus is similar and is focused on the individual, social and country-specific ways in which the Greek Cypriots are dealing with the fact that, since 1974, the country is divided into two separate states and their strategies for developing a "new identity" bases on this fact, specifically related to the status of the Greek part, i.e. being a full member of the EU since 2004. In this paper I will show some outcomes of these projects. It is an attempt to connect the approaches in biographical research with the processes of social transformation. The aim is to bring theoretical issues and approaches from biographical research and life history work into adult education research and practice.

## Stories and Structures

To understand how I handled the data and the aims of the projects, it is necessary to first give some theoretical background. Biographical research projects seek to determine how individuals compose their memories in particular ways and how the processes of remembering could be a key to understanding the ways in which certain individual and collective versions of the past are active in the present. There is strong multivalency of individual memory and the diversity of versions of the past provided by different speakers (as well as different documentary sources). But the distortions of memory could be a resource as much as being a problem. In recent years biographical researchers have become more interested in exploring the relationships between (collective) memory and subjectivity as well as between remembrance and the processes of acting in different modes of societies. Biographical self-reflection is an attempt to find and "build up" stories in which one can reconstruct oneself. Creating an adequate (auto)biography is always part of the constantly ongoing process of identity building throughout life; this happens in everyday life and in the process of learning and taking action. Dealing with the subject's world means, in a constructivist view, that people are narrative constructors of their world. This focus includes the influences of the "real world", but our own constructions have a tremendous impact on this world. In these dialectical relations between "stories and structures" we create our world in the environment of our everyday existence. Narrations are much more than mere subjective reconstructions of the "real world". Methodologically speaking, they are the king's way of understanding reality because the disposition to tell a story (or to interpret history) is always from the perspective of the actor. There is no other way to describe history, and particularly life history, apart from in the form of a narrative. However this does not mean that the narrative is identical with real actions and events that happened in the past. It means that there is a characteristic relationship, a structural similarity between things happening in the "real world" and those that are told in a story; Paul Ricoeur has powerfully argued this in his book Time and Narrative (1984).

Stories make up the unity of our individuality, but they are also inter-subjective in character because they create the social contexts in which we live. Every historical description is also fundamentally a narrative because it looks at historical events as elements within chains of events, in a quite unpretentious sense, as "stories". The future exists only on the horizon of expectations. To that extent, every successful approach to looking at societies is based on narrations, even if we are dealing with structural social issues. On the other hand the everyday narrator is also a holder of "structures" because the narrative links him with the social and historical lifeworld in which he takes part. Narrators always have a kind of "lay concept" of the world in the sense of the everyday world or lifeworld. To use narrative forms they need a system of references which gives access to collectively obtainable knowledge. It is thus clear that "stories and structures" cannot be separated from each other (Alheit/Dausien 2000).

## Territories are Stories: Kosovo

My main work in Kosovo was teaching the methodology of qualitative empirical social research (the technique of the narrative interview) and to establish several interpretation groups for the structural analysis of life stories. After an expanded introduction to the principles of biographical research (Schütze 1984) and grounded theory (Strauss/Corbin 1996) students were asked to conduct narrative interviews. Most of them were not familiar with the possibilities for and the conditions of qualitative social research so I had to come up with some points for the process of interpretation. One of the frequently asked questions was about the truth of the story and the relationship between the story and the culture. I developed a small and easily understandable system which allows for differentiation between the different text levels.

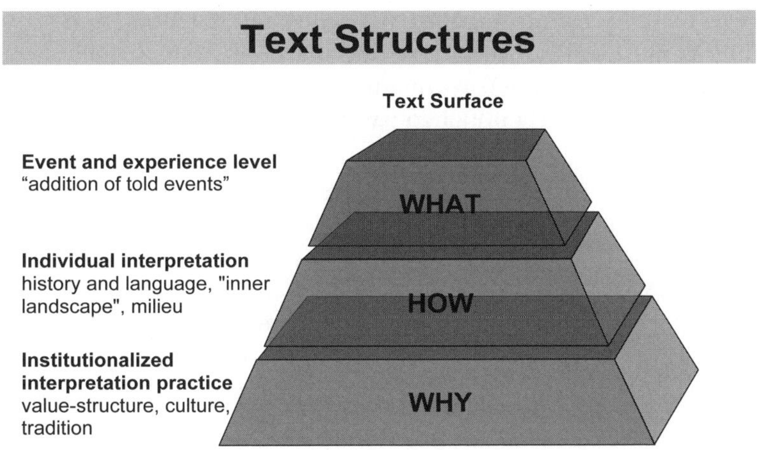


The event and experience level represents the framework of the selected events in the narration. All the experiences and stories are used as constituent and essential parts of the life story in the interview. On the level of individual interpretation, it is the perspective of the narrator, his/her language and the "inner landscape" of a person that characterise the story. All these narratives are formed by institutionalised interpretation practices which are fed by cultural traditional and normative social orientations.

In working with biographies, the question about the truth and the actual correctness of told stories emerged consistently in every interpretation process. Did the events, the narrated situations, the experiences actually take place as they were presented in the interview or are they simply a kind of fiction, half lies or expressions of permanent image management which the biography-holder offers for his or her own reasons? This question about the truth can also be analysed on different levels.

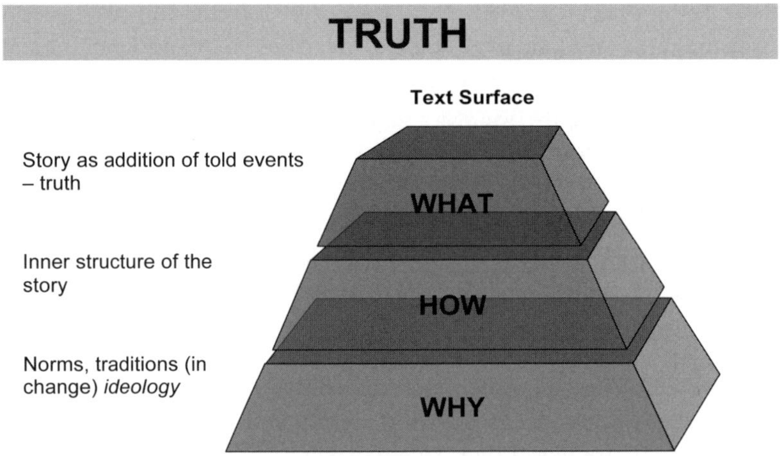


On the WHAT level (actually concerning the told events) this question can be answered quite pragmatically because we can determine the life events that actually happened and this can usually be proven on the basis of other narrations, other people's stories or with the help of historical sources. On the HOW level it is quite different because the production of the "inner landscape" depends not only on the external events but also on the meaning of these actions and situations in the eye of the narrator. On this level it is important to reconstruct the "mechanism" of this "map". So truth here means the subjective side of the facts, the individual structure of the story, and not the historical truth. On the traditional or cultural level we have to figure out the links between the individual story and the structure, i.e. the social realm. The question about truth cannot be limited by classical correct or wrong patterns. It has to be seen as an intermediate form between the individual story and the social structure, between the social world and ideology. (A good example concerning these processes can be found in the novel 1984 by George Orwell in which he stresses the structure of reality. Things and feelings which have no linguistic counterpart don't really exist.) So our language is also a pool of words, terms and phrases in a cultural context.

These distinctions have a great impact on the processes of interpretation of life stories because we want to analyse and reconstruct the relevance systems of the subjects. We want to see how experiences in biographies are linked to the social structure. In a narrative interview, the interviewees have to construct the horizon of the possible narrations for themselves. They have to decide which topics or themes should (selectively) be narrated and in which way. This is why we have to follow these processes in the analysis of the texts. The hidden working control mechanism of the total view, the mechanisms of the selection of stories, as well as the topic frame of the narrator are significant for a single event. In the interpretation phase we work with abductive conclusions (Peirce 1991). In the course of a sequential analysis we systematically follow the inherent sense of the narration. In a line by line analysis we open up the text and find categories, indicators and dimensions as outlined by Glaser and Strauss (Strauss/Corbin 1996) in their coding procedure.

The second goal of my work in Kosovo was to establish a life course archive. Students of different faculties made recordings of the life stories of different groups within Kosovar society. These interviews were then transcribed and archived. In cooperation local partners at the university and at KODI (Kosovar Research and Documentation Institute), some of the interviews have been translated into English to allow them to be used as learning materials for the processes of interpretation with interpretation groups (by both Kosovar students and others from all over Europe). The archived material is currently being used by students to learn the principles of qualitative research methods. In the future the collected narratives and the results of the interpretation can also serve as "pathfinders" or as a "store of ideas" for new investigations. Lastly, this archive should be a resource for humanitarian and research projects in the analysis of conditions of and possibilities for social change in a post war society. Since 2003, 84 interviews have been made, documented and stored in a digital archive (all in Albanian – 34 have been translated into English). Due to the sensitive nature of the qualitative data, we prepared a detailed protocol regarding anonymity and data protection. The strategies to ensure anonymity are based on a rule that personal details like names, addresses and places are left out when the interviews are transcribed in order to prevent the identification of the interviewee concerned. It is nonetheless clear that detailed analyses of interviews are hardly possible without an awareness of biographical details. For the structure of the case it is necessary to know the whole context of the narration. The question under which conditions this collected qualitative data can be given to other researchers or interested persons is answered this way: our data may only be used for learning, research and humanitarian purposes. It's forbidden to pass on the material to a third parties, data must remain anonymous, personal details may not be quoted or published and a notification of the end of the project must be given and the data which has been made available must be destroyed. The use of archived data for (re-)analysis and secondary analysis has many social, political and methodological advantages – even in a society after a war.

In the work with the interpretation groups it became clear that the frames of reference (which represent narrative reconstructions of social reality) not only act as a "system of rules" – it is more like a biographical action perspective. Any remembering of an experience or event that must necessarily precede the narrative situation opens up not only a narrower or wider horizon but also refers back to changes in the narrator's self. An event worth being remembered is obviously one that has left traces; it has marked the narrator and left behind an "impression", altering the structure of his experience to a greater or lesser degree. "Any impromptu narration of one's own experience is also a new remembering of this more or less unnoticeable process of change" (Schütze 1984: 82). This statement is of explicit theoretical importance because everyone has to confirm this narrative plan in his narration. How these consequences unfold as a "cognitive frame of reference" for narration in impromptu autobiographical narrative has been described in detail by Fritz Schütze (1984). In this sense we have to deal with the different meanings of history, of life stories (individually and collectively) because the "collection of memories", of events, doesn't produce meaning in itself. The "red line" of a story can be built by different "stones" of (what we call) memory. The space in which memory can be filled up with meaning is a highly stressed area in which meaning is produced by different "voices" of culture, mythology, race and gender. These processes of "negotiation" are linked to biographical educational processes in which in the reconstructions we see how our roots fix the possibilities of our routes into the future and also into the past. It is vital in the situation of Kosovo to look at how these processes are underlined by the so-called collective memory in this country. All the historical suffering of this "fate community" produces extremely long memory cycles, and the degradations and also the demands from periods of long term repression can make this memory work very painful. In our work with the students we tried to widen the possibilities for interpretation of the past in a methodologically based way. Narration was thereby never only used as a reproduction of the past but also as means of production of new plots, new areas of historical experience and views of the horizons of expectation. In the concrete work with the interviews (and in many discussions inside and outside of the university setting) we always came to the same questions: how to cope with history and how to create and develop new possibilities and resources to handle the past. Almost every Kosovar (student or interviewee) raised the question of the "real truth" about what happened in recent decades. They declared that only this truth can build a bridge to the future. It was hard to learn that this necessary truth is a condition of living, but in the scientific work we're only looking for the constructions behind these facts. In the following passages I'll briefly present some details from an interview interpretation from our first workshop.

## Puzzles from an Analysed Interview

The interview begins with the words (lines 4 to 11):

> My name is V. H., I am from Priština and I was born 1977. Life, what is life for a young man? I will start with the first steps of my childhood, speaking of my grandfather H. H., from whom I learned a lot in 1981 when I was 4-5 years old. I don't forget the first Albanian riots. I remember as it was today when he told me about the Serbs. And later that how the Serbian conquest had come to its end and a war would be opened pretty soon I don't forget that we were living a modest life with our father working to maintain the whole family.

The interview begins with a formal introduction in the sense of "normal-biography" of a young man. What is life like for a young man in Kosovo? Which paths can he take? What are the individual and the political situations for a young man in general? Which are the worthy goals to best prepare for the future? The interviewee finds his reference in the presentation of his grandfather whom he designates with his full name. Not only the family relationship is important here but also his relationship to a long-established family in the region from which he comes. For the Kosovar students the fact that he mentioned the full name of his grandfather is an honest testimony of the respect for his position in a culture tied to genealogy. At the same time he mentions the history of the Kosovar people in general. The story of his childhood is related to the historical continuum of suffering and fear. The crucial words are: "*I remember as it was today when he told me about the Serbs.*" In this short sequence it is clear that he is still tangled up in an old story about the Serbian conquest and his role in the beginning of a new war. He connects his own experiences with the courageous history and the mythological environment of Kosovar citizens. There is a high level of emotional participation by the interviewee in this narrative. He describes a specific form of his enculturation with the grandfather's message (that is in a way an underlying subtext), which can have several meanings. On the one hand it is a kind of prophecy which determines the way of life of the Kosovar people in the culture of Serbian suppression. This prophecy could be regarded as a certain kind of social-historical concept for the conditions and possibilities of the individuals in this state. At the same time it includes this "concept" of different recommendations for his actions in the future. The words of his grandfather become a burden because he has to fight for the freedom of his nation. He has to fulfil the historical task, the historical mission of each Albanian which is linked to all aspects of mythology, genealogy and family. In the discussion of these interpretations with the students, we worked out the processes of this production of history and tried to explain the different roles (as the graphic below shows).

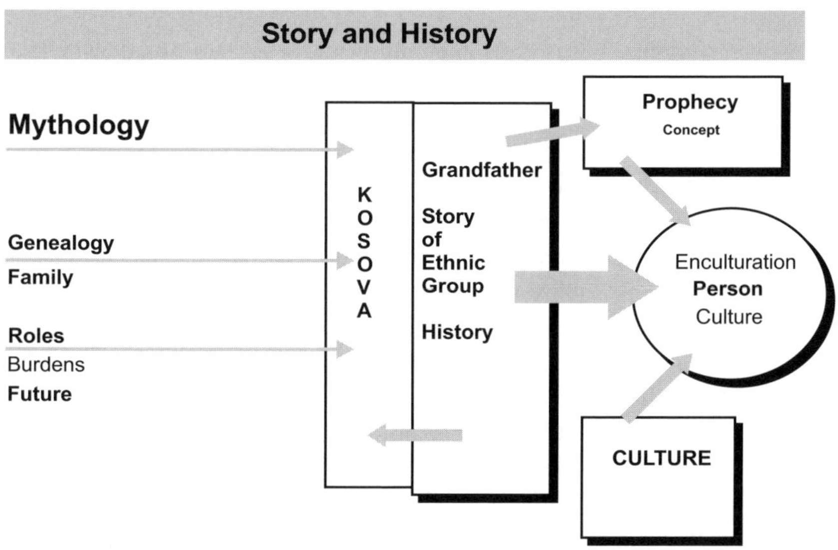


For the Albanian students it was very clear that he could act in only one way to find out something about his role. He had to take over the role of a fighter because enculturation means to carry the burden and to fulfil the story. Similarly we went on to the second segment (lines 12 to 18):

> My education was following it's normally course until 1989 or 1990, when the protest started. Then I remember when the curfew began to be imposed, I remember that in front of our house just one minute past the curfew time, a neighbour of us killed a one right before our eyes. I don't know how he could do it, he has been a retired member of at Serbian MUP but he killed a man.

Again the narrator begins with his orientation at the level of normality with a formal statement. The crucial date for the ending of his general education is linked to the decline in the living conditions of Kosovar people. The curfews are in the end the last visible step in the processes of exclusion from normal life. The story of the murder is temporally set one minute after the entry of such a curfew which shows how brutal the exclusionary practices were handled in the eyes of the interviewee. At the same time, yet another incident became painfully real for him because it was a neighbour who killed a man in front of him "like it was nothing". We discussed this event at length in the group and we looked for interpretation scenarios. In the end the point that explains the act was reconstructed on several levels.

1. First of all is the level of civil rights, of the legal basis which determines responsibility and justification. This includes the topics of the state and the judicial system, ideology and the political system.
2. Secondly there is the part concerning the actor's roles which the students divided into four ranges: the ethnical part (the Serbian aggressor), the state function (the policeman), the human/ethical being and the social function (the neighbour).

For the Kosovar students it was clear that the crime was committed with the aim of ethnic cleansing. There was an extended discussion with the foreign students about this interpretation. In this debate students learned a lot about the correlation between the concepts we have in our head and our actions in daily life, between the dominant inherent concepts and our way of explaining our daily life. If we think in terms of ethnical concepts, we see everywhere ethnically coded actions. In addition, Kosovo is not only a post-Serbian but also a post-communist society, but the fact is that 40 years communism in this country plays no role in the discussions. In the analysis of this interview we finally tried to create different modes of interpreting this scene – at least theoretically. The resistance from the Albanian students against this interpretation work was enormous, but in this confrontation all students opened up a substantial learning field in handling their own experiences in the processes of understanding history. In this discussion about different historical means of explanation, the students came to the question: "When does history actually begin?" In the processes of interpreting and in the discussion of the statements, the students had some important emotional and also cognitive experiences regarding how history is "produced" and associated with a special kind of future. This particularly understandable way showed the structure of the differences which make a significant difference when looking at history. With this work we also gained good insight into the ethnical view of the Balkans states and the "inner logic" of these communities.

## Narratives are Borders: Cyprus

My starting points in the project in Cyprus were nearly the same as in Kosovo. The goal was to find out how Greek Cypriots cope with the border in their country and how these people are entangled in the categories of space, national territory, political organisation and life-world in the contexts of narratives. In the analysis of the narratives we could see very clear that the Cypriot "model" is still strongly determined by a mode of genealogy (as in Kosovo) which defines the role of people and their stories in an ethnical sense. This ethnic space in which people live their lives is on the one hand determined by national constructions. On the other hand Cyprus is (especially since its EU membership) involved in a process of modernisation in which new social and physical spaces and boundaries are being developed. In the analysis of the empirical material we can see how difficult it is to integrate the old stories into the new social and physical space.

To understand the subjective and collective identity constructs in the Greek Cypriot society we have to analyse the main underlying recognition structures which influence the social and subjective space in which memories are created. The dominant memory of the "invasion of the Turks" is the main aspect, the "big wound", of the grand narrative of Greek Cypriots. It seems to be endemic that the Turkish Cypriots are seen as "foreigners" who are not compatible with the dominant civilisation and cultural patterns of the "real Cyprus". For Greek Cypriots, the existing ceasefire line is not an acceptable border. The Turkish argument, that two hostile ethnic groups which cannot live together, must be separated from each other, is vehemently rejected (even though the Greek Cypriot arguments are dealing with a similar concept of ethnical groups). The category Greek (or Turk) is for both of them the most important justification for the segregation. But as in any other nationalistic conflicts, it depends on the "real perspective" on which this justification is grounded. That means, that it is a conflict in the "history of memory" and shows the trivial and often forgotten insight that memory itself has a history, a historical space. In order to avoid further disasters, this separation could (for both nations) only be justified if it corresponds to the historical truth. This specific long-term memory of generations or even epochs builds up the horizon of the Greek Cypriots and proves their historical awareness that each generation has to paint the same picture of the past for itself; it asks the old questions of the past and appropriates it anew with the internal traditional map of the border. In the stories I collected and analysed, people always marked their specific ethnic position in Cyprus as the foundation of their identities. But the basis of (historical) identity and current legitimacy is fundamentally made erroneous by the fact that the national integrity is not guaranteed, as a man said in an interview:

> This is sometimes the case that you're a stranger in your own country. I was in my father's house in the Turkish part, and I had to apply for a visa and had to have an auto insurance policy, and pay money for it and then I yelled in my own country, at the birthplace of me and my parents and their parents, you know this is really bad.

All these stories are based on individual or related experiences of losing historical, local and regional relations. It's the same situation as in Kosovo where people are also looking for a nationalistic identity or "natural ethnic boundaries" which can anchor their lives in a coherent memory space.

Since joining the EU in 2004, the discussion of Cypriot identity building was encouraged by another factor that asks about new values. In these discussions of the ethnic and geographic extension of their homeland, Greek Cypriots are not clear about how to cope with these new tasks. On the one hand they see the prevailing arguments that Cyprus is an original part of Europe, including in particular an ancient heritage, and everywhere you can find the story of Aphrodite. Cyprus is without doubt one of the economic winners in the European consolidation process. Beside these surfaces, many Greek Cypriots feel an ambivalence toward the EU which is not able to be developed into a natural profile of a bigger state that could be fixed to objective criteria. There is no better story in the context of EU than the Greek story, though even this European integration process misses the memory of nations. The case of the Greek Cypriots can also show how much hidden transfers from generation to generation influences the conditions and expression of historical conceptions and new life circumstances.

## That's History. So What?

These small projects describe how the reconstruction of narrations could help to encourage understanding of the dominant values of societies. What we call history is always an interpretation of the past and the future and can only be understood and reconstructed in the process of constant translation between the desires, conceptions, ideas and scripts of people in their concrete life. From Schleiermacher we can learn that this interpretation is an endlessly turning interpretative circle which looks for new ways and which nonetheless recognises that the given feel is just a guide and not a fixed point. The work in Kosovo and in Cyprus may contribute insight into the fact that this hermeneutic circle of interpretation doesn't end and that the interpretation of our world will always be open to discussion because in ongoing discussions we have to realise that one's own thinking is "culturally produced" in a socio-historical environment. A dialogue with open debate and mutual criticism could also help enhance the understanding that cultural differences are never only where we believe we see them – they are already written into the point of view from which we look at world. The reconstruction of the visible and invisible structures could sensitise students to the linkage of the individual story with the larger, structural perspective in society and ideology. Data and its relation to the real world are substantial, and that's why the interpretation folios we worked out could also help in comprehending the special role of social scientists. The mode of the treatment is however again culturally conditioned; this could also be seen clearly. One example is the big difference between American and south-eastern European colleagues and students. If the Americans say "that's history", they usually mean that something is gone and it is no longer relevant. If south-eastern Europeans define something as history they mean that it now becomes an absolutely important and indelible fact. Both aspects (or better said coping strategies) of handling history have different and specific ways of dealing with the past. The "so-what?" strategy of the Americans fades out the past in favour of the present and the view ahead; the constant reference to the present and the future is the driving force. On the other hand the unavoidable look into the hard and violent events in the past of the south-eastern Europeans narrows the view to specific modes of the production of the present. Both are in the long run forms of ideologies which structure history and connect present and future in a special way. National differences in the clarification of significant historical events are normal, but we have to understand how to behave with regard to these differences. It is ridiculous to ignore "another" memory, to imagine that it does not exist. It is irrational to deny its justification or to try to exploit discrepancies in national images of the past. We should be convinced that people can be encouraged by their own civic responsibility in terms of being members of a historically formed community, but as work on the new and the old borders in Europe can show, all these stories tell us about the fear of losing one's position in the world and how much time and strength it needs to discover others. There are so many narratives and routes that make us aware how far old borders can reach and how they destroy the aims of cohesion.

## References


Alheit, Peter (1992): The Biographical Approach to Adult Education. In: Mader, Wilhelm (ed.): Adult Education in the Federal Republic of Germany: Scholarly Approaches and Professional Practice. Vancouver: The University of British Columbia/ International Council for Adult Education. pp. 186-222.

Alheit, Peter (1993): Transitorische Bildungsprozesse: Das „biographische Paradigma" in der Weiterbildung. In: Mader, Wilhelm (ed.): Weiterbildung und Gesellschaft. Grundlagen wissenschaftlicher und beruflicher Praxis in der Bundesrepublik Deutschland. Bremen, 2. erweiterte Aufl. pp. 343-418.

Alheit, Peter/ Dausien, Bettina (2000): Die biographische Konstruktion der Wirklichkeit. Überlegungen zur Biographizität des Sozialen. In: Hoerning, Erika M. (ed.): Biographische Sozialisation. Stuttgart: Lucius & Lucius. pp. 257-283.

Alheit, Peter/ Kammler, Eva (1998) (eds.): Lifelong Learning and its Impact on Social and Regional Development. Bremen: Donat.

Egger, Rudolf (1995): Biographie und Bildungsrelevanz. Eine empirische Studie über Prozeßstrukturen moderner Bildungsbiographien, Wien/München: Profil.

Maleski, Denko (2008): The borders of our minds. http://www.newbalkanpolitics.org.mk/editorials/the_borders_of_our_minds.html [12.04.2011].

Peirce, Charles Sanders (1991): Schriften zum Pragmatismus und Pragmatizismus. In: Apel, Karl-Otto (ed.), Frankfurt am Main: Suhrkamp.

Ricoeur, Paul (1984): Time and Narrative, 3 Vols., translated by Kathleen McLaughlin and David Pellauer. Chicago: University of Chicago Press.

Schütze, Fritz 1984: Biographieforschung und narratives Interview. In: Neue Praxis, H. 3. pp. 283-293.

Strauss, Anselm/ Corbin, Juliet (1996): Grounded Theory: Grundlagen Qualitativer Sozialforschung, Weinheim: Psychologie Verlags Union.

Thompson, Paul (2000): Re-using Qualitative Research Data: a Personal Account [48 paragraphs]. http://www.qualitative-research.net/fqs-texte/3-00/3-00thompson-e.htm [18.01.2006].

# Imagining and Re-imagining Transcultural Spaces – The 'Mitteleuropa' Discourse and Deconstructing the 'British Isles'

*Fergal Lenehan*

## Abstract

*This chapter argues that linguistic processes and nomenclature are essential to the imagining and creation of spaces, including macro-regional transcultural spaces beyond the confines of the nation-state. These linguistic processes may be inclusive and result in the imagining of new, or reinvigorated, spaces that seek to elicit a sense of belonging and a sense of place beyond the nation-state. The 'Mitteleuropa' discussion of the 1980s, it is argued, is an example of an inclusive transcultural spatial imagining that sought to create a trans-national sense of belonging based upon the linguistic sign itself and its inherent idea of a distinct transcultural space. Such linguistic processes may also act as a force of separation and may undermine conventional trans-cultural spatial notions that are no longer deemed by some to retain validity. The 'British Isles' discussion of the 1990s and the 2000s, it is argued, is an example of a divisive transcultural spatial imagining that sought to destabilise and question this conventional sign and the trans-cultural space it was deemed to signify.*

## Introduction

Linguistic processes and nomenclature are essential to the imagining and creation of spaces. This is also true of transcultural spatiality that exists beyond the confines of the nation-state and that often defies easy categorisation. These linguistic processes, it is here argued, may be inclusive and result in the imagining of new, or reinvigorated, trans-national spaces that seek to elicit a sense of belonging beyond the narrow margins of the nation-state, such as the 'Mitteleuropa' discourse of the 1980s. Such linguistic processes and spatially oriented discourses may also act as a force of separation and may be used to deconstruct established trans-cultural notions now held to be no longer valid, seen for example in relation to the discussion surrounding the term 'British Isles' in the 1990s and the 2000s. Nomenclature and linguistic processes are it is here argued central to the formation and transformation of trans-cultural spaces.

## Space, Language, Intellectuals and Scholars

Space, language and notions of social reality are complexly intertwined. According to the spatial theorists Henri Lefebvre and Edward Soja space is a necessary component of *all* social reality. Edward Soja, in *Thirdspace*, argues that: "Social reality is not just coincidentally spatial, existing "in" space, it is presuppositionally and ontologically spatial. *There is no unspatialized social reality*". Even in pure abstraction there is, he argues, "a pervasive and pertinent, if often hidden, spatial dimension" (Soja, 1996: 46). While Lefebvre, in *The Production of Space*, maintains that, in the same way that social reality is unavoidably temporal, social relations "have a social existence to the extent that they have a spatial existence; they project themselves into a space, becoming inscribed there, and in the process producing that space itself" (Lefebvre, 1991: 129). Therefore, spatiality and social reality are indelibly intertwined and any social reality is not only temporal but also spatial.

Social reality is also entangled with linguistic processes. John Searle, in his publication *The Construction of Social Reality* (Searle, 1995: 1-69), maintains a distinction between "brute facts", "intrinsic to nature", that can exist independently of all mental states, e.g. the rocks and soil of material reality, and "institutional facts", which require "human institutions" and mental states for their existence, and are "observer-relative features" of reality. The feature of language is necessary for, and partly constitutive of, "institutional facts", as are symbolic devices, such as words, which represent or symbolise something beyond themselves. Through the use of language and symbols, the "brute fact" "intrinsic to nature", can become an "institutional fact", "observer-relative" and dependent on mental states and linguistic devices. Thus, for example, the "brute fact" of wood that has been cut from a tree can become an "institutional fact" designated by the word "table"; the "brute fact" of the rocks and soil of material reality can become the "institutional facts" of the 'British Isles' or 'Mitteleuropa'.

Thus, spatiality is intertwined with social reality and language and words are partly constitutive of, and have a constructive function in relation to, social reality, which remains partly "observer-relative". If 'geography' is seen not as a given that just 'is', but as, as Gearóid O'Tuathail notes, "a conflict between competing images and imaginings", a "contest between different ways of envisioning the world" (O'Tuathail, 1996: 14f.), then language and nomenclature are essential instruments in the conflict of these imaginings, in the 'battle' to interpret and give meaning to the spatial contours of social reality. Language, according to Roland Burkart, is a system of "man-made signs" ("künstliche Zeichen") that depend upon historical societal conventions within a certain community, was created to facilitate communication between humans and each individual sign within this system is given a conventional meaning (Burkart, 2003: 25). Sometimes these meanings constitute a source of conflict, however, and have an excluding function and sometimes they may be inclusive, if still, nonetheless, wavering in meaning.

Public intellectuals are central to the discourse surrounding spatiality and its meanings and the imagining and re-imagining of trans-cultural spaces. Yet, as Liam O'Dowd (1996: 5) points out, "the problem of definition pervades any study of intellectuals". The Swedish sociologist Ron Eyerman (1996: 33) provides the definition that will be used here. He states that:

> The role and practise of the intellectual is bound up with communicating ideas to an audience, with 'education' and with persuasion (...) intellectuals arouse and stir public debate around issues fundamental to society and, in the process, they help create the concepts through which we understand society.

The intellectuals and scholars examined here communicate their idea of alternative linguistic signs and meanings of signs that couch the perceived reality of particular transcultural spaces. This is undertaken in a manner that is either consciously inclusive or exclusive and the intellectuals and scholars will deal with attempt to recreate certain concepts through which their readers understand and perceive their reality.

## 'Mitteleuropa'

'Mitteleuropa', as a German word, concept and geographical construction has a long, and indeed, well-researched, history. In the early 20th century the term attained connotations of a specifically German dominated central European space, as famously depicted in Friedrich Naumann's *Mitteleuropa* from 1915. Naumann's 'Mitteleuropa' concept was imagined as "eine Art Oberstaat über den Staaten, ein Reich über den Reichen" (an over-state above the states, an empire above empires) (Naumann: 1915: 2), a German dominated buffer zone in the centre of Europe, created by the merging of the German and Austrian empires.

'Central Europe' re-emerged as a positively denoted 'discursive concept' from Hungarian, Czech, and Polish intellectuals in the 1980s. As the Danish historian Peter Bugge maintains, even if one takes a "sceptical stance" and rejects the notion as a "nostalgic historical mirage" or "an abortive project of identity building", "the continuous regularity of the concept's appearance suggests that it does fulfil a function" (Bugge, 1999: 22f.). The debate was initiated and carried forward especially by 1980s Czech and Hungarian intellectuals such as Milan Kundera, György Konrad and Václav Havel. They saw the positive advantages of 'moving' to the 'centre' of Europe, especially as German occupation of the term was at an end. They also sought to establish some distance from Russia and to acquire a positive designation for the former community within the Habsburg Empire. The term for these Czech, Hungarian and Polish intellectuals undoubtedly held an inclusive resonance and conjured a new, or reinvigorated, image of a trans-national, trans-cultural historical space that could elicit a sense of belonging to those within its boundaries beyond the narrow margins of the nation-state, facilitating a return to 'Europe'. The linguistic sign itself was central for the imagining of this space.

The 'Mitteleuropa' concept was reintroduced into German debate in the 1980s from these non-German sources. 'Mitteleuropa' was seen within German intellectual discourse before this as somewhat poisoned by its nationalist misuse and was, therefore, only used "very cautiously" (Ash, 1990: 2). Timothy Garton Ash distinguishes "tentatively" between four "intersecting circles of Central European discussion" in West German intellectual-political debate of the late 1980s: cultural-historical rediscovery of the term, a historical-geopolitical right-national viewpoint, a historical-geopolitical left-national viewpoint and a mainstream social democratic concept, which he labels as "arguably the most important circle of intellectual-political 'Mitteleuropa' debate" (Ash, 1990: 4-6). For reasons of space we will deal chiefly with the initial cultural-historical usage and the social democratic use of the term.

One of the first German usages of the expression in the 1980s came from the historian Karl Schlögel (1986) in his essay *Die Mitte liegt Ostwärts – Die Deutschen, der verlorene Osten und Mitteleuropa* (The Centre lies in the East – The Germans, the Lost East and Mitteleuropa); the concept was used in a cultural-historical and highly nostalgic fashion. The author imagined 'Mitteleuropa' as a network of historical but vanished cultural interaction with Austro-Germany at its centre. He was influenced by György Konrad, distanced himself explicitly from Friedrich Naumann and saw the term as offering not only a new possibility and way of thinking but as a perspective that truly encapsulated reality. Schlögel (1987: 18-29) saw the term in three ways: as constituting a political overcoming of the Cold War East-West fixation, as representing a common and intertwined history and, rather nostalgically, as a historical civilisation in which vital, independent city centres existed alongside the imperial capitals, such as Vienna. Thus, 'Mitteleuropa' represents here a trans-national lens with which to view a macro-region, but also as a possibility for contemporaneous accord.

The 'Mitteleuropa' concept and term was also strongly linked to the peace movement in Germany, and 'Mitteleuropa' was often imagined as a demilitarised and peaceful area of détente, straddled between the USA and the Soviet Union (Rider, 1994: 12). Thus, the term not only conjured an imagining of a trans-cultural space but also acquired connotations of a utopian, alternative space of hope beyond the Cold War. The author Peter Glotz was the leading exponent of the German social-democratic 'Mitteleuropa' idea (Ash, 1990: 6; Bugge, 1999: 26; Rider, 1994: 12). In an interview with Eric Hobsbawn in the British communist magazine *Marxism Today* from 1986 Glotz (1986: 14f.) elucidates his idea of a 'Mitteleuropa'. He states that he is sceptical of ideas put forward for the "restoration of the small-German Bismarckian empire in the name of reunification", preferring instead to put his faith "in a real European solution", namely that of "Central Europe". His 'Central Europe' is described in terms of disarmament, economics and culture. He believes "we can make 'Central Europe' a disarmament zone", a "chemical weapon-free zone" and a "nuclear free corridor", while "intensified economic contacts" and "joint ventures between east and west" would also be of importance, especially as we "should not allow the Americans to force us into curbing the transfer of technology between west and east". Glotz also emphasises that "cultural discussions should play a much larger and more crucial part", along with the "mutual exchanges of our intimately related European cultures", especially as "Warsaw, Prague and Budapest are profoundly European cities", a fact that is often "suppressed and forgotten". The social democratic author Peter Bender (1987: 87, 91f.) also saw 'Mitteleuropa' as a protest against the division of the continent and the authority of the Americans and the Russians, as a further expression of a new state of perception that placed Europe into the centre.

Yet, there were also critical voices within the 1980s discourse that could not quite disengage the term from Friedrich Naumann and fears of German dominance in Central Europe. The French-based Professor Joseph Rovan (1987: 55) saw 'Mitteleuropa' as a dangerous and potentially explosive concept that could disrupt political integration within Europe. He also detected some arrogance in the term, as it seemed to provide the Germans with a birth right in relation to close contact with Eastern Europe. The sociologists Hans-Albert Steger and Renate Morell (1987: 12) perceived 'Mitteleuropa' as not being an actual place, as a signifier without a signified, yet the expression allowed for the widening of the horizon of one's thinking. The sociologist Sven Papcke and the political scientist Werner Weidenfeld (1988: viii) criticised the term for its "spatial mysticism" ("Raummystik"), its lack of clarity and its ideological dubiousness, yet also praised it for evoking a discussion that allowed the two halves of the continent to rediscover each other. While in a collection of essays translated into German from Czech, Slovak, Polish and Hungarian authors concerning 'Mitteleuropa' the literary critics Hans-Peter Burmeister, Frank Boldt and György Mészáros (1988: 7) see the concept as encapsulating an (undefined) common culture and reality, while they also link it to the broader European idea.

Thus, the term 'Mitteleuropa', encapsulating an ambiguous trans-cultural macro-region, became the centre of a wide-ranging intellectual debate in late 1980s Germany. Because of this process of intense reflection, the conscious distancing of the term from earlier Austro-German nationalist intentions, encapsulated by Friedrich Naumann's usage, and the adoption of 'Mitteleuropa' by Czech, Hungarian and Polish intellectuals, the concept, in its German language use, completely lost its earlier connotations. The term is now used regularly and retains "a positive ring" while 'Eastern Europe' "signals dissociation and rejection" (Bugge, 1999: 16). The geographers Wolfgang Natter and Hans-Dietrich Schultz (2003: 290f.) have shown that the expression 'Mitteleuropa' retains a presence in German geography schoolbooks and is one of many "utilitarian signifiers of territory".

The term has undoubtedly gained a wide currency in the German-speaking world as an unquestioned signifier. It has, indeed, become an "institutional fact" based upon convention language usage. It has, for example, been used unreflectively in a German-language Reader's Digest 'coffee table book' containing images and short informative texts concerning Germany, Switzerland, Austria, Liechtenstein, the Czech Republic, Slovakia, Poland and Hungary (Brauns, 2010). Thus, 'Mitteleuropa' represents a linguistically conjured, ambiguous trans-cultural space that has acquired conventional societal relevance as a macro-region with ambivalent, unclear borders. The linguistic sign intrinsic to its existence invokes an inclusive, trans-national and trans-cultural space beyond the nation-state.

## 'British Isles'

Spatially oriented discourses and linguistic processes may also act as a force of separation and may be used to deconstruct long established, conventional trans-cultural spatial signs that are deemed by some to be no longer valid. This may be seen in relation to the discussion surrounding the term 'British Isles' undertaken by British and Irish intellectuals and scholars during the 1990s and 2000s. The term has been attacked as colonialist and archaic when used to describe the reality of trans-island spatiality containing the two nation-states of the United Kingdom of Great Britain and Northern Ireland and the Republic of Ireland. Some of the alternatives proffered have included the 'Atlantic Archipelago', 'the Isles', 'these islands' and 'Britain and Ireland'. These attempts to discredit and deconstruct the term have been so successful that the 'British Isles' is heard decreasingly in contemporary trans-island public discourse. Thus, linguistic processes and nomenclature have been used in this context in an act of trans-cultural spatial separation.

This discussion has occupied the minds of scholars and intellectuals but also the common person, chiefly in Ireland, as represented by letter writers to Irish and British newspapers (Lenehan: 2010). Presently some scholars and intellectuals who have offered alternative terms will be examined.

The New Zealander and historian of ideas John A. Pocock engaged with this topic as early as 1974. For Pocock (2005: 26, 27) the problem of British history was that it largely constituted the expanding of "English" history onto a wider canvas, that the term "Britain" is, in itself, a multifaceted and extremely indistinct term. Pocock points out the problematic nature of the existing nomenclature and "we should start with what I have called the Atlantic archipelago since the term 'British Isles' is one which Irishmen reject and Englishmen decline to take quite seriously". The British historian Norman Davies also engaged with the problematic nature of nomenclature and decided upon a term that is also the name of his bestselling 1999 history: *The Isles*. He maintains that: "the Isles ceased to be British precisely fifty years ago when the Republic of Ireland left the Commonwealth, though few people in the British residue have yet cared to notice" (Davies, 1999: xxii). The British historian Ian Hazlett also distanced himself from the term 'British Isles' when writing a trans-island history of the Reformation. According to Hazlett (2005: 17) the older term retains colonial baggage but "nowadays, however, 'Britain and Ireland' is the more favoured expression".

Not all historians who wrote trans-island histories during this period adopted alternative terms, however. Prominent British historian Hugh Kearney's *The British Isles – A History of Four Nations*, published originally in 1989, is an influential work in which the author looked towards a decentralisation of British history, away from the "nation paradigm" and towards the "'Britannic melting pot'" (Kearney, 1995 (1989): 1, 5). In the "Preface" to the second edition of *The British Isles* from 2006 he approaches the problem of terminology directly and suggests an alternative. He discusses the term 'British Isles' and states that he is well aware that "almost inevitably many within the Irish Republic find it objectionable, much as Basques or Catalans resent the use of the term 'Spain'". Yet what, he asks, is "the alternative to 'The British Isles'?" He criticises "attempts to encourage the use of such terms as 'The Atlantic Archipelago' and 'The Isles'" due to their "vagueness", suggesting that perhaps "one solution is to use 'the British Isles' in inverted commas" (Kearney, 2006: xvi). This usage would point to the problematic nature of the term yet would also provide a distinct and obvious geographical orientation for the reader. It would also, of course, retain the sense of 'natural' interconnectedness and British essentialism associated with the term that suggests the existence of a mono-cultural space rather than a trans-cultural space.

British and Irish scholars within literary studies and literary theory have also discussed the problematic and ideologically loaded 'colonialist residue' inherent in the term 'British Isles'. The Irish literary scholar Siobhán Kilfeather (2000: 9) decides that, in response to such difficulties, 'Britain and Ireland' is becoming a "preferred usage" although there is "also a growing trend amongst some critics to refer to Britain and Ireland as 'the archipelago'". The British literary studies academic Glenda Norquay and the Irish cultural historian Gerry Smyth (2002: 4) describe their publication as a response to the "contentious practise of 'archipelagic historiography'" and as being a contribution to an "archipelagic cultural studies" or an "archipelagic cultural criticism". The authors themselves favour the term 'Atlantic archipelago' which "may be of no greater use in the long run, but at this stage it does at least have the merit of questioning the ideology underpinning more established nomenclature". The Irish literary critic Joan Fitzpatrick (2004: ix) also decides upon the expression 'Atlantic Archipelago' as, within the term 'British Isles', "is encoded a history of colonial oppression of Ireland by its neighbour". Yet, as the British literary theorists Philip Schwyzer and Simon Mealer (2004: 2) state, the term 'Atlantic Archipelago' "will probably never roll easily off the tongue". They maintain, however, that this difficulty is "part of the point" as it allows for a new perspective upon "a geographical entity whose story we may imagine we already know all too well".

These questions regarding transcultural spatial nomenclature were also highlighted by British and Irish public intellectuals, who, unlike the majority of the 'scholars' already mentioned, write for a wider audience and in publications with a more extensive distribution. Thus, for example, the Irish philosopher and public intellectual Richard Kearney, in an article for the *Edinburgh Review*, writes of the "Irish-British archipelago" when arguing for "a postnationalist paradigm of intergovernmental power" (2000: 21, 33). The British left-wing thinker and author Simon Partridge, in a text originally from 1999, also challenges what he calls the "Anglo-Saxon-Cornish-Welsh British hegemony of the 16$^{th}$ century which felt free to name these isles 'British'". In a pamphlet for the British decentralist, social democratic think tank Catalyst Partridge (1999: 16) writes: "The classical Greek name for these islands, 'Pretanic', has been suggested. For the time being it seems we will have to live with the hyphenated 'British-Irish' or 'Irish-British' and learn to say goodbye to the mutual linguistic colonialisms of the 'British Isles' and 'Republic of Ireland'". Thus, Partridge not only views the term 'British Isles' as a linguistic colonialism but also the 'Republic of Ireland'; this expression seeking to encapsulate all Irishness within the southern Irish state, thus excluding Irishness existent in Northern Ireland.

Linguistic processes are central to the creation of transcultural spaces but discussions regarding nomenclature may also result in the disintegration of trans-cultural spaces or, at the very least, their questioning. The term 'British Isles', as a conventional linguistic sign or as an "institutional fact", has undoubtedly been destabilised as a result of these discussions from the late 1990s and the early 2000s. This is to be seen, for example, when comparing the different editions of James O'Driscoll's introductory book to British culture and society for learners of English; a book that has been enormously successful, has sold in large quantities and has moulded the image of Britain and British culture for large amounts of people around the world. In the 1995 edition O'Driscoll (1995: 8, 10) writes, for example, that "in the British Isles there are two states" and "England is only one of the four nations of the British Isles". Thus, in the 1995 text O'Driscoll uses the term 'British Isles' in an unreflective fashion that suggests an essentialism or ultimate collectiveness in what is, he admits, a transcultural space; albeit a transcultural space that is, ultimately, a 'British' space. The 2009 edition, however, is different. In the later text, after the public discussion regarding the term in the late 1990s and the early 2000s, he writes that it is "not easy to keep geography and politics apart". There is no agreed single name for the two islands he states although during the "nineteenth and the twentieth centuries they were generally called 'The British Isles' but "most people in Ireland and some people in Britain" regard it as outdated because it reflects "the time when Ireland was politically dominated by Britain" (O'Driscoll, 2009: 9). Thus, this linguistically oriented discourse questioning the term 'British Isles' has been somewhat successful and has acted as a force of separation helping to deconstruct a conventional and established trans-cultural sign and notion that is no longer seen by many to retain validity.

## Conclusion

This chapter has argued that linguistic processes and nomenclature are essential to the imagining and creation of spaces, including macro-regional transcultural spaces beyond the confines of the nation-state that defy easy categorization. These linguistic processes, when intellectuals and scholars suggest new nomenclature, may be *inclusive* and result in the imagining of new, or reinvigorated, spaces that seek to elicit a sense of belonging and a sense of place beyond the nation-state. The 'Mitteleuropa' discussion of the 1980s is an example of an inclusive transcultural spatial imagining that sought to create a trans-national sense of belonging based upon the idea of a distinct trans-cultural space. Such linguistic processes may also act as a force of *separation* and may undermine conventional trans-cultural spatial notions that are no longer deemed by some to retain validity. The 'British Isles' discussion of the 1990s and the 2000s is an example of a divisive trans-cultural spatial imagining that sought to de-stabilise and question this conventional sign and the trans-cultural space it was deemed to signify.

## References


Ash, Timothy Garton (1990): Mitteleuropa? In: Daedalus. Vol. 119. No. 1. Winter. pp. 1-21.

Bender, Peter (1987): Mitteleuropa – Mode, Modell oder Motiv? In: Spannenberg, Dietrich (ed.): Die blockierte Vergangenheit – Nachdenken über Mitteleuropa. Berlin: Argon. pp. 85-103.

Brauns, Patrick (2010): Mitteleuropa. Stuttgart: Reader's Digest.

Bugge, Peter (1999): The use of the Middle: Mitteleuropa vs. Strední Evropa. In: European Review of History-Revue européenne d'Histoire. Vol. 6. No. 1. pp. 15-34.

Burkart, Roland (2003): Kommunikation als soziale Interaktion. In: Bolten, Jürgen/ Ehrhardt, Claus: Interkulturelle Kommunikation. Sternenfels: Brauner Verlag. pp. 17-38.

Burmeister, Hans-Peter/ Boldt, Frank/ Mészáros, György (1988): Vorwort. In: Burmeister, Hans-Peter/ Boldt, Frank/ Mészáros, György (eds.): Mitteleuropa Traum oder Trauma? Bremen: Edition Temmen. pp. 7-10.

Davies, Norman (1999): The Isles. London: Macmillan.

Eyerman, Ron (1996): Intellectuals in Historical and Comparative Context. In: O'Dowd, Liam: On Intellectuals and Intellectual Life in Ireland. Belfast: Baird. pp. 31-51.

Fitzpatrick, Joan (2004): Shakespeare, Spenser and the Contours of Britain – Reshaping the Atlantic Archipelago. Hertfordshire: University Press.

Glotz, Peter (1986): Deutsch-böhmische Kleinigkeiten oder: Abgerissene Gedanken über Mitteleuropa. In: Die Neue Gesellschaft / Frankfurter Hefte, Juli. pp. 584-585.
Hazlett, Ian (2005): The Reformation in Britain and Ireland. London/New York: T and T Clark.
Hobsbawn, Eric (1987): Interview with Peter Glotz. In: Marxism Today. August 1987. pp. 14-19.
Kearney, Hugh (1995): The British Isles – A History of Four Nations. Cambridge: University Press.
Kearney, Hugh (2006): The British Isles – A History of Four Nations. Cambridge: University Press.
Kearney, Richard (2000): Towards a postnationalist archipelago. In: Edinburgh Review. 103. X. pp. 21-34.
Kilfeather, Siobhán (2000): Disunited Kingdom – Irish, Scottish and Welsh writing in the postwar period. In: Davies, Alistair/ Sinfield, Alan (2000) (eds.): British Culture of the Postwar – An Introduction to Literature and Society 1945-1999. London. Routledge. pp. 9-30.
Lefebvre, Henri (1991): The Production of Space Malden. (Translated by Donald Nicholson Smith). Oxford/Victoria: Blackwell Publishing.
Lenehan, Fergal (2010): From the 'British Isles' to 'These Islands': Nomenclature, Language and Changing Social Reality? In: Jänicke, Nadine/ Lenehan, Fergal (eds.): Language and the Moulding of Space. Leipzig: Meine Verlag. pp. 45-62.
Naumann, Friedrich (1915): Mitteleuropa. Berlin: Georg Keimer.
Natter, Wolfgang/ Schultz, Hans-Dietrich (2003): Imagining "Mitteleuropa": Conceptualisations of "Its" Space in and outside German Geography. In: European Review of History- Revue européenne d'Histoire. Vol. 10. No. 2. pp. 273-292.
Norquay, Glenda/ Smyth, Gerry (2002): Introduction: crossing the margins. In: Norquay, Glenda/ Smyth, Gerry (eds.): Across the Margins – Cultural Identity and Change in the Atlantic Archipelago. Manchester: University Press. pp. 1-11.
O'Dowd, Liam (1996): Intellectuals and Intelligentsia: a Sociological Introduction. In: On Intellectuals and Intellectual Life in Ireland. Belfast: Baird. pp. 1-31.
O'Driscoll, James (1995): Britain – The Country and its People. Oxford: University Press.
O'Driscoll, James (2009): Britain – For Learners of English. Oxford: University Press.
O'Tuathail, Gearóid (1996): Critical Geopolitics. Minneapolis: University of Minnesota Press.
Papcke, Sven/ Weidenfeld, Werner (1988): Vorbemerkung. In: Papcke, Sven/ Weidenfeld, Werner (eds.): Traumland Mitteleuropa? Beiträge zu einer aktuellen Kontroverse. Darmstadt: Wissenschaftliche Buchgesellschaft. pp VII.
Partridge, Simon (1999): The British Union State – imperial hangover or flexible citizens' home? London: Aldgate Press.
Partridge, Simon (2007): The British-Irish Council: the trans-islands symbolic and political possibilities. www.britishcouncil.org/studies/england/partridge.htm [06.06.2007].
Pocock, J.G.A. (2005): British History: a Plea for a New Subject. In: The Discovery of Islands. Cambridge: University Press. pp. 24-43.
Rider, Jacques Le (1994): Mitteleuropa. Auf den Spuren eines Begriffes. Wien: Deutike.
Rovan, Joseph (1987): Betrachtungen zu Mitteleuropa. In: Spannenberg, Dietrich (ed.): Die blockierte Vergangenheit – Nachdenken über Mitteleuropa. Berlin: Argon. pp. 45-57.
Schlögel, Karl (1986): Die Mitte liegt Ostwärts – Die Deutschen, der verlorene Osten und Mitteleuropa. Berlin: Siedler.
Schlögel, Karl (1987): Nachdenken über Mitteleuropa. In: Spannenberg, Dietrich (ed.): Die blockierte Vergangenheit – Nachdenken über Mitteleuropa. Berlin: Argon. pp. 11-33.
Schwyzer, Philip (2004): Introduction. In: Philip Schwyzer/ Mealer, Simon (eds.): Archipelagic Identities – Literature and Identity in the Atlantic Archipelago. 1550-1800. Hampshire: Ashgate. pp. 1-7.
Searle, John R. (1995): The Construction of Social Reality. London/New York/Victoria/Toronto: Penguin Press.

Soja, Edward W. (1996): Thirdspace – Journeys to Los Angeles and Other Real-And-Imagined Places. Cambridge (Mass)/Oxford: Blackwell Publishers.
Steger, Hanns-Albert/ Morell, Renate (1987): Einleitung. In: Steger, Hanns-Albert/ Morell, Renate (eds.): Ein Gespenst geht um … Mitteleuropa. München: Eberhard Verlag. pp. 10-12.

# Presencia Centroamericana en la Frontera Sur de México: un Espacio en Construcción Transnacional

*Germán Martínez Velasco*

## Resumen

*Desde una visión panorámica, en este capítulo se presentan las interacciones sociales ocurridas en la frontera mexicana de Chiapas con Guatemala. Las interacciones han sido de distinta naturaleza y han estado marcadas por su tiempo histórico, comenzando con la conformación de la Frontera Sur de México en la que pueblos guatemaltecos quedaron geográficamente divididos. Otras han ocurrido por la atracción de mano de obra guatemalteca para el cultivo y desarrollo de la cafeticultura en territorio chiapaneco. Otro episodio reside por las situaciones conflictivas en Guatemala que derivaron en una migración de refugiados a México, principalmente a Chiapas, cuando numerosas poblaciones rurales de ese país, estuvieron interactuando en plena connivencia con poblaciones, también rurales mexicanas. Por último, una fase que ha propiciado otro medio de contacto ha derivado de una migración proveniente no solamente de Guatemala, sino de casi toda Centroamérica que dirigiéndose a los Estados Unidos, por diversos motivos, algunas poblaciones de hombres y mujeres, en calidad de transmigrantes, quedan estacionados en la región más fronteriza del estado que es El Soconusco Chiapas. Este último evento, constituye otro acontecimiento histórico reciente que ha modificado, no solamente el devenir de las vidas de los propios migrantes, sino de los escenarios sociales fronterizos en México. El titulo arriba enunciado, en una perspectiva de larga duración, alude a la entidad chiapaneca, especialmente a la región de El Soconusco, como un espacio en construcción trasnacional, en tanto que las manifestaciones culturales de origen centroamericano, o especialmente guatemaltecas que se presentan son todavía muy incipientes aún cuando su presencia es de larga data y de arraigo histórico. Esto se debe, en gran parte, al carácter hegemónico que la cultura mexicana tiene, y que como campo minado se disemina en todo el territorio nacional y allende sus frontera, y por otra, a las circunstancias de vulnerabilidad social en que los distintos segmentos de población guatemalteca que han llegado a Chiapas y en las que permencen, hace que sus manifestaciones culturales se tornen furtivas.*

## Introducción

La formación histórica de la frontera sur de México, socialmente nació siendo binacional en razón de que al establecerse el pacto de demarcación de la línea divisoria entre los gobiernos de México y Guatemala en 1882, en lo que corresponde a la demarcación del estado mexicano de Chiapas, multitud de poblaciones de origen guatemalteco quedaron al instante convertidas en chiapanecas, y por tanto en mexicanas debido a que sus asentamientos geográficamente quedaron formando parte del territorio nacional.

A este primer acontecimiento le continuó un flujo constante de población rural guatemalteca debido al inicio y consolidación de la plantación cafetalera en el estado fronterizo de Chiapas, México, que hasta la fecha esa actividad sigue incorporando grupos familiares originarios de poblados fronterizos de Guatemala que de manera temporal, en su mayoría, se emplean en distintas labores agrícolas del café, además de otros grupos de personas que eventualmente se asientan de manera indefinida en dichas unidades agrícolas de corte empresarial.

Otro elemento detonador de la presencia centroamericana en la frontera sur de México, consistió en la presencia de miles de familias que en calidad de refugiados se asentaron a lo largo de toda la franja fronteriza del estado de Chiapas con Guatemala a finales de la década de 1970 y a principios de la de 1990. Este evento constituyo un parte-aguas en las relaciones sociales de las poblaciones de ambos países, en tanto que por la fuerza de los hechos, las poblaciones refugiadas de manera intempestiva entraron en intensa interacción social con las poblaciones receptoras, generando así una serie de intercambios materiales y simbólicos.

Con las crisis política y económica permanentes en Guatemala desde el decenio de los 80's, y los procesos de pérdida de cohesión intra-familiar, producto del proceso modernizador acaecido en las sociedades latinoamericanas, se originaron cada vez mas desprendimientos de mujeres adolescentes y adultas de sus respectivas unidades familiares, con fines de contribuir a la reproducción familiar, por lo que hacia finales de la década de 1980, se afianza la presencia de ellas en ciudades fronterizas de Chiapas, principalmente en la mas importante ciudad llamada Tapachula en labores de baja remuneración en calidad de trabajadoras domésticas.

De manera simultánea, otro segmento importante de mujeres, no solamente guatemaltecas sino de casi toda Centroamérica, principalmente de origen urbano, habrían de insertarse en el comercio sexual también en las ciudades de la frontera sur de México, con su consecuente estigmatizacion por parte de las sociedades locales. Lo inmediato anterior, sería el preludio de una masiva corriente migratoria de población centroamericana que ocurre en los años 90's que habrían de llegar a la frontera sur de México en calidad de indocumentados con intenciones de pasar por Chiapas, recorrer el territorio mexicano y llegar a los Estados Unidos de Norteamérica. En tal contexto, la entidad chiapaneca, se habría de convertir en un primer filtro mediante el cual, algunos segmentos de población indocumentada sin posibilidades de continuar la travesía, optarían por permanecer en la región en espera de tiempos mejores.

La conjunción de una serie de procesos tanto de larga como de corta duración configurada en la región fronteriza de Chiapas, han desplegado un proceso gradual de construcción de un espacio transnacional a partir de las distintas dinámicas de interacción fronteriza.

Lo que aquí se expone son levantamientos de información de campo con población local originaria de la entidad, así como de inmigrantes, unos residentes y otros de paso, así como de conversaciones con actores locales y regionales de los organismos de la sociedad civil e instancias gubernamentales mexicanas y centroamericanas (consulados) así como de aquellos únicos estudios que tangencialmente han abordado el tema.

## Geografía y destino guatemalteco: primer contacto transnacional

A tono con la construcción de los estados nacionales en América Latina en la era poscolonial, se impuso la necesidad de establecer los límites territoriales entre los nacientes estados-nación. En ese sentido México y Guatemala iniciaron lo propio concluyendo con el tratado de límites en 1882 que acreditó la posesión de México de un territorio, considerado en tiempos coloniales como parte del Reino de Guatemala, consistentes en porciones geográficas del Departamento de San Marcos que junto con sus numerosos pueblos y habitantes, sin ningún cambio residencial de un día a otro, fueron designados por ambos gobiernos como nuevos mexicanos (González Navarro, 1974; Cossío Villegas, 1972; Martínez Velasco, 1994).

De acuerdo a Martínez Velasco (op. cit.) esta población que quedó del lado mexicano serían los que habrían de convertirse en la mano de obra inmediata y mas importante para los inicios de la plantación cafetalera en el estado mexicano de Chiapas; detalla los procedimientos y vicisitudes experimentados cuando el gobierno mexicano emprendió la nacionalización de estos guatemaltecos residentes en su territorio nacional. Señala como factor determinante la imperiosa necesidad de otorgar cartas de naturalización a los jornaleros agrícolas guatemaltecos, que junto con el campesinado mexicano, tiempo atrás habían iniciado un movimiento agrario en la región de Mariscal y Soconusco y su inevitable resolución a través del otorgamiento de parcelas agrícolas por parte del gobierno mexicano, previa acreditación de ostentar la nacionalidad mexicana. También expone las dificultades que tuvo la instancia gubernamental llamada Comisión Demográfica Inter-secretarial para la cesión de la ciudadanía mexicana, ya que dentro de estos contingentes agraristas, también se habían incorporado otros grupos de guatemaltecos que siendo residentes de ese territorio, incursionaban en calidad de jornaleros temporales a las plantaciones de café en Chiapas, y que ante la expectativa de obtener tierra en México, se adscribían también como mexicanos de origen guatemalteco no reconocidos. Sin duda que el interés de grandes núcleos de población rural residente en Guatemala consistía en alcanzar dos oportunidades históricas: a) escapar de las condiciones y relaciones de servidumbre en que se encontraban derivado del peonaje por deudas[1] impuestos por el Estado guatemalteco en beneficio de terratenientes de ese país; y b) convertirse en propietarios de parcelas agrícolas con aspiraciones de alcanzar libertad de movimiento laboral, y mejoras domésticas con base en el usufructo de la tierra. Este proceso concluyó con la entrega de tierras a mexicanos de nacimientos y mexicanos de origen guatemalteco por naturalización, así como de guatemaltecos que – en sentido estricto – encontraron la oportunidad de asumirse como residentes en México que difícilmente las autoridades mexicanas en situación de convulsión agraria podían diferenciar claramente.

Se tiene entonces la existencia de un primer e intenso contacto entre mexicanos y guatemaltecos dado por tres grandes eventos históricos: a) los acuerdos de los límites fronterizos entre Guatemala y México; b) las interacciones laborales entre guatemalte-

---

1 El peonaje por deudas consistía en un sistema, que mediante deudas, arraigaba a la población rural a las haciendas fincas o ranchos y con ello, garantizar la disposición de mano de obra según las necesidades de esas unidades agrícolas.

cos y mexicanos en los espacios de trabajo de las plantaciones cafetaleras, y c) la incorporación de guatemaltecos en la demanda por la tierra y su consecuente acceso a la misma, en plena interacción con los mexicanos de origen, producto de la lucha y de la posterior vecindad rural.

Sin embargo, la política de mexicanización que el gobierno mexicano impuso para las poblaciones guatemaltecas residentes en México, no permitieron que estos hechos históricos se convirtieran en los detonantes de procesos de diversidad cultural, sino todo lo contrario, de negación de la identidad guatemalteca. Basado en el discurso de la lealtad nacional proclamado por el Estado mexicano, la integración y la asimilación forzada hicieron lo suyo para proceder a la homogeneización cultural, evitando en la medida de lo posible, la "migración" de la identidad guatemalteca, su reproducción en el nuevo lugar de residencia, o la re-creación cultural con base en la matriz de origen. El trabajo de Hernández Castillo (2008) sobre la aculturación emprendida por el Estado Mexicano a dicha población indica de la existencia de un desplazamiento lingüístico y la sustitución de lenguas mayas como el jakalteko, kaqchikel, mam, mochó, q'anjoba'l y chuj, por el castellano.

Pasado el tiempo, guatemaltecos y mexicanos a la fecha siguen interactuando en el ámbito laboral, a través de su participación en el cultivo del café chiapaneco teniendo como escenario social no solamente a las grandes plantaciones de café como antaño, sino a un sinnúmero de comunidades campesinas mexicanas, en las que se incluyen a las nuevas generaciones de mames de padres o abuelos naturalizados, y que en determinadas épocas del año estas comunidades requieren de la mano de obra de sus compañeros de etnia provenientes del otro lado de la frontera.

## El refugio guatemalteco: segundo contacto.

Otro gran proceso de interacción fronteriza lo constituyó la traumática guerra intestina al interior de Guatemala durante mediados de la década de los 80's y principios de los 90's que generó masivas corrientes de migraciones forzadas a distintos puntos de la frontera Chiapas-Guatemala. Agravios y resentimientos sociales acumulados en contra de las comunidades indígenas de Guatemala, desde épocas coloniales y pos-coloniales, y las respuestas organizadas incubadas desde mediados de la década de los años 50's mediante la intermitente aparición de grupos insurgentes, alcanzaron su forma más estructurada a finales de los 70's mediante actos de resistencia y apropiación de tierras, lo que hizo de estas comunidades rurales un blanco sangriento por parte del Estado guatemalteco.

El resultado de la estrategia de "tierra arrazada" por parte de la élite militar guatemalteca propició la intempestiva llegada de refugiados guatemaltecos a territorio mexicano en casi toda su franja fronteriza, en un número acumulado en 1984 de 46,000 personas según fuentes oficiales de la Comisión Mexicana de Ayuda a Refugiados (*comar*), mientras que hacia 1989 la cifra alcanzaba a los 53,000 refugiados según *comar* y *cirefca*, (Conferencia Internacional sobre Refugiados Centroamericanos), citado en Martínez (op. cit.: 55). Ahora bien, es importante aclarar que las cifras arriba señaladas, correspondían solamente a las personas refugiadas que por iniciativa propia habían sido dadas de alta en los registros de la comar, sin tomar en cuenta un número indeterminado de personas, que también habían llegado a territorio mexicano como escape a la muerte, pero que por algún motivo optaron por permanecer en el anonimato y en consecuencia, no ser acreedor de la ayuda mexicana e internacional. Este grupo de personas se les denominó refugiados dispersos, y mediante una asociación llamada ardigua (Asociación de Refugiados Dispersos de Guatemala) se estimaba su número en una cifra que ascendía a 150,000 personas (Martínez Velasco 1994, op. cit.).

La diseminación de la población refugiada se presentó en situación precaria a lo largo de 300 kilómetros de la línea divisoria entre Guatemala y el estado mexicano de Chiapas, en ejidos, tierras comunales, ranchos, fincas y poblados en general. En una reunión celebrada en 1999, en San Cristóbal de Las Casas, se hizo un balance de la situación de los refugiados reconocidos por distintas instancias tanto gubernamentales como no gubernamentales, publicándose un documento de esa reunión en 2002 (Kauffer, 2002), en que se aprecia, que hacia finales de los años 90's casi 20 años después de haberse iniciado el refugio, y que una parte de refugiados se había trasladado- a iniciativa del gobierno mexicano, a otros estados del país como Campeche y Quintana Roo, se planteaba la cuestión de que la población refugiada se encontraba en el dilema de quedarse a vivir de manera permanente en México o bien retornar al país de origen. Se convertía en un conflicto, porque para ese entonces, la mitad de la población refugiada de origen guatemalteco, había nacido ya en tierras mexicanas y esa situación hacía difícil el desarraigo para las poblaciones jóvenes, de tal suerte, que al final de cuentas, hubieron familias que sí aceptaron el retorno y otras que refrendaron su asentamiento definitivo en México (Kauffer, op. cit.).

Para los propósitos de este documento, cabe mencionar que la publicación en referencia, aún cuando su título consiste en "La Integración de los Exrefugiados Guatemaltecos en México", de la *integración*, solamente se refiere a los mecanismos legales mediantes los cuales la *comar* instrumentó la legalización indefinida de la población en el país, es decir, de la puesta en marcha de un programa de estabilización migratoria que consistió en el otorgamiento de visas, que para los que deseaban establecerse en México se les brindaba la FM-2, y FM-3 para los que deseaban regresar a Guatemala. A esto y la asistencia emanada por los gobiernos locales y la *comar*, se le llamó integración, sin mayor análisis del plano sociocultural de las poblaciones refugiadas con las mexicanas.

La experiencia guatemalteca en México, principalmente para el estado de Chiapas, constituyó una ambivalencia por parte de las poblaciones exiliadas como las receptoras, ya que por una parte, si bien por cuestiones de vecindad y humanitarismo les fueron abiertas las puertas, también fueron muy bien conocidas las condiciones que se les impusieron a las familias guatemaltecas en relación a los contra-pagos que tenían que cubrir en servicios colectivos a las comunidades mexicanas, los bajos salarios obtenidos por largas jornadas en las parcelas de los ejidatarios y comuneros, la extrema limitación en el uso de los recursos naturales disponibles como la leña y el agua, y por último, los celos colectivos en las comunidades mexicanas causados por la ayuda nacional e internacional que los refugiados recibían.

Así, el fenómeno del refugio constituyó otra posibilidad de interacción bicultural, multicultural, intercultural o transcultural con las poblaciones fronterizas mexicanas, pero debido a circunstancias totalmente asimétricas y de desgaste psico-social por parte de las guatemaltecas, no permitieron tener mas y mejores expresiones de sus culturas originarias, quedando integradas por la fuerza de los hechos a la cultura nacional hegemónica de México.

## Centroamericanos a Estados Unidos: La espera transmigrante en Chiapas, México, tercer contacto.

Los graves conflictos suscitados en Guatemala, concluyeron con la firma de paz en diciembre de 1996, suscritos por los representantes del Estado guatemalteco con los representantes de la Unión Nacional Revolucionaria de Guatemala (unrg). Por su parte, el conflicto de El Salvador, después de 12 años de guerra civil se puso fin con los Acuerdos de Paz de Chapultepec, en enero de 1992 firmados por el Gobierno salvadoreño y los representantes del Frente Farabundo Martí de Liberación Nacional (ffmln). Se refiere como *Chapultepec* a un lugar histórico de la Ciudad de México debido a que este país tuvo una notable participación en la creación y posterior gestión del llamado Grupo de Contadora compuesto por los países de México, Colombia, Panamá y Venezuela.

Antes, en 1991, Nicaragua había emprendido un largo proceso de paz, culminado en 1997 que también ponía fin a 20 años de los cuales los primeros 10 habían sido de guerra civil contra el poder de la familia Somoza, y los restantes, del gobierno sandinista que siempre tuvo enfrente la fuerza a los contra-revolucionarios agrupados en la llamada resistencia nicaragüense.

No es casualidad que cuando los procesos de paz se habían cristalizado en Centroamérica, es cuando ocurren las migraciones masivas de carácter laboral fuera de la región Centroamericana. Las devastadas economías centroamericanas, producto del desaliento a la inversión productiva de años precedentes; el desempleo también causado por los altos montos de bajas de miembros tanto de los ejércitos oficiales como el de los insurgentes; un mercado interno nada dinámico, más las severas crisis en sus productos de agro-exportación como el café y banano; gobiernos con infladas deudas públicas, aparte de los impactos sociales de las políticas de ajuste estructural inspirados en los dictados del Fondo Monetario Internacional, hicieron de Centroamérica el santuario de la migración a los Estados Unidos de Norteamérica. Su paso por México, inevitable.

Según estadísticas del Instituto Nacional de Migración (inm), organismo encargado de controlar y deportar a los grupos de inmigrantes que llegan a México, reportó que entre 2001 y 2010 se registraron 1,344,946 eventos de deportación, de los cuales aproximadamente el 96.6 por ciento corresponden a nacionalidades centroamericanas. Según la misma fuente, se tiene que los guatemaltecos se encuentran en primer lugar, los hondureños en segundo, en tercero los salvadoreños y en cuarto los de origen nicaragüense. En concordancia con lo anterior, de acuerdo al siguiente gráfico 1, del total de centroamericanos deportados entre 2009 y 2010, cerca de la mitad le corresponde a los guatemaltecos; poco más de un tercio a los hondureños; en un 15.0 por ciento a los salvadoreños, y menos del 5.0 por ciento los nicaragüenses. También se puede apreciar la poca importancia que tienen en el flujo otros países centroamericanos como Belice, Costa Rica y Panamá.

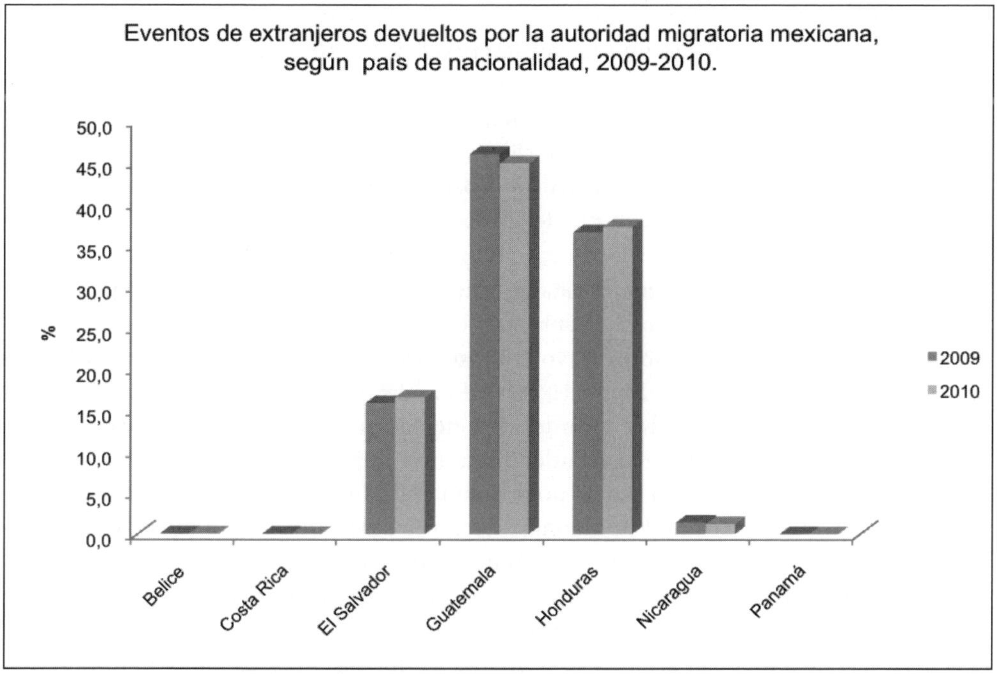


Fuente: Instituto Nacional de Migración. Serie histórica 1999-2010

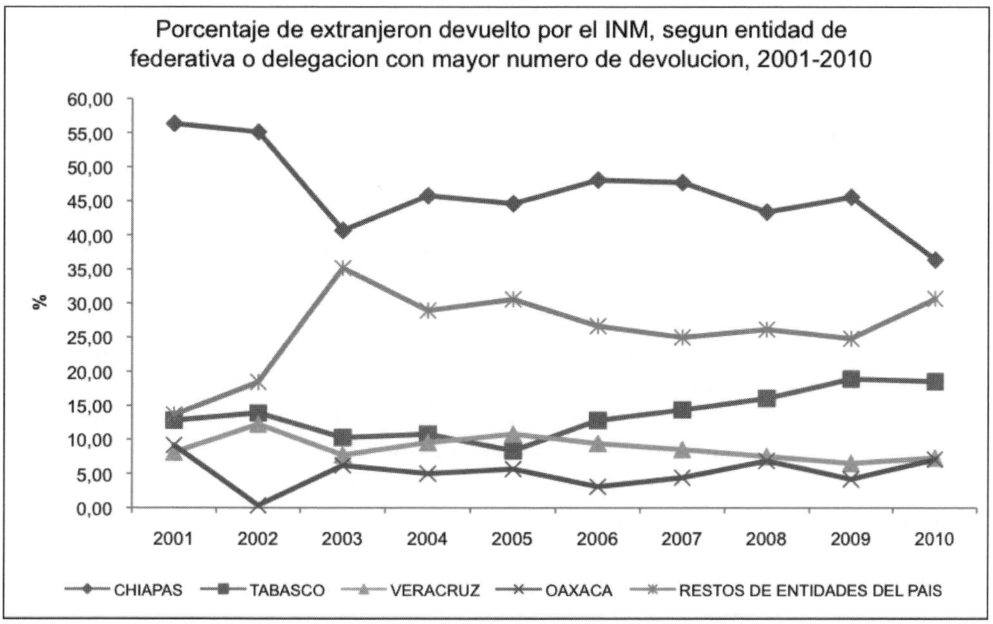


Fuente: Instituto Nacional de Migración. Serie histórica 1999-2010

El mayor contacto fronterizo que tiene la entidad mexicana de Chiapas con Centroamérica, se demuestra en que una mayor cantidad de personas de esa región pasa por el territorio chiapaneco y también en esa medida se realizan ahí un mayor número de aprehensiones y deportación de indocumentados (gráfico 2). En términos cuantitativos esta es la única evidencia con la que se prueba la posición que las entidades del país tienen respecto a su importancia de ser un espacio de transmigrantes.

De la gráfica anterior, también puede apreciarse, que el estado de Chiapas ha tenido una baja en el número de deportaciones, situación que está relacionada con una menor presencia de transmigrantes por el estado, mientras que otra entidad fronteriza como lo es Tabasco ha asumido una destacada participación a raíz de la reorientación de los flujos centroamericanos. La razón de lo anterior reside en que en el estado de Chiapas se reforzaron las medidas de control terrestre por las principales vías que comunican con el centro de país, pero sobre todo por los efectos que el huracan Stan dejó en 2005 en las comunicaciones terrestres en la entidad, que imposibilitaron el funcionamiento del medio fundamental usado por la población centroamericana: el ferrocarril mexicano, llamado la 'bestia'. Por ambas razones, los grupos de indocumentados comenzaron a trasladarse al interior del territorio guatemalteco por la región de El Petén, y así ingresar por otra de las puertas de entrada a México, siendo ésta la zona fronteriza del estado de Tabasco llamado Tenosique. Esta reorientación de una parte del flujo centroamericano ha tenido un gran costo humano, ya que ha sido por esa región de El Petén-Tabasco, en donde se han establecido con mayor presencia y crudeza bandas del crímen organizado que asolan la región con actividades ilícitas como lo es el secuestro y la extorsión a migrantes. Las localidades fronterizas de mayor cruce es Tenosique en territorio mexicano y la localidad de El Ceibo en territorio guatemalteco.

*El espacio transnacional: El Soconusco chiapaneco*

Como se mencionó al inicio del documento, la mayor interacción fronteriza entre Centroamérica y Chiapas ha sido la región fronteriza de El Soconusco; y Tapachula ha sido la ciudad-capital regional en donde la población centroamericana despliega una serie de actividades de sobrevivencia cotidiana. Como también se dijo, es por aquí por donde actual e históricamente, la población centroamericana ha incursionado su travesía ya sea sólo al interior de la región o bién por todo el país. Desde principios de los años 90's la región se conviertió en el santuario de la inmigración centroamericana a México, unos con fines de establecerse en la región, la mayoría con intenciones de usar el territorio para llegar a la frontera México-Estados Unidos. Es en esta década cuando comienza a identificarse el ferrocarril como el fundamental medio de transporte, y con esto, la ocurrencia de miles de mutilados como consecuencia de sus movimientos improvisados ya sea en su intento por subir al tren, o, una vez arriba, en su adormilado viaje, caer súbitamente a tierra entre las vías y ruedas de la 'bestia'.

A esta primera población frustrada de su viaje, se le suma otra población que habiendo optado por el automovil o tractocamión con la guia de un 'coyote' es aprehendida por los cuerpos de seguridad y control migratorio como la Policia Federal Preventiva (pfp) o bien del Instituto Nacional de Migración (inm). Despues de ser deportados, en la mayoría de las veces retornan a México con la esperanza de que en un nuevo intento alcancen sus propósitos de vida, sin embargo, esta población puede ser de nuevo aprehendida y, después de mas intentos, sin dinero, decide permanecer transitoria o indefinidamente en la región. Debido a la ola de asaltos y secuestros a migrantes ocurridos en todo México, principalmente en el corredor del Golfo de México: Tabasco, Veracrúz y Tamaulipas, se torna en un motivo más para que cientos de indocumentos decidan permanecer temporalmente en Chiapas, mientras se allegan de nuevos recursos económicos para continuar el recorrido.

Estos rostros migratorios son los que deambulan y pueblan en casi toda la región de El Soconusco, pero con mayor preponderancia en la ciudad de Tapachula, debido al volúmen de población que representa ésta y las posibilidades de acceder a empleos de diversa índole, así como también de ser alojados en los varios albergues y casas del migrante ahí ubicados.

La presencia centroamericana en El Soconusco, Chiapas, se centra básicamente en tres nacionalidades: guatemalteca, hondureña y salvadoreña. La primera la que históricamente tiene los lazos comunes en relación a historia, geografía y paisanaje, su presencia no solamente es a través de su asentamiento residencial, sino en el 'ir y venir' cotidianos de la población fronteriza guatemalteca que reside en los pueblos adyacentes a la línea fronteriza. La población residente consiste en aquellos pequeños grupos que día con día vienen a la región, con fines de compra-venta de mercaderías, es decir, son personas que traen productos guatemaltecos como verduras, al tiempo que llevan productos mexicanos industrializados como aceite, pastas, bebidas, cigarrillos, etc. Otro flujo también consiste en mujeres guatemaltecas que estando en México, se dedican a la reventa de productos mexicanos y que en una esquina, o de casa en casa deambulan por la principal localidad que es Tapachula. Otro flujo importante de mujeres guatemaltecas es aquel que se dedica al trabajo doméstico, que vienen y regresan semanalmente, empleándose fundamentalmente en la citada ciudad. Existen hombres, que aparte del trabajo agrícola inicialmente mencionado, desarrollan actividades laborales urbanas en la industria de la construcción, músicos y vendedores, unos regresan diariamente y otros aguardan en casas de parientes guatemaltecos en territorio mexicano.

Por su parte, la población residente de origen guatemalteco en la región, ha facilitado su consolidación residencial principalmente a través de la inserción en el comercio establecido y en toda clase de actividades del sector informal, estableciendo alianzas con grupos – también de comerciantes mexicanos y guatemaltecos – en la lucha por el control de los espacios comerciales y en la cuotas del derecho de piso que se exige a otros grupos mas desprotegidos, sean guatemaltecos o mexicanos. También se dedican en el trasiego de mercancías y personas en la línea divisoria, que en alianza con grupos de comercio de contrabando y de tráfico de indocumentados, sean éstos mexicanos o centroamericanos les representa significativas ganancias que les permite adquirir lotes de terreno e edificación de viviendas.

Las interacciones sociales en el ámbito cultural con las poblaciones mexicanas se establecen a través de la participación en la fe religiosa. Además de la frecuente socialización en los rituales cotidianos, también ocurre en la organización, diseño de estrategias y operación para la cooptación de más adeptos y en el engrandecimiento y consolidación de las innumerables iglesias pertenecientes a los credos no católicos en las que ellos militan. Quizás sea este el eje principal de mayor intensidad en la interacción transnacional entre guatemaltecos y mexicanos, ya que ambos grupos, en simetría organizacional, despliegan sus actividades tanto al interior de México como en el de Guatemala.

El deporte también es un ámbito de socialización, principalmente entre hombres, que unidos a través de los ámbitos laborales y/o del vecindario propician interacciones amistosas que se recrean en los campos deportivos, principalmente en la práctica del futbolsoccer y otros de menor cuantía como en son en los billares y en el basquetbol.

Cabe señalar que esta socialización de la población guatemalteca se presenta de manera bilateral con la población mexicana, sin que existan mayores nexos con otras nacionalidad, sin embargo, es a través del sexo-servicio en que la socialización se convierte en multilateral, ya que es esa actividad la que propicia la interacción con las nacionalidades hondureña y salvadoreña, sin obviar la mexicana que participa en su calidad de jefaturas de puesto, trátese de hombres o de mujeres, posicionados al frente de la operación y administración de los establecimientos, así como en la destacada participación masculina, también mexicana, como consumidora de dicho servicio.

En el colectivo masculino de origen mexicano, el ejercicio de la prostitución de centroamericanas se concibe como el toque "exótico" de la vida nocturna, en este caso, no solamente de Tapachula, sino también de Tuxtla-Chico, Cacahoatán y otras localidades técnicamente limítrofes, así como otras más al interior de la región, en la costa chiapaneca, y otras regiones fronterizas donde se ubican las localidades de Frontera Comalapa y Comitán de Domínguez. Asi, la vida nocturna en la región, se desliza para los consumidores mexicanos entre un centro nocturno a otro, unas veces en busca de mujeres previamente conocidas, en otras, en busca de nuevas mujeres, mejor aún si se trata de menores de edad. Para las poblaciones femeninas, la noche transcurre en la espera de algún cliente, para tomar bebidas alcohólicas y cobrar por eso y/o establecer acuerdos monetarios por su efímeros servicios sexuales.

Los estereotipos mexicanos en la definición de lo *fronterizo* en Chiapas, más que por la interculturalidad o multiculturalidad que pudiera existir, se define por lo más tangible y visible de la vida cotidiana: la prostitución centroamericana, los pequeños grupos de maras que eventualmente llegan a la región, y las empleadas domésticas, estas últimas haciéndose visibles mediante su día recreativo que es el domingo, circunscrito al parque central de Tapachula. Otro grupo importante que se mueve en los claroscuros cotidianos consiste en los indocumentados, unos en tránsito y otros varados, que se hacen visibles en su andar en busca del tren, el coyote, o en búsqueda de un alojamiento *exprofeso*. Esta es la grafía o el conjunto de signos que envuelve la vida fronteriza en Chiapas, develándose como los *íconos* representativos de la región, al tiempo que en términos maniqueos se convierten en insumos para la *nota roja* de los diarios locales.

Guatemaltecas, hondureñas y salvadoreñas son el grueso de la población involucrada en el sexo-comercio, y que unas por azahares del proceso migratorio quedaron enganchadas en las redes de la prostitución en espera casi permanente de tiempos mejores para continuar su marcha hacia los Estados Unidos. Fernández-Casanueva (1999) presenta la variedad de situaciones y vicisitudes experimentadas en sus trayectorias migratorias desde sus lugares de origen hasta las que hicieron posible estacionarse en las localidades desempeñando tal actividad. La autora (op. cit.) refiere que aun cuando se trata de mujeres indocumentadas laborando en una actividad como el sexo-servicio, lo que las ubica en una situación de marginalidad, no por eso dejan de tener una serie de redes sociales que en determinado momento utilizan para mantener su estancia o para librar las aprehensiones por parte de los cuerpos de seguridad migratorios. Los apoyos vienen tanto de las mismas compañeras de trabajo como de las amistades mexicanas, principalmente hombres, que muchas de las veces pueden propiciar un desenlace amoroso.

Sin embargo, otras centroamericanas, aún cuando también se encuentran en situaciones vulnerables, su espectro de opciones se antoja distinto. En el caso específico de Dalia, de 25 años de edad, inmigrante hondureña corrobora las opciones distintas al sexo-servicio, ya que ha tenido oferta de trabajo en bares, pero ella ha decidido por un *trabajo digno*

> Hemos salido a buscar trabajo, nos piden ser legales con el FM3 (…). Nos han ofrecido mucho ese trabajo (sexo-servicio), pero mejor vamos a seguir buscando otro trabajo haber si encontramos (…). Una señora quería de mesera de cantina y me iba a pagar 50 pesos de 4 a 2 de la mañana: ¡eso es explotación! y 'si quieres puedes tomar' (alcohol) me dijo; no, yo no acostumbro ni tomar en mi país, menos acá (…) tampoco, casi no tratamos con hombres preferimos estar solas (…). Pues (prefiero) como mesera de restaurantes, o de cocinera; (…) no conozco la comida de aquí, pero aprendo! (Entrevista con Dalia, julio de 2010)

Dalia había trabajado hasta inicios del 2007 como operaria en una maquiladora de ropa, ubicada en San Pedro Sula, su ciudad natal en Honduras. Narra que el salario mínimo que ganaba (menos de 100 dólares mensuales) apenas le alcanzaba para su propio sostenimiento y el de su grupo familiar: "Ah yo me dedicaba a las maquilas, pero el problema del país como te has dado cuenta esta muy mal, desempleo, están cerrando fábricas. ¡Es el problema!"

Después de estar varios meses radicando en Tapachula, señala "me gustaría quedarme acá pero cuesta mucho hacer los trámites. Pero dios sabe, El dispone (…)." De esa forma, con esa incertidumbre dejada a la inercia pasan los días en la eterna espera, pudiendo ser que de un momento a otro cambie, o que el tiempo imperecedero tenga que definirlo.

En otras entrevistas, se pudo identificar las dificultades que tiene la población centroamericana para responder a las circunstancias a través de la constitución de redes, por ejemplo, un entrevistado señaló: "No, a veces, no es muy bueno entablar conversación con cualquier persona, sin mucha confianza porque uno no sabe con qué intenciones viene (…), tal vez si puedo hablar pero tranquilo (con cautela) y todo pero hasta ahí nada más" (Entrevista con Efrén, junio 2010).

También hubo quienes dijeron que es mejor viajar sólo cuando se transita por la región con destino hacia la frontera norte, ya que de esa manera se evita ser vistos por los asaltantes de migrantes, e igualmente evitar platicar y omitir si uno lleva dinero o no durante el viaje. Esto responde a que muchas de las veces, dentro del mismo grupo de inmigrantes en tránsito se han camuflajeado integrantes de la delincuencia organizada, sea de los propios centroamericanos o de mexicanos, o bien de grupos mixtos, que dentro de la misma ciudad o en el trayecto hacia el destino norte, con esa información, sus golpes hacia cada uno de los inmigrantes serán más certeros.

Lo anterior, parece indicar que los inmigrantes no tienen una relación sólida con los de su misma nacionalidad, en este caso, entre hondureños, ya que aún estando en la ciudad de Tapachula, se previenen de sufrir de algún tipo de agresión por parte de sus mismos connacionales: "No quiero saber de ellos, porque ellos van a decir hey vos chele – porque así nos decimos allá en Honduras – o me van a decir hey vos güero veni vamos a echarnos algo; nada de nada, me siento bien como estoy, al contrario en vez de andar a la bebida me siento súper bien, aquí solo (...)" (Entrevista con Hugo, Julio de 2010).

En cambio, los inmigrantes prefieren construir o formar relaciones sociales con otras nacionalidades, dependiendo del tiempo y la confianza que estos se tengan durante el tiempo de permanencia en Tapachula, Neftalí inmigrante, manifestó que la red se va construyendo a partir del primer momento que se establecen en el albergue. "Depende de cómo esté la gente en el albergue, si no hay problemas, por ejemplo en este albergue nos ha dado bastante confianza no hay problemas, ni nada, platicamos bastante y todo (...)" (Entrevista con Efrén, Julio 2010).

Sin embargo, otros escenarios se tornan difíciles, como el que se relata:

> (...) uno encuentra de todo tipo sean paisanos (connacionales) pero hay unos que les gusta beber bastante utilizan drogas o a veces uno mejor evita ese andar con ellos porque de repente se consigue la muerte porque no es nada seguro ni en el camino ni en la calle o por donde quiera que vayas en la línea del tren siempre los problemas están a la orden del día pues cualquier cosa le puede pasar a uno, entonces lo mejor es evitar acercarse aunque sean personas tuyas pero si usted ve que el usa droga o es alcohólico mejor lo haces a un lado y buscar de otra manera (Entrevista con Carlos, Julio 2010).

Producto de las circunstancias que les acontece a lo migrantes en la frontera en la que se incluye la población varada en Tapachula y en otras pequeñas localidades de la región, en cierta forma, éstos espacios han dejado de ser solamente lugares de tránsito de indocumentados para convertirse en lugares de paulatino asentamiento. En el caso de las mujeres que se dedican a la prostitución, un primer paso es el bar, la casa de cita, o como también se constató, el alojamiento breve en un cuarto sea de una amiga o de algún hombre conocido con pago de favores mutuos: "vivo en una colonia aquí en Tapachula, un barrio no sé cómo se llama con un señor de aquí de Tapachula que es bien lindo" (Entrevista con Jackelinne, Julio 2010).

En contraste, en el caso de los transmigrantes hombres que las circunstancias acaecidas en el camino hicieron que su estadía sea en la región, una primera y única opción son las casas o albergues del migrante. Si no se consiguen estos alojamientos, entonces optan involuntariamente por los lugares riesgosos debido a la ubicación y del conocimiento que de ellos tienen por parte de los asaltantes. Cuestión de género.

> La verdad que cuando llegamos veníamos con poco dinero, igual estábamos aquí en Tapachula no hallábamos donde agarrar para donde, estuve allí en el parque empecé a buscar algunas ayudas que me dijeran por lo menos que qué podía hacer, ya habíamos decidido dormir en la calle pero un señor, no sé si pastor de la iglesia me dijo que en la parte de abajo hay un albergue y nos venimos práctica-

> mente caminando y de ahí pues no hallábamos para donde agarrar no dábamos con el albergue, agarre un taxi que me vino a dejar a este lugar (Entrevista con Carlos, Julio de 2010).

Cabe resaltar aquí la importancia de las organizaciones civiles que fungen como apoyo a los inmigrantes como los albergues el Buen pastor y albergue Belem. Es el caso de Carlos, como cuando llegó por primera vez a Tapachula, Chiapas en que las organizaciones civiles fueron sus anfitrionas.

Si después de algunos días, no obtienen alojamiento en otros sitios, algunos consiguen prolongar su estancia en los albergues de paso, negociando con sus respectivos responsables, en donde por reglamento se hubieran quedado únicamente por tres días. Durante el día, pueden emplearse en trabajos de la construcción, en talleres mecánicos, en el comercio o en restaurantes y cantinas; otros de limpia-parabrisas en los cruceros de la ciudad: el objetivo es reunir el dinero suficiente para proseguir su viaje. Los menos se quedan en fincas de café o de otros cultivos ocupandose en labores agrícolas.

En los dias de trabajo de campo realizado en la ciudad de Tapachula, se tuvo la oportunidad de encontrar a inmigrantes de origen hondureño, que se autodenominaban exiliados políticos debido al golpe de Estado ocurrido en Honduras en junio de 2009 que derrotó al presidente Zelaya.

> como esa feria fue al amanecer (la feria de Tapachula), si de hecho ahí encontré a un paisano que trabajaba en un restaurante pues él nos dio comida y la cena; y cuando el restaurante cerro fue como las 3 de la mañana nosotros le ayudamos a recoger las bancas y todo y nos tendió una colcha y nos quedamos a dormir (...) al siguiente día fuimos a COMAR y también al siguiente día, y entonces a partir de ese momento COMAR empezó a llevar nuestro caso para tramitar nuestros papeles (Entrevista con Tomás, Julio 2010).

En estos casos, los inmigrantes pueden demorar en un albergue durante semanas, mientras la *comar* (Comisión Mexicana de Ayuda a Refugiados) determina la situación migratoria del solicitante (González Hernández, 2010).

La percepción laboral del migrante centroamericano, en este caso, el hondureño, está basada en el optimismo de encontrar un trabajo en México y así permanecer aquí: Hugo dice: "sí me encantaría quedarme y trabajar aquí"; y Tomás comenta "Pues yo hablé con la licenciada de *comar* pienso que ellos pudieran a hacer algún trámite porque tengo mi hija allá (Honduras) entonces quiero tenerla cerca de mí y a mi esposa también, y así salir de Tapachula ya que esta forma parte de la frontera sur y prefiero no quedarme" (Entrevistas con Hugo y Tomás, Julio 2010).

En definitiva, existe una ambivalencia en parte de esta población, en relación a quedarse en México, pero no en Tapachula, lo que significa no solamente cambiar de lugar, sino principalmente de escenario social, deseo compartido en otras entrevistas, en donde se presentó la inquietud por salir de la región. Es probable que estar en la "frontera" simbólicamente se rechace ya que puede revelarse como mantenerse enganchado a la suerte que la trajo a ella, mientras que salir de ahí posibilita abrir nuevos horizontes y escenarios de socialización, y sobre todo, de movilidad territorial, para cualquier propósito que en un momento determinado se persigan. Este deseo debemos enmarcarlos en la ausencia de muy pocos sentimientos de solidaridad y de confianza entre – al menos – los hondureños en Tapachula.

> Si, lo he pensado, claro que si, porque no, no pienso regresar a mi país, pero no me quiero quedar en Tapachula porque estoy muy cerca de la frontera y aquí pasan demasiado los migrantes de todos los países, es una de las ciudades más transitadas para poder pasar para arriba (norte de México), pues si me quiero ir a una ciudad donde me puedan pagar más (Entrevista con Tomás, Julio de 2010).

En otros casos, como el siguiente testimonio nos ejemplifica una forma de desechar la idea de ir a los Estados Unidos que alguna vez se arraigó en el migrante, que después de vivir la cadena de vicisitudes en el tránsito, viene la resignación o revaloración residir en el país de origen.

> Sí, me decían allá que me dan papeles, allá en Veracruz (México) (...) les agradezco mucho, tengo hijos la más grande tiene 14 años están pequeñitos todos, pero yo ya no tengo idea de irme a los Estados Unidos, para que? uno pasa en su país como a dios lo ha mandado, come pero no se muere de hambre. Lo que pasa es que hay mucha ambición y no se sabe lo que le puede a uno pasar, así. (...) esta dura la vida, mejor estar en su país (Entrevista con Hugo, Julio 2010).

*La nacionalización como la otra opción*
Por otra parte, cierto segmento de la población centroamericana asentado en la región, después de un tiempo de incertidumbre, especulación, expectación y de cavilar sobre el futuro personal o familiar que les depara, comienzan a contemplar seriamente su residencia documentada e indefinidamente en el país. Haber tomado esta opción, inherentemente ha pasado por los siguientes procesos:

a. Contar con un tiempo considerable de estancia en la región
b. Disponer de un espacio de residencia en la región, que puede ser alquilado o propio.
c. Contar con una actividad laboral que le garantiza, al menos, al cónyuge varón, o en otros casos, a la madre-soltera la sobrevivencia diaria.
d. Haber interiorizado, producto de la socialización en el escenario cotidiano, de un estilo de actuación en la vida cotidiana, acorde a los patrones del lugar de acogida.
e. Aceptar un estilo de vida y de reproducción sociocultural y material distinto al que se esperaba cuando se arribara a los Estados Unidos.

En una muestra de registros de aquellas personas que desean legalizar su estancia en la región (gráfico 3) se aprecia que la nacionalidad guatemalteca alcanza total primacía en volumen, seguida por la hondureña y después por la salvadoreña, y por último, por la nicaragüense. Sin embargo, al establecer la tendencia entre 2009 y 2010, parece ser que, con excepción de la guatemalteca, cuya tendencia es a la disminución, el resto de nacionalidades tienden estar a la alza, con especial preponderancia la hondureña.

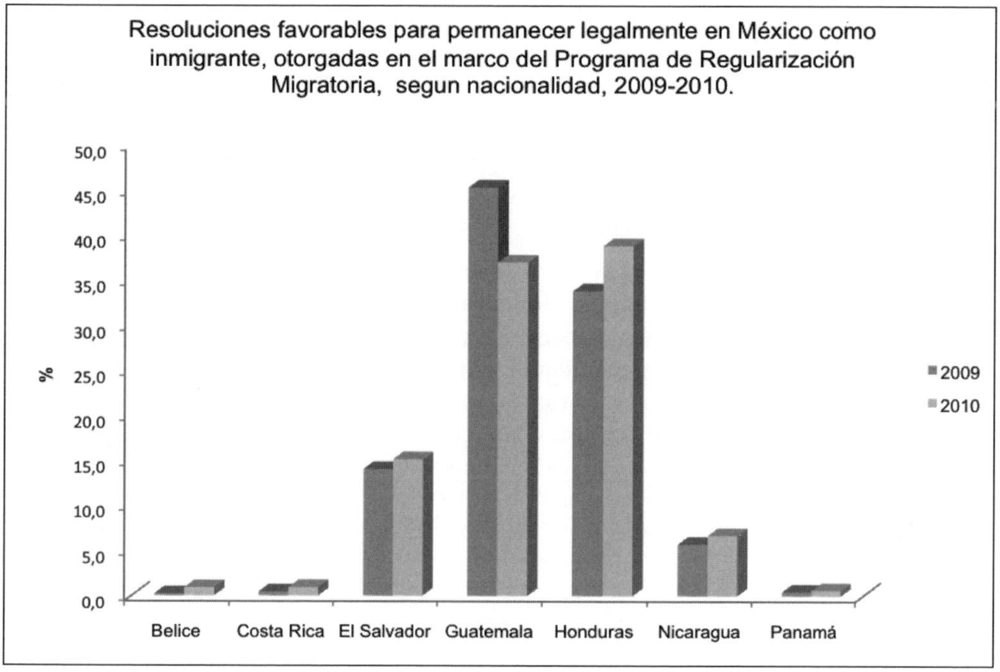


Fuente: Instituto Nacional de Migración. Serie histórica 1999-2010[2]

*Comunicaciones con el lugar de origen*

La frecuencia con la que ocurren las comunicaciones entre los centroamericanos con sus respectivas familias en sus países de origen, está condicionada de acuerdo a los recursos económicos. Al tiempo que esto está asociado a otros factores, tales como: a) el tiempo que haya transcurrido de permanencia en Tapachula, y b) la devastación económica en la que se encuentre el inmigrante según su experiencia que haya tenido con las bandas delincuenciales en su cruce y tránsito por la región.

Las dos formas más utilizadas para comunicarse son las llamadas por teléfono y el uso del Internet, las llamadas son a través de las casetas telefónicas de monedas localizadas en parques o esquinas de la ciudad de Tapachula y, en el caso del Internet, lo realizan a través de mensajes electrónicos o mediante una página-web llamada "abriendo brecha" que ellos conocen. "Si, es en el teléfono del parque, donde están esas casetas frente al chorro de agua, ahí es en donde me comunico, de vez en cuando, con mi mamá". "Ahorita por el momento solamente es por vía de Internet, por el correo electrónico" (Entrevista con Santiago y Luis, Julio de 2010).

En otros casos los inmigrantes debido a circunstancias específicas han dejado de mantener contacto con sus familias. En alusión al caso de Hugo y Carlos, argumentan que los primeros días, después de salir de su lugar de origen, la comunicación con su familia era frecuente, pero después de transcurrir un tiempo, tras hacer varios intentos re-

2 Graficas elaborado por Juan Sántiz Girón.

cientes de comunicación, la familia ha dejado de contestarles las llamadas, por lo que los intentos cada vez son más lejanos, y de esa forma, se presenta una paulatina extinción en la comunicación. En gran medida esto obedece a la intencionalidad de las llamadas. Además de interesarse por el saludo familiar, también las comunicaciones se hacen con la expectativa de que la familia en el lugar de origen pueda enviarles pequeños recursos económicos, por lo que la familia, ante la situación precaria por la que también atraviesa, tampoco puede cumplir tal expectativa.

> No, no he tenido dinero para hacer llamadas a Honduras allá tengo mis documentos, mis cedulas de allá de Honduras, las primeras veces que he llamado mi mamá, si hijo yo te voy a ayudar con tus documentos, y nada. Mi hermana me mandaba 50 o 30 dólares para ver si yo podía ayudarme en la comida o ropa. Yo necesito comunicarme con mi mamá, pero al principio mi mamá me contestaba pero después yo intenté comunicarme como 3 o 4 veces, si, lo intente, y allá en la casa ya solo me salía en el celular "comunícate por favor (...) deje un mensaje", solo así me salía, a la cuarta, quinta vez o sexta vez yo ya me enojé por eso y dije, 'yo ya no voy a seguir llamando, mi mama ya no quiere saber nada de mí' (Entrevista con Carlos, Julio de 2010).

En otros casos como Dalia tienen comunicación con su familia por medio del teléfono de moneda pero ella argumenta que la comunicación es únicamente para informar de su estado de salud, ella prefiere que solo sea en ese sentido y no para solicitar apoyo económico: "Si, hablamos, por teléfono de moneda. Si, ellos saben que estoy aquí pero no les quiero pedir dinero, porque quiero trabajar, quiero un trabajo honrado" (Entrevista con Dalia, Julio de 2010).

## Conclusiones

A lo largo del presente texto hemos documentado los tres principales procesos históricos que han sido el escenario en el que se han suscitado los mayores contactos entre las poblaciones centroamericanas con las poblaciones fronterizas mexicanas. Se ha señalado que la principal sociedad de contacto por parte de la población mexicana ha sido la que se ha ubicado en la franja fronteriza del estado de Chiapas, principal estado fronterizo del Sur. Por su parte, de las sociedades centroamericanas, ha quedado señalado que ha sido la guatemalteca la que mayor contacto ha tenido con la mexicana, debido a su posición limítrofe con Chiapas, México; y del carácter histórico compartido. Sin embargo, recientemente, otras nacionalidades como la hondureña y la salvadoreña, han presentado una actuación inusitada debido a la crisis económica permanente en que la región centroamericana se ha desenvuelto y el consiguiente intento de llegar a los Estados Unidos.

En el contexto actual, la región fronteriza de Chiapas, presenta un proceso de construcción trasnacional en tanto que de manera paulatina se han venido asentando cada vez más personas solas y/o familias completas de origen centroamericano que después de considerar como imposible la travesía hacia los Estados Unidos, han determinado residir de manera definitiva en dicha región. De esta suerte, la región, y principalmente la ciudad más importante que es Tapachula, ha pasado de ser solamente de tránsito para convertirse en un espacio de inmigración, lo que ha propiciado la creación de un perfil sociodemográfico diverso con implicaciones en la vida cotidiana que la convierte en un espacio dicotómico: por una parte un lugar de acogida, en tanto que ahí se asientan albergues y casas de migrantes, pero por otra parte, ahí también se generan mecanismos de exclusión y estigma social, principalmente en lo concerniente al consumo sexual al que se ven sometidas las mujeres.

De esta forma, tambien hemos apreciado que en la región fronteriza aparte de las poblaciones que han quedado varadas, también confluyen poblaciones de diversos perfiles sociales que residen en lugares adyacentes a la línea fronteriza compuesto por hombres y mujeres, los primeros para laborar en distintas actividades de la vida urbana y rural y las mujeres en distintas actividades comerciales, incluyendo otras como el trabajo doméstico. En el transcurrir del tiempo, también esta población ha sido parte de los grupos humanos que por convenir sus intereses también gradualmente van conformando núcleos en el medio urbano y rural de la región, que con el paso del tiempo, por la vecindad geográfica, han de ser los enlaces móviles entre México y Guatemala.

## Bibliografía


Cossío Villegas, Daniel (1972): Historia Moderna de México. El Porfiriato, la vida política exterior. Primer volumen. México, D.F: editorial Hermes.

Fernández-Casanueva, Carmen (1999): Experiencia de mujeres migrantes que trabajan en bares de la Frontera Chiapas-Guatemala. En: Papeles de Población. Vol. 15. Núm. 59. Toluca, México: Universidad Autónoma del Estado de México.

González Hernández, Lucio Apolinar (2010): Redes sociales de los inmigrantes hondureños en Tapachula, Chiapas. Tesis de Licenciatura en Sociología. México: Universidad Autónoma de Chiapas. pp. 173-192.

González Navarro, Moisés (1974): Población y Sociedad en México, 1900-1970. 2 volúmenes. Facultad de Ciencias Políticas y Sociales (serie estudios, 42). Universidad Nacional Autónoma de México: México, D.F.

Hernández Castillo, Rosalva Aida (2008): Procesos contemporáneos de conformación de identidades indígenas en la frontera sur de Chiapas. Comisión Nacional para el Desarrollo de los Pueblos Indios. México, D. F.

Instituto Nacional de Migración (2010): Serie Estadística 1999-2010, México, D.F: Instituto Nacional de Migración.

Kauffer, Michel Edith F. (2002): La integración de los exrefugiados guatemaltecos en México. Una experiencia con rostros múltiples. México, San Cristóbal de Las Casas, Chiapas: El Colegio de la Frontera Sur.

Martínez Velasco, Germán (1994): Plantaciones, trabajo guatemalteco y política migratoria en la Frontera Sur. Instituto Chiapaneco de Cultura, Gobierno del Estado de Chiapas. México, Ocozocuatla de Espinosa, Chiapas.

# National Identity Formation in Transnational Spaces: The Case of the Sahrawis of Western Sahara

*Sidi M. Omar*

## Abstract

*The chapter analyses the situation of the Sahrawis, the people of Western Sahara, by examining how a strong sense of collective national identity has been nurtured and institutionalised among Sahrawi communities living in refugee camps in south-west Algeria and in the wider diaspora. Special emphasis is laid on the role played by the Sahrawi State, SADR, in institutionalising and normalising the Sahrawi national identity amidst the refugee community through the active deployment of its various state apparatuses and by inculcating a feeling of common citizenship. The discussion also focuses on the transnational experiences of Sahrawi diaspora and the political role played by these small but politically active groups. Overall, the chapter will seek to demonstrate that the Sahrawis have been able to construct and institutionalise a Sahrawi national identity despite separation and dispersion across various exilic and diasporic spaces. It will further argue that the Sahrawi experience of forging and sustaining a national identity across different transnational spaces may help to problematize the centrality of territoriality as an essential component of the nation and national identity formation.*

## Introduction

The political developments that took place in Western Sahara in the seventies had left their mark on the people of the territory and particularly on their nation-building political project. Owing to the mass trauma of the Moroccan invasion and annexation of their territory in 1975, many Sahrawis had to leave their country and seek refuge or exile abroad. It was in these exilic and diasporic spaces that they continued building their nation in exile and reinforcing their national identity, whilst being attached to their homeland as an enduring referent that provides them with a sense of anchorage across place and time. The discussion that follows will include the formation of national identity amid the Sahrawi refugees and the diaspora. The 'Sahrawi refugees' will refer specifically to those Sahrawis that live in the refugee camps near Tindouf, in south-western Algeria. The diaspora will refer to the Sahrawis who live outside the refugee camps and the Sahrawi occupied territories. The chapter will begin with a brief introduction to the key concepts that frame the discussion, which will be followed by the examination of the processes whereby a national identity has been nurtured and normalised in the Sahrawi refugee camps and the diaspora. Methodologically, the discussion will draw on literature on nationalism, diaspora and identity construction as well as on transnationalism. Primary sources including interviews will also be used. Though the focus is on 'Sahrawi national identity' in the singular, this does not mean however that it is a unified and historically uniform identity. As will be discussed later, the expression 'Sahrawi national identity' is employed here as mainly a generic term for highly differentiated identitarian trajectories and narratives constructed across various national and transnational spaces and locations.

Overall, the chapter will seek to demonstrate that, despite the fact that they have had to live in various exilic, diasporic and transnational spaces, the Sahrawis have been able to construct a national identity through their everyday performance of that identity and their engagement in the political struggles attached to it. It will further show that the discussion of the processes whereby a Sahrawi national identity has been forged and sustained across different transnational spaces may help to problematize the overemphasis laid on territoriality as an essential component of the nation and national identity formation. This way, it may contribute to a richer discussion of identity construction in transnational contexts.

## Nation, National Identity and Transnationalism: Preliminary Remarks

Before addressing the issues raised above, it is perhaps useful to begin by providing some working definitions of the 'nation', 'national identity' and 'transnationalism'. Given that defining these concepts remains a matter of long-standing debate, the aim here is not to map out all the academic treatments of these notions, but to provide brief working definitions to frame conceptually the discussion that will follow.

A useful starting point for defining the 'nation' is perhaps Benedict Anderson's widely quoted remark that the nation is "an imagined political community" because "the members of even the smallest nation will never know most of their fellow-members, meet them, or even hear of them, yet in the minds of each lives the image of their communion" (Anderson, 2006: 6). However, the necessarily imagined nature of the nation in no way undermines its discursive, material or political effectiveness, because 'nation-ness' remains "the most universally legitimate value in the political life of our time" (ibid.: 3).

Given the emphasis laid above on the imagined and contingent nature of the nation, 'national identity', as any other form of identity, can only be understood as a construct in a process of construction and reconstruction in specific historical and institutional sites within specific discursive formations and practices. Stuart Hall (1993: 394) argues that "identities are the names we give to the different ways we are positioned by, and position ourselves within, the narratives of the past". Nonetheless, it should be recalled that the constructed nature of identity does not diminish its material effectiveness, not least in ideologically motivated nationalist contexts. As Anthony Smith (1991: 143) points out, "national identity is perhaps the most fundamental and inclusive" of all the collective identities which human beings share today.

Another key term related to our discussion is obviously 'transnationalism', a concept whose emergence has been accompanied by mounting theoretical ambiguity and analytical confusion in the use of the term (Guarnizo and others, 2003: 1212). However, since the analysis will focus mainly on how a Sahrawi national identity has been constructed and normalised within and across various transnational spaces, I will introduce the term 'transnationalism' to refer loosely to the processes whereby migrants, refugees or exiles forge and sustain multi-stranded social relations between their societies of origin and settlement. The emphasis laid on the links or relations that span more than one place suggests that the 'transnational' is to be construed as more of a relational than a physical space.

In summary, in view of the discussion above, it is obvious that my understanding of identity stems from a constructionist perspective that looks at it not as a 'natural' given, but as something that is constructed by the very acts of narration and explanation. My interest, therefore, lies in the ways in which national identity is constructed and normalised through daily routines and interactions, institutional practices as well as ritualised and significantly symbolic celebrations of nationhood.

## The Formation of Sahrawi National Identity: A Brief Background

Anderson's remark, which suggests that nations are 'imaged communities', implies that the analysis of the nation should focus on the processes and ways in which a given nation has been and continue to be imagined. In this sense, the discussion will now present a brief historical background to the historical, social and political processes whereby a Sahrawi collective 'self' or nation has been imagined and constructed over time and space, along with the national identity associated with it.

Historical studies on Western Sahara (Hodges, 1983; Aguirre, 1988) demonstrate that in precolonial times, the Sahrawis lived as one independent community and developed their own socio-political structures that were distinctly different from those established by neighbouring peoples that inhabited northwest Africa. Fredrik Barth (1998: 13) argues that in defining ethnic groups as a form of social organisation, the critical feature becomes "the characteristic of self-ascription and ascription by others." In his treatise on the history of the Sahrawis, Joaquín Portillo Pasqual del Riquelme (1991) points out that all the inhabitants of the Sahara were generically called by the Europeans as 'Sahrawis'. "However, the inhabitants of Western Sahara called themselves Sahrawis, and have managed that not only Spain but also the rest of the world would accept to call them Sahrawis" (1991: 101; emphasis in original).

By ascribing to themselves this appellation, the inhabitants of the territory demonstrated also that they were collectively aware of their existence as one people. The constitutive elements of this collective awareness consisted in their socio-political structures, their common culture and territory, their language, Hassaniya, and the self-identification of themselves as Sahrawis, which progressively gave rise to the Sahrawi identity as "a unique and complex regional hybrid – a mixture of autochthonous, Arab and sub-Saharan African factors" (Zunes and Mundy, 2010: 95).

Colonial rule in Western Sahara began in 1884 when the territory was declared a Spanish protectorate as a result of the Berlin Conference of 1884-5 (Hodges, 1983: 43) that divided Africa among the European powers. The evolution of the Sahrawi indigenous population from the nomadic to the 'modern' era, due to the colonial sedentarisation policy, reinforced the sense of belonging to a larger community that went beyond traditional kinship ties. However, it was during the colonial era that a strongly articulated Sahrawi national consciousness emerged. The emblematic moment of this historical process was the creation of the *Frente popular para la Liberación de Saguía El Hamra y de Río de Oro* (or the Frente POLISARIO) as an anticolonial liberation movement, which immediately gained overwhelming support among the population and was later recognised as the sole and legitimate representative of the Sahrawi people.

Spain terminated its colonial presence in Spanish/Western Sahara in February 1976. As I pointed out elsewhere (Omar, 2008: 46), although Spain withdrew without fulfilling its responsibilities in decolonising the territory, it nevertheless created the conditions and structures on which a national Sahrawi entity would be founded. First, Spain delimited the borders of the territory through a series of international agreements. Second, it contributed, through its colonial policy, to the emergence of a relatively homogeneous demographic community conscious of its own distinctive self: the Sahrawi people. The role played by the colonial administration in the formation of Sahrawi national identity is also recognised by Zunes and Mundy (2010: 95) who argue that "Spanish domination specifically and regional colonization generally played a profound role in shaping the Western Saharan's self-conception".

It was in this context that the Frente POLISARIO proclaimed the Sahrawi Arab Democratic Republic (SADR) on 27 February 1976, which has become a memorable day for the Sahrawis not only for its symbolic value but also for the fact that it signalled the commencement of the project of their nation-state building, which continues to date. The process of fostering Sahrawi national consciousness was further entrenched during and after the war that erupted in 1975 owing to the Moroccan and Mauritanian joint invasion and forcible annexation of Western Sahara, following Spain's withdrawal from the territory. John Comaroff and Paul Stern (1995: 5) suggest that national ties become stronger when a population realises that its common interests or its integrity are under threat. The Moroccan invasion and annexation of Western Sahara, notwithstanding its political and economic motives, implied a denial of the existence of a distinctive Sahrawi national identity entitled to exercise its own right to self-determination (Omar, 2009: 9).

In his theorisation of identity building processes, Manuel Castells (2010: 9) discusses 'identity for resistance', which "constructs forms of collective resistance against otherwise unbearable oppression, usually on the basis of identities that were, apparently, clearly defined by history, geography, or biology". The process of consolidation of the Saharawi political identity can thus be appreciated in the context of the ongoing Moroccan-Sahrawi confrontation. However, this confrontation cannot alone explain what in fact is a rather complex process historically and socio-politically. As Bernabé López García (2005) has argued, reducing the conflict in Western Sahara to a question of irreconcilable identities or to a clash of nationalisms is perhaps a simplification, although such an assumption can help to understand the reality.

In summary, the brief background to the formation of Sahrawi national identity demonstrates that, though a national consciousness had emerged in the territory in the precolonial and colonial times, it was mainly in the neo-postcolonial period following Morocco's invasion and annexation of Western Sahara in 1975 that the Sahrawi national identity was further generalised, solidified and institutionalised.

## The Sahrawi Refugees: Nation-building in Exile

The Moroccan occupation of Western Sahara forced the major part of the Sahrawi population to flee the country and seek protection in southwest Algeria, where they established their refugee camps near the town of Tindouf in one of the harshest desert environments.

The camps are home for roughly 150,000 refugees that have been living there for over three decades. The refugees are entirely dependent for survival on international aid organisations and on the host country. There are four main refugee camps (vast tent cities) that are named after towns in the occupied Western Sahara. The camps are self-managed by the refugees and administered by the Sahrawi State, the SADR.

The shared mass trauma of the Moroccan invasion and the collective experiences of displacement, exile and dispossession have had considerable impact on the Sahrawi identity in the refugee camps. These common experiences have cemented the refugee community, and in the process, they have led to the development of a common national identity, albeit on a "borrowed territory" (Farah, 2010: 62). Worthy of note is also the efforts made by the SADR, since the early days of exile, to embark on a national project aimed at creating a cohesive and ordered society with modern institutions, in which the erstwhile tribal differences were absorbed into a code of larger significance, namely the Sahrawi nation-state. By establishing an institutional framework of governance and inculcating a feeling of common citizenship, the SADR has managed to engender a growing sense of common identity and belonging to a unified Sahrawi nation. Moreover, by establishing self-determination as a marker of collective identity (Farah, 2010: 65), the SADR has been able to rally great support for its national strategy amid Sahrawis in the refugee camps and beyond.

Anthony Smith (1991: 16) highlights the role played by standardised and public mass education systems in the inculcation of national devotion and a distinctive, homogeneous culture. It is in this sense that we can understand the great importance accorded by the SADR to education, where free and compulsory education is provided for all children in mixed schools from pre-school to preparatory level. In particular, to counter Morocco's denial of the existence of a Sahrawi nation, a Sahrawi official history has been reconstructed to educate the younger generations on the basis of their common culture and history.

An entire generation of Sahrawis were born in the refugee camps and they have never been to their 'home' country, Western Sahara. When asked about how they relate in their everyday life to that remote homeland and how does this influence their self-conception as Sahrawis, a great part of the respondents pointed out that they relate to their home country 'indirectly'. This relationship is nurtured by the stories of their parents, the accounts emanating from people living in the occupied territories or the exposure to Sahrawi geography and history in school. As an interviewee said, "I was born in the refugee camps. I have never been to my homeland, and this fact saddens me. I want to know my land and to discover every corner of it"[1].

1 Interview (1) via email with Zahra Abdallahi Lefdil, 14 March 2011.

Kath Woodward (2002: 156.) observes that the imaginary constructions of place play a large part in the formation of identities in exile. To confront their forced 'homelessness,' Sahrawi refugees have articulated and maintained a sense of home by imagining and memorialising the homeland in their everyday experiences and practices. The fact that the refugee camps are named after existing towns in the occupied Western Sahara, for example, implies an attempt to create a space in which exile is displaced or deferred, albeit imaginatively, and home is relocated to accommodate the shifting experiences of its dwellers.

A key strategy for fostering the belonging to the nation entails that the national territory be produced and reproduced on a daily basis through 'national socialisation' (Paasi, 1996: 55). The increasing importance accorded by the SADR to the free zones of Western Sahara, over which the SADR exercises its full sovereignty, demonstrates how national territory is brought into the collective consciousness. Significant political, social, economic and cultural events have taken place in those territories in which significant infrastructure has been built. Moreover, apart from the small population that dwells in those zones on a relatively permanent basis, many refugees would spend varying periods in those territories especially during the rainfall season. What may seem as a temporary break from the refuge life in fact represents an experience of reconnecting to one's home and to one's sense of being at home.

In conclusion, as observed before, the creation of the SADR was a milestone in the solidification and institutionalisation of Sahrawi national consciousness. Through its management of the refugee camps, in which its state apparatuses are actively deployed, the SADR has contributed significantly to institutionalising and normalising the Sahrawi national identity among the refugee community.

## Sahrawi Diaspora: Politically Engaged Transnational Communities

A large group of Sahrawis have left the refugee camps in recent years and migrated to the neighbouring countries, Europe (mainly Spain) and other regions. This emerging diaspora is attributed less to the 'ideology of movement' characterising the Sahrawi society (Chatty, 2010: 52) than to the political conflict itself and its ramifications. The formation of a Sahrawi diaspora has thus been intertwined with the Sahrawi nationhood and the nation building in exile, and hence it has been politically active since its inception.

The predominantly political character of the Sahrawi diaspora has had a great bearing on the formation of the identities of its members, and their practical and virtual relation to their home country. Stuart Hall (1993) suggests that diaspora refers to people "who have succeeded in remaking themselves and fashioning new kinds of cultural identity by consciously or unconsciously drawing on more than one cultural repertoire" (cited in Woodward, 2002: 63). The interviews conducted with some Sahrawis living in the diaspora demonstrate that they continue to maintain a strong sense of belonging to their 'ancestral home' even as they establish new relationships with new social spaces and geographies.

An interviewee who was born in Western Sahara and is currently living in Ohio (US) pointed out that "After having lived in many places, I started getting closer to my true self as a Sahrawi. I then started preserving my identity against whatever seems to be alien or foreign to me"[2]. Asked about how her transnational experiences have impacted her sense of identity as a Sahrawi, a female respondent, who was born in the refugees camps and is now studying in Stockholm (Sweden), replied that "Living abroad has definitely contributed in my sense of national identity. Now I feel more patriotic and nationalistic especially of feeling the duty to represent my fellow countrymen and women abroad"[3].

The relation between this sense of identity and the larger political context is manifest in the replies given by the respondents when asked about how they are involved in the polity back home. One of the most common themes appearing in their responses is their 'commitment to the Sahrawi cause'. An interviewee, who was born in Western Sahara and is now living in Spain, specified that "I participate actively in the activities we do for Western Sahara here. I also write to media about the issue. These activities make me feel the connection to the cause of my people and their plight, and prepare me psychologically to do my utmost for them"[4]. It is perhaps interesting to note that the transnational experiences of some of the respondents described above resonate with the author's own trajectory and diasporic experiences of having lived in exile for over three decades and for having lived and worked across different continents.

Worthy of note is also the transnational experiences of some Sahrawi students studying abroad. This is the case of the "Cubarawis", a term that commonly refers to Sahrawi students that studied and lived in Cuba and then returned to the refugee camps. As noted earlier, the SADR has accorded special importance to education and it is in this context that Sahrawi students were sent on scholarship basis to countries such as Algeria, Libya, Spain and Cuba, among others, in order to complete university degree programmes. As a result, many doctors, lawyers, engineers and teachers have graduated from Cuba and are now working in the refugee camps.

Asked about how his experience in Cuba has affected his sense of identity, an interviewee who studied for many years in Cuba, pointed out that, "The experience of studying in Cuba has undoubtedly affected my identity, because it has changed my ideas about the world and about me. My identity is now a mixture of Sahrawi and Cuban cultural elements. Although it seems that the two cultures have nothing to do with each other, but through me, they complement and interact with each other in a way that enriches me and my vision of the world. It is a privilege"[5]. The experience of the respondent resonates with the transnational experiences of thousands of Sahrawi students (Cubarawis) whose identities have been forged in the overlapping context of their experiences in Cuba and their sustained engagement with the shifting 'homes' that they had left behind and to which they have returned after many years.

---

2 Interview (2) via e-mail with Salah Mohamed Abdallahi, 10 March 2011.
3 Interview (3) via e-mail with Senia Bachir Abderahman, 12 April 2011.
4 Interview (4) via e-mail with Sid Hamdi, 6 March 2011.
5 Interview (5) via e-mail with Limam Boisha Omar, 27 March 2011.

## Conclusion

The chapter has sought to demonstrate that, though they have had to live in various exilic, diasporic and transnational spaces, the Sahrawis have been able to construct a national identity through their everyday performance of that identity and their engagement in the political struggles attached to it. Overall, defying many physical barriers, Sahrawis in their respective 'exiles' have been engaged in and shaping various transnational linkages and complex networks encompassing the refugee camps, the relatively small but active diaspora and the occupied territories as well. The increasing use of the new technologies of communication has allowed the continuation of these social connections that reinforce their collective belonging to one nation, as a project for both the present and the future.

Anthony Smith (1991: 9) argues that the Western or 'civic' model of the nation is a predominantly spatial or territorial conception. However, in a condition of transnationalism that is marked by, among other things, the growing disjuncture between territory, subjectivity and collective social movement (Appadurai, 1995), the centrality of territoriality becomes problematic, not least in terms of its bearing on the formation of national identity. The discussion of the processes whereby a Sahrawi national identity has been formed across different transnational spaces may therefore help to problematise the overemphasis on territoriality as an indispensable element to the nation and the national identity formation. This way, it may contribute to a richer discussion of identity construction in transnational contexts.

The complex ways in which Sahrawi refugees and exiles have forged their identities in relation to their territory also demonstrates that the relationship between space and national identity is more variegated and multi-scaled than what is commonly assumed. As discussed above, the majority of the Sahrawis continue to live unrelated physically to their homeland. However, since national identities are always constructed in reference to what is taken to be home – however far and imaginary that home may be – for the Sahrawis, Western Sahara, as both an imagined home and actual geography, continues to represent an enduring referent that provide them with a collective sense of being a situated community. Their experiences seem to replicate Gloria Anzaldúa's articulation of her multiple habitable locations. As she succinctly states, "I am a turtle, wherever I go I carry 'home' on my back" (Anzaldúa, 1989 :21).

## References


Aguirre, José R.D. (1988): Historia del Sahara Español: La verdad de una traición. Madrid: Kaydeda Ediciones.

Anderson, Benedict R. (2006): Imagined Communities: Reflections on the Origin and Spread of Nationalism. Revised edition. London: Verso.

Anzaldúa, Gloria (1989): Borderlands/La Frontera. San Francisco: Spinsters/Aunt Lute Press.

Appadurai, Arjun (1995): The production of locality. In: Fardon, Richard (ed.): Counterworks: Managing the Diversity of Knowledge. London: Routledge. pp. 204-225.

Barth, Fredrik (ed.) (1998): Ethnic Groups and Boundaries: The Social Organization of Culture Difference. London: Allen & Unwin.

Castells, Manuel (2010): The Power of Identity. Oxford: Blackwell Publishing Ltd.
Chatty, Dawn (ed.) (2010): Deterritorialized Youth: Sahrawi and Afghan Refugees at the Margins of the Middle East. Oxford and New York: Berghahn Press.
Comaroff, John L./ Stern, Paul C. (1995) (eds.): Perspectives on Nationalism and War. Amsterdam: Gordon and Breach Publishers.
Farah, Randa (2010): Sovereignty on Borrowed Territory: Sahrawi Identity in Algeria. In: Georgetown Journal of International Relations. Summer/Fall 2010. pp. 59-66.
Guarnizo, Luis E., and others (2003): Assimilation and Transnationalism: Determinants of Transnational Political Action among Contemporary Migrants. In: American Journal of Sociology. Vol. 108(6). pp. 1211-1248.
Hall, Stuart (1993): Cultural Identity and Diaspora. In: Williams, Patrick/ Christman, Laura (eds.): Colonial Discourse and Post-Colonial Theory. A Reader. New York: Harvester Wheatsheaf. pp. 392-403.
Hodges, Tony (1983): Western Sahara: the Roots of a Desert War. Connecticut: Lawrence Hill & Company.
López García, Bernabé (2005): Entidad saharaui, identidades y nación. In: El País. 23.04.2005, http://www.elpais.com/articulo/opinion/Entidad/saharaui/identidades/nacion/elpepiopi/20050423elpepiopi_7/Tes, [26.10.11].
Omar, Sidi M. (2008): The Right to Self-determination and the Indigenous People of Western Sahara. In: Cambridge Review of International Affairs. 21:1. pp. 41-57.
Omar, Sidi M. (2009): Mapping of the Conflict in Western Sahara. In: Strategic Studies Group (El Grupo de Estudios Estratégicos). http://www.gees.org/articulo/6705/, 10 September 2009 [13.05.2011].
Paasi, Anssi (1996): Territories, Boundaries and Consciousness. The Changing Geographies of the Finnish-Russian Border. Chichester: John Wiley and Sons.
Pasqual del Riquelme/ Joaquín Portillo (1991): Historia de los Saharauis y Crónica de La Agresión Colonial en el Sahara Occidental, Tesis Doctoral, Departamento de Periodismo III de La Facultad de Ciencias de La Información de La Universidad Complutense de Madrid. http://eprints.ucm.es/tesis/19911996/S/3/S3017901.pdf [30.05.2011].
Smith, Anthony D. (1991): National Identity. London: Penguin Books.
Woodward, Kath (2002): Understanding Identity. London: Arnold.
Zunes, Stephen/ Mundy, Jacob (2010): Western Sahara: War, Nationalism and Conflict Irresolution. New York: Syracuse University Press.

# Migration Moves and Shapes Society

*Marc Hill and Erol Yildiz*

## Abstract

*A token of our time is the "opening of places to the world." Migration movements have significantly contributed to this phenomenon. This is evident in particular in urban everyday life. Urban development and urbanity are today scarcely conceivable without migration. Nonetheless, this fact appears to be but weakly anchored in public consciousness. Negative attributions continue to stamp discourse on migration. Migrants are labeled as aliens and criticized for being resistant to integration. This paper reverses the perspective, discussing the relevance of migration-linked diversity in the urban context as exemplified in everyday life in Cologne. Our main thesis is that diversity through migration is an urban resource.*

## Urban Life in its Rich Multiplicity

To introduce the topic, we would like to begin with an everyday observation by the Russian author Vladimir Kaminer (2000), who has a humorous take on urban living in Berlin:

> Berlin is a city full of mystery. Nothing here is as it might initially appear (...). Once fate would have it that I went to Wilmersdorf (...), and found myself in a small Turkish restaurant. (...). The salespeople tell us: "Look, those aren't Turks, they're Bulgarians, just pretending to be Turks (...)." Berlin is too diverse. You don't have to complicate that situation unnecessarily. The consumer expects that in a Turkish restaurant, he'll be served by Turkish personnel, even if they're actually Bulgarians. The very next day I went to a Bulgarian restaurant I had recently discovered. And I thought the Bulgarians they're were actually Turks. But this time the Bulgarians were genuine. However, the Italians in the Italian restaurant next door turned out to be Greeks. They told me that after they'd taken over the place, they went to night classes to learn Italian. The guest in an Italian restaurant expects to be spoken to at least a little in Italian. A short time after that I went to a "Greek" place, and my feeling did not deceive me. The help there turned out to be Arab.
>
> From day to day I learned ever more. The Chinese from the small restaurant across the street from me are Vietnamese. The Indian on Rykestraße is in reality an honest-to-God Tunisian from Carthage. And the boss of the Afro-American bar with all the voodoo stuff on the walls, well, he's a Belgian.

Kaminer's conclusion: "Nothing's genuine here, every person is himself and at the same time someone else" (Kaminer 2000: 97f.).

To characterize contemporary societies, we use the metaphor "opening up of places to the world". What we mean by that is that we are constantly being confronted in our everyday lives with different, contradictory elements that are connected in a worldwide mesh of communication. The concepts "cosmopolitanizing everyday life" or "transnationalizing how people live their lives" express this transformation. From this perspective, globalization is a process happening here and now. It appears as something ordinary, everyday. Globality is a set of quite everyday experiences. It can be seen as a transformation of the contexts in which our life unfolds. In the meantime, our spaces of experience and conception have been global in scope, especially as a result of technological and electronic possibilities for transport and communication. A kind of *mobile sedentary* life or *sedentary mobility* appears to be a characteristic feature of global societies. It sparks trains of thought, increasingly influencing how our lives are shaped.

As a consequence of radical individualization and the dissolving of traditional forms and patterns of living, many biographies are now in motion. Their trajectories have lost the former straight line, they've become more risky. The itinerary of a life is breaking up more and more into individual phases and segments (Beck-Gernsheim 1997: 65ff.), extending beyond previous familiar reference points like place of birth or profession learned. The 'reflexive turn' brought about by radical individualization, which forces a person to think more and more about their own biography, has transformed individual life history into a space of learning. We can observe in this connection a kind of generalizing of education connected not only with social spaces and groups but with the temporal structuring of social life. An expression of this development is the topicality of the concept of what we have come to call lifelong learning.

It was precisely a migration across borders in the wake of industrialization which stamped the character of large cities right from the start, contributing significantly to making our everyday life more cosmopolitan and pluralistic. Basically, urban development and urbanity are inconceivable without in-migration. Looking at the most important benchmarks of European migration history, we can see that being sedentary over several generations is a kind of myth. Experiences of mobility and their associated diversity and heterogeneity have also left their formative stamp on urban life. Already 110 years ago, half of the 400 million residents of Europe changed their place of residence at least once in their lifetime, across national borders or from one continent to another. That tendency increased in the upheavals of the two great wars.

More and more people are on the move, traveling on through: pupils, students, scholars, computer specialists, artists, staff of global firms. And of course labor migrants, refugees, including the undocumented, the so-called illegals. So it is not only the existence of migration which is new today. Rather it's the fact that at the beginning of the 21st century, migration is affecting almost all countries on the planet. And most migration is not taking place, contrary to official perception, in Europe, but rather in the so-called 'developing world'.

To visualize mobility, the artist Morgan O'Hara, born in Los Angeles, has developed a method we find interesting and would like to briefly present. She calls the drawings she makes protocols of movement. Her mapping and charting of peoples' trajectories in space and time traces the paths persons traverse in their life. To create these portraits, O'Hara places the same piece of paper on the map of the world, countries and cities, tracing the paths taken by an individual. The web of lines produced creates individual world maps, inclusive of a person's own boundaries. In her cartographic portraits, she depicts the trajectories of her subjects through actual time and space. Traces of movement become visible here which are all equal in value, no matter whether traced as the result of a trip around the world, a change in residence, commuter paths, a path of flight and escape, or emigration. With these portraits, O'Hara emphasizes that in the 20th and 21st century, traveling has significantly shaped biographies or set them in motion. She sees movement as a marker of life.

However, along with the possibilities which such worldwide connections offer the individual in everyday life, there are national boundaries of nation-states and the associated controls on mobility, as well as economic and political discrimination that hamper migration.

## Movement through Migration: Keupstraße in Cologne as a Success Story

As a result of an influx of migrants after WW II and labor migration since the 1960s, neighborhoods have arisen in Cologne that are shaped by this migration process. One such 'quarter', is exemplary in its development and public perception in the city, is Keupstraße in Cologne-Mühlheim. At the end of the 19th century, the neighborhood developed into an important industrial area and a classic working-class neighborhood through the influx of workers who sought to live near the factories where they worked.

Persons of differing origin and beliefs moved in and settled in Keupstraße over the years, only to move on and out of the area. The last group of migrant workers to come in consisted largely of Turkish migrants. As a result of economic crisis and the de-industrializing of the neighborhood, many were left jobless. The last German shop owners closed their stores and moved elsewhere. The empty apartments, restaurants and shops were then gradually taken over by in-migrating Turks. Opening an independent business was for most the only way out of joblessness. Stores were renovated and reopened, small service outlets, shops and restaurants stand one next to the other. Soon the facades of buildings and apartments were also renovated and remodeled.

However, the discrepancy between this everyday reality of reinvigoration and public perception is striking. For years, the municipality and mass media in the city warned about the ghettoization of this neighborhood, about how it was becoming a 'slum'. Keupstraße in Cologne became a watchword and metaphor for the "parallel Turkish society in town", playing a role only in negative critique. Everyone in Cologne knows its reputation, but most Cologne residents have never ever even seen Keupstraße, which lies on the other side of the Rhine River from most of town. As a result of this construction of a negative image in the media and public perception, the Social Services Ministry in the state of North Rhine-Westphalia commissioned a study in 1999 about life in Keupstraße (Stadt Köln 1999). This study issued a sharp word of warning about the danger of a ghetto in formation and called for a "balanced mixture in the local population" in order to put a halt to processes turning the neighborhood into a virtual slum.

Turkish supermarket in the Keupstraße neighborhood. Old halls are recycled and reused, photo © Marc Hill.

It becomes clear that the spatial segregation of migrants is perceived as a central political and social problem in urban development. This view, distorted by ethnic and culturalizing blinders, degrades this residential area (and other neighborhoods in the city marked by in-migration) into a social problem space. Constructing migrants as strangers makes it at the same time difficult to see and better grasp experiences specific to migration and related resources.

Fixed categories such as ethnic identity and homogeneous culture, repeatedly ascribed to the neighborhood's residents, lose their meaning when scrutinized under a more powerful lens. In any interviews we see diverse social and cultural experiences that overlay and cross over one another. Most of the residents identify with the neighborhood, emphasize the high quality of life there, and even in discourse of the "old-timer" German residents, most express a sympathetic distanced attachment. People have come to terms with developments on the ground, and see the situation as quite positive, though somewhat 'exotic' from their German vantage (Bukow/Yildiz 2002: 102ff.).

Many residents maintain family, social, and economic relations across borders. These worldwide networks are qualitatively new circumstances which arise in local contexts on the basis of a globalized society (Yildiz/Mattausch, 2009). Cosmopolitan intercultural competence consists specifically in the ability to absorb local concrete processes and to recode them on a transnational basis. We have urgent need of that ability in today's everyday world.

In contrast with public "ghetto discourse", migrant neighborhoods like this are not only evidence for the ways in which everyday life is rendered cosmopolitan and pluralistic. They also corroborate successful strategies for dealing with the challenges of our era, and for successfully reinvigorating urban neighborhoods through in-migration.

Carnival procession on Keupstraße ('d'r Zoch kütt'), photo © Peter Bach.

Cologne juxtaposition: Catholic/
Turkish facade on Weidengasse,
photo © Erol Yildiz

## Migration as a Resource: Diversity as a Basis for Intercultural Learning

First attempts in the educational sphere in the late 1960s and early '70s initially reacted to the situation of immigration as deficit-laden and in need of compensatory action, ascribing to the migrants a mode of socialization deemed incomplete. This perspective acted to direct attention away from educational institutions and concepts, and toward a focus on migrant families and children (Bernstein, 1973: 24).

Even if intercultural and transcultural concepts were brought in later on, they all remain focused down to today on the cultural factor as the real problem (hypothesis of cultural difference). Although these approaches have been criticized for several years due to their excessive orientation to a kind of 'special education' perspective and/or the culturalizing and ethnicizing of the problem complex (Bukow, 1996), this deficit-oriented interpretation is still widespread today, and in Germany at least is regarded as educational normalcy and common wisdom. Even if in scholarly debate in recent years new approaches have been developed, where diversity due to migration has been rediscovered and viewed as a resource for educational processes, this perspective still seems to be a 'minority position', and thus has not managed to make its way into everyday practice.

It is interesting how this traditional view of things can radically change when viewed as pragmatically necessary. Cologne's candidacy in 2004 as the "cultural capital of Europe 2010" is a telling example. Cologne's bid bore the motto that was something of a riddle for outsiders: "We live it". Reference was to the practical everyday relevance of interculturality in living together in Cologne, and the natural way in this was accepted. In the application, Cologne presented itself as a city "open to the world", multilingual, multi-religious and transnational.

For the sake of submitting an application, the history of Cologne was reinterpreted as a history of migration. In the course of reinterpreting the past and its reconstruction, migration was showcased as a resource for the development of Cologne into a new transnational locality. At the same time, the urban space for people became a field for new action and a didactic project for intercultural learning. Simultaneously, the way the media dealt with migration changed radically. The local media presented their new discovery of cultural diversity in the city on a daily basis. In this reinterpretation, Cologne became a space of possibilities, a place for learning, and the history of migration became a history of success. Migration, which keeps cities alive and in motion, opening up new spaces for action, becomes a process full of opportunities, which in turn stimulates innovation and reflection.

This symbolic upgrading of the value of urban spaces through migration – and thus the new, unfortunately temporary habitus of the city as a migration city (the application was unsuccessful and Essen was chosen instead) – created a new public consciousness in Cologne, opening up fresh perspectives on different groups living together. It sparked intercultural processes of learning or at least showed how such processes could appear.

It is recognized that this opening to the outside is not only viewed as something positive. Rather, specifically in the form of migration, it is regarded as something threatening, a phenomenon that throughout Europe goes hand in hand with tendencies toward political re-nationalization. Sections of cities where a larger number of (im) migrants reside are viewed with suspicion; they are quickly categorized as 'foreigner neighborhoods' or 'parallel societies'. New boundaries are drawn between locals and in-migrants, social insecurity and conflicts are viewed from a national and ethnic perspective.

## Back to Cologne in Motion

Cologne likes to style itself as Italy's most northern city. And the attitude toward life does in fact have in many spheres a touch of Mediterranean influence. Concrete examples show just how successful immigrants were despite the restrictive conditions and structural barriers (habitus of the art of survival). Solely in view of the fact that among migrants joblessness is twice as great and general qualifications are half of what they are in the rest of the population, these neighborhoods, as illustrated in Keupstraße, constitute a success story. They show that immigrants have a high degree of desire to integrate even under extremely unfavorable conditions, and develop new competencies which ultimately should be recognized as a prerequisite for living and learning, as cultural capital.

Instead of reducing migrants to an ethnic dimension, stripping them of their biographies, the multiplicity of possible designs for living, and this within a group defined as "ethnic", are made visible. Migrants are viewed as experts on their own everyday life, as discoverers and inventors of their reality.

In the context of these mobility movements, the so-called ethnic ascriptions become more and more complicated. The number of those who for various reasons leave their places of origin, or are compelled by circumstance to leave – for a shorter or longer period, or permanently as emigrants abroad – is constantly growing. To be born here, to grow up there, to work and live there, and to spend the last years of one's life somewhere else, becomes everyday normality. Transposed to everyday life in the neighborhood, imagine the following combination:

One example: A woman in Cologne-Ehrenfeld, from Brazil, is married to a homosexual man and lives in a commune with four Salsa music fans, and has intimate relations with one of them. A lawyer, she works in a citizen's action group. Her homosexual husband, with whom she is married for reasons of a visa to stay in Germany, was born and raised in Munich and now lives in Cologne. He has a Bavarian accent, knows some Turkish and Arabic. His father is from Syria, his mother from Turkey.

Migration generates transnational networks, designs for living and competencies; here only one of countless examples: Family M. has lived for five years in the Cologne neighborhood Nippes and runs a Turkish pastry shop on Market Square in Nippes. The father initially emigrated from southern Turkey to Switzerland at the age of 18. Later he met his current wife in Strasbourg and then moved there. She is the daughter of a guest worker family from Turkey, born in Strasbourg and raised there. Five years ago, the family moved to Cologne, following the suggestion of their relatives, since the store at that time on Market Square was vacant, and shops there are in great demand. The family decided to open a Turkish pastry shop, because the husband in Turkey had been trained as a pastry baker. They "imported" Turkish and French recipes for pastries, cakes and desserts. All the family members are French citizens. They often have visitors from Strasbourg, former neighbors and friends, but also from the Netherlands, where another part of the family is living. For that reason, different languages are spoken in the shop: French, German, Turkish, Dutch. The children are growing up trilingual, a daughter is now attending high school.

We see here the creative potential of life constructions that have come about as a result of migration movements, and today represent normalcy in urban everyday life. Through transnational family networks and their utilization, new competencies are developed, social and cultural capital is accumulated. Transnational spaces becomes spaces of possibility and promise (Schiffauer, 2006: 169ff.). In this manner, "affiliations in motion" (*'bewegte Zugehörigkeiten'*) (Strasser, 2009) and multiple global connections become a complex, multilayered and hybrid phenomenon, and thus a biographical resource in a globalized world. Locality appears here as the result of different family relations which can extend far beyond the local place, and even encompass the entire planet (Massey, 2006: 26). New forms and inventions spring from these networks and concepts for living; locally, these bind together the parties concerned coming from different elements in a reflexive manner. Such concepts for living point to an everyday life praxis which does not lag behind the reality of the globalized world, but rather is a force which drives it onward (Apitzsch, 1999: 482). "The illusion of the sedentary is that you have to commit yourself spatially and culturally to a territory in order to find an answer to the question of identity" (Römhild, 2003: 14).

## Conclusion

A look at urban worlds shows that everyday life is more geared to an *undramatic social grammar* strongly more oriented to concrete processes and contexts of experience than the all too simple cultural ascription would suggest. Differing strategies of incorporation and practices of location developed in urban spaces should be viewed as new and creative achievements. Diverse and in part global (cultural) elements and ties are utilized as transnational social capital, and are fused together depending on context into hybrid conceptions of life.

Thus, urban spaces become transnational stages, points of departure and interfaces for numerous strategies of location that extend beyond the local world. In the process, local places become multi-centers for different traditions, cultures, memories, events and experiences. A *social grammar* becomes visible, which permits new spaces for possibilities; there, differences are rethought, activated and combined with one another in various ways. These forms of redesign and restructuring do not emerge in mythical concepts of integration but rather principally in the lowlands of everyday life: as Mark Terkessidis notes, "a policy to shape diversity must take these everyday experiences seriously" (2010: 88).

## References


Apitzsch, Ursula (1999): Biographieforschung und interkulturelle Pädagogik. In: Krüger, Heinz-Hermann/ Marotzki, Winfried (eds.): Handbuch erziehungswissenschaftliche Forschung. Opladen: Leske + Budrich Verlag, pp. 471-486.

Beck-Gernsheim, Elisabeth (1997): Stabilität der Familie oder Stabilität des Wandels? Zur Dynamik der Familienentwicklung. In: Beck, Ulrich/ Sopp, Peter (eds.): Individualisierung und Integration. Neue Konfliktlinien und neuer Integrationsmodus? Opladen: Leske + Budrich Verlag, pp. 65-81.

Bernstein, Basil (1973): Der Unfug mit der „kompensatorischen" Erziehung. In: Bernstein, Basil/ Grauer, Gustav/ Holzkamp, Christine (eds.): Familienerziehung, Sozialschicht und Schulerfolg. Weinheim: Beltz Verlag, pp. 21-36.

Bukow, Wolf-Dietrich (1996): Feindbild Minderheit: Zur Funktion von Ethnisierung. Opladen: Leske + Budrich Verlag.

Bukow, Wolf-Dietrich/ Yildiz, Erol (2002): Der Wandel von Quartieren in der metropolitanen Gesellschaft am Beispiel Keupstraße in Köln oder: Eine verkannte Entwicklung. In: Bukow, Wolf-Dietrich/ Yildiz, Erol (eds.): Der Umgang mit der Stadtgesellschaft. Ist die multikulturelle Stadt gescheitert oder wird sie zu einem Erfolgsmodell? Opladen: Leske + Budrich Verlag, pp. 81-111

Kaminer, Vladimir (2000): Russendisko. Munich: Manhattan.

Massey, Doreen (2006): Keine Entlastung für das Lokale. In: Berking, Helmuth (ed.): Die Macht des Lokalen in einer Welt ohne Grenzen. Frankfurt am Main/New York: Campus Verlag, pp. 25-31.

Römhild, Regina (2003): Welt Raum Frankfurt. In: Bergmann, Sven/ Römhild, Regina (eds.): Global Heimat. Ethnographische Recherchen im transnationalen Frankfurt. Frankfurt am Main: Institut für Kulturanthropologie und Europäische Ethnologie, pp. 7-20.

Said, Edward W. (1978): Orientalism. New York: Random House.

Schiffauer, Werner (2006): Transnationale Solidaritätsgruppen, Imaginäre Räume, Irreale Konditionalsätze. In: Berking, Helmuth (ed.): Die Macht des Lokalen in einer Welt ohne Grenzen. Frankfurt am Main/New York: Campus Verlag, pp. 164-180.

Stadt Köln (ed.) (1999): Dokumentation. Veränderungsprozesse und Konfliktebenen in der Keupstraße. Cologne: Stadt Köln.

Strasser, Sabine (2009): Bewegte Zugehörigkeiten. Nationale Spannungen, transnationale Praktiken und transversale Politik. Vienna: Verlag Turia + Kant.

Terkessidis, Mark (2010): Interkultur. Frankfurt am Main: Suhrkamp.

Yildiz, Erol/ Mattausch, Birgit (eds.) (2009): Urban Recycling. Migration als Großstadt-Ressource. Basel/Boston/Berlin: Birkhäuser Architektur.

# III

# Spaces of Tensions: Local – Global

# Private Sentiment and Public Issues – Irish Medium Education and Complex Linguistic and Political Identification

*Simon Warren*

## Abstract

*Is it possible to construct a non-essentialist politics of place? This is a central question explored in this chapter. The empirical focus of the chapter is the cultural politics of language surrounding the Irish-medium education policy of a secondary school in an Irish-speaking region of Ireland. The primary objective of the chapter is the development of a theoretical framework for thinking through the possibility of a non-essentialist politics of place. The chapter is organised around three related theoretical discussions of space/place, social/political and public/private. Identity (of place and politics) is seen as formed at the intersection of history, economics, culture and politics producing contingent but temporarily stable identities. Drawing on the contributions of Doreen Massey, Ash Amin and Chantal Mouffe the chapter argues that local identity is formed from the 'throwntogetherness' of place or the collision of 'micro-worlds'. The diversity of perspectives and values concerning the 'common good' that arise from such 'throwntogetherness', rather than fixed, essential identity, is seen as forming the basis for a politics of place. Therefore, it is argued that it is possible to construct a non-essentialist politics of place that holds open the possibility of overcoming oppositions between the particular and the cosmopolitan, the local and the global.*

## Introduction

### *Depiction 1*

*Experience the magic of the Dingle Peninsula*
*located in the Southwest of Ireland*

Once cited as 'the most beautiful place on earth' by the National Geographic; was voted among the top 100 destinations in the world by Trip Advisor; CNN recently recommended it as a very favourable winter destination; it is listed as one of the top 10 places to be on New Year's Eve – all of these accolades refer to the stunningly beautiful Dingle Peninsula.

Tá clú agus cáil bainte amach ag Leithinis Chorca Dhuibhne mar cheann scríbe de bharr a cuid litríochta, teangan agus cultúir. Ó thaobh áilleachta, saibhreas oidhreachta agus imeachtaí ní féidir Corca Dhuibhne a shárú agus tá a hainm i n-airde le lóistín, bia, ceardaíocht, ceol is tithe tábhairne.

Is Gaeltacht í Corca Dhuibhne, áit ina bhfuil an Ghaeilge nó *Gaelainn* mar theanga labhartha í dtithe áirithe, san ionad oibre agus sna scoileanna go léir.

Much of the Dingle Peninsula or Corca Dhuibhne is a *Gaeltacht* or an area where the Irish language (*Gaeilge* or *Gaelainn*) is widely spoken in the home, workplace or school (Dingle Peninsula Tourism, 2011a)[1].

### *Depiction 2*

In June 2009 a case was brought to the High Court in the Republic of Ireland by a group of parents, acting for 12 children[2], against the language policy adopted by the Board of Management of the community secondary school – Pobalscoil Chorca Dhuibhne, in Dingle, on the West Kerry peninsula, south west Ireland. As claimed by the parents the central issue at stake in this case was that the civil and human rights of their children to education were being denied to them because of the school's policy of Irish-medium education. This referred to the policy of the school, in line with its statutory duties under the Education Act 1998, and by virtue of its location in one of the officially designated Irish-speaking regions (Gaeltacht) of Ireland, that the medium of education and the business of the school would be conducted through Irish. The parents maintained that the opportunity to succeed educationally, and therefore economically, was denied their children by being required to undertake their secondary school education through the medium of Irish rather than English. Pobalscoil Chorca Dhuibhne was formed as a new co-educational community secondary school, amalgamating the previous boy and girl's schools in the town. This is the only post-primary school in the area and serves both the Irish and English-speaking communities on the peninsula. The other nearest secondary school is 21 kilometres away. However, the nearest alternative Irish-medium secondary school is 40 kilometres. The new school opened in 2007 and was immediately confronted with a group calling itself the 'Concerned Parents of Corca Dhuibhne' campaigning against the school's language policy. Within the first months of the new school year the Concerned Parents group organized two public meetings, a petition, a student strike, campaigned for the Department of Education to conduct a parent and student survey, and initiated court proceedings. At both public meetings those speaking in Irish were heckled and jeered. At the first meeting one of the key protagonists likened the school's policy, and that of Irish language activists generally, to the genocidal actions of Adolf Hitler (Creedon, 2007). At the second meeting a key member of the group reportedly referred to the school's policy as 'ethnic cleansing'. This was followed by an editorial in one of the national newspapers, the Irish Examiner, comparing the schools' language policy with Islamic extremism and the London bombings in July of that year (Irish Examiner, 2007). This campaign has caused bitter divisions between people in the area. The parents who took their case to court

1 Dingle Peninsula Tourism, a marketing co-operative owned and managed by its members, have produced this website to provide the visitor with the information they need to plan and enjoy their visit.

2 Pobalscoil Chorca Dhuibhne has approximately 465 pupils.

and the school eventually made an out of court settlement. This settlement has maintained Irish as the language of instruction and business, but in addition extra supports have been put in place for those students whose competence in Irish might restrict their access to the curriculum and achievement.

These are depictions of the same place, yet they convey radically different images. The place is Dingle[3], in West Kerry on the south west coast of Ireland. The first depiction, produced by the local tourism organisation, depicts Dingle as a space of natural beauty, a place to unwind. The local language, Irish, is portrayed as a community language. Importantly, it is portrayed as a public language, the language of education and business. There is no sense of the language as troubling, of local identity as troubling. The second depiction, therefore, could not be more different. Here the language is placed at the centre of a heated dispute, and its place as a public language of education contested. The idea of Irish as a 'community' language is disrupted by this second depiction.

How are we to understand these different depictions of the same place? Doreen Massey (1995; 2004; 2010) would suggest that both are practices of place-making, that geographical locations are constructed as particular places through discursive and material practices, out of social interaction and the collision of history, culture, economics and politics. Furthermore, she would argue that processes of place-making are never finished, rather places represent what might be termed a flux of 'stories so far' (Massey, 2010). This is not to question the placeness of place, but to emphasise that we need to examine the specific configuration of events and processes that give places their particularity. The first objective of this chapter is to formulate a framework for understanding how both depictions of Dingle can be produced simultaneously – how are we to understand what makes Dingle a particular place. Transnationalism is not the primary focus of this chapter but explores some of the social effects of historic and contemporary transnational formation. Transnationalism has been associated with the reconstitution of place (Vertovec 2001) as a result of the links and negotiations between "sending nation and hometown", between place of departure and place of settlement (Portes, 1999: 217). It is proposed that the analytical model developed here can enable us to understand the particular modalities of transnational formation as the affect vulnerable sections of host communities.

The second objective is more applied. This chapter has a history, in fact three histories. The rationale for asking the questions that structure my discussion in this chapter arose from a personal and political engagement with the cultural politics of language captured by the second depiction. As a parent I was confronted with having to take a position in relation to the Irish-medium language policy of the school in Dingle as a result of my own children attending the school. The situation forced upon me the requirement to transform private sentiments into public political acts. Eventually this took the form of me publically defending the school's language policy, making me a

---

3 An Daingean was the official Irish language name for the town under the Official Languages Act 2007. Subsequently a local campaign persuaded the Irish Government to amend the place names order so that the town would be officially known by a bilingual version *Dingle/Daingean Uí Chúis*. The town is more popularly known through its English name of Dingle. For the purposes of this article I will use the English language version.

participant in the cultural politics that later became an object for my sociological study. The decision to make the cultural politics of language and identity an object for academic study arose from my need to understand the nature of this cultural politics and the positions I was adopting within it. Was I supporting a parochial, backward looking and exclusive policy? Was I positioning myself against the necessary modernisation of Ireland in the face of increasing multiculturalism? These troubling questions forced me to make my own involvement an object of study. This second strand of history fed into my involvement in a series of academic seminars organised at the Catholic University of Leuven in Belgium and later symposia at the European Conference for Educational Research in Helsinki and Berlin[4]. These seminars and symposia were concerned with issues of the construction of public spaces for democratic learning. I was prompted therefore to link my reflections on the cultural politics of language and identity with issues of democratic politics and the public sphere. More specifically I was concerned that my academic reflections should feed into a practical cultural politics of language and identity that did not rely upon essentialist notions of identity but were premised upon the idea of identity as formed at the nexus of history, economy, culture and politics, and of identity as being constantly made and re-made through cultural practices.

This chapter is based on one proposition – a relational understanding of identity, and two objectives – to develop a framework for understanding how place is produced, and to link this understanding to a practical cultural politics of place. I do this through an elaboration of an analytical framework through three related discussions of *space and place*, *social and political*, and *public and private*. Although I draw upon further depictions of Dingle as a space of tourism and Dingle as a space of cultural politics, these are for illustrative purposes and help me to build up my developing argument. The choice of material is therefore highly selective and should not be misunderstood as a form of data analysis. The concluding section '*re-imagining a politics of language, place and identity*' draws the three theoretical discussions together and addresses the two objectives for this chapter. Specifically I argue that it is possible to construct a cultural politics of language and identity without relying on essentialist conceptions of identity, but, paraphrasing Stuart Hall, this is a politics without guarantees.

## Thinking Through a Possible Cultural Politics of Place and Identity

*Space and place*

The two depictions of Dingle presented above seek to portray it as authentic but each involves different visions of that authenticity – authentically beautiful, authentically Irish speaking. Authenticity, in this sense, is seen as located in a particular locale. For instance, the tourist Dingle links it with a particular place on the map marked by natural features:

4 The seminar series was organised under the auspices of 'Dealing with Difference and Otherness in Urban Environments. Emergent Learning and Democratic Citizenship' supported by the Fonds voor Wetenschappelijk Onderzoek – Scientific Research Foundation, Flanders. The symposia were organised by Professor Gert Biesta (who also participated in the Leuven seminars) at the ECER conferences in Helsinki (2010) and Berlin (2011).

> The peninsula is dominated by the range of mountains that form its spine, running from the Slieve Mish range to Mount Brandon, Ireland's second highest peak. The coastline consists of steep sea-cliffs, broken by sandy beaches, with two large sand spits at Inch in the south and the Maharees to the north. The Blasket Islands lie to the west of the peninsula. (Dingle Peninsula Tourism, 2011c)

The place is constructed as an escape from the modern world, a place to wind down and recharge the batteries. I have already noted above that the touristic depiction of the area defined in terms of the Irish language sits in tension with Dingle as a site of cultural antagonism. Tourist brochures, of course, are written to attract visitors to the locality, not to record the cultural politics. It is interesting, however, that Irish is invoked as a pre-modern language enabling the visitor to 'step back in time':

> The Dingle Peninsula / Corca Dhuibhne is a unique storehouse of Irish cultural heritage. Until recently, the peninsula was remote from the influences of the modern world, and this meant that the language and traditions of the area have survived intact to a greater degree than in most of Ireland. (Dingle Peninsula Tourism, 2011b)

This discussion of the construction of place through imagining Dingle as a particular kind of space defined by natural beauty and history as heritage helps us to grasp the complexity of place and how places are made. For the people of Dingle it is a place of work, of servicing a modern tourist economy, of generating income from the hills and the sea through farming and fishing, and home for those for whom Irish is not a throwback to a former pre-modern time but a living culture, a central feature of their identity and their link to this place. But Dingle imagined as a tourist space involves a complex mix of social relations that relate to each other in specific ways. Fáilte Ireland (Fáilte Ireland, 2010)[5] estimates that tourism generated € 3,9 billion in 2009. For towns such as Dingle tourism is an essential element of the economy. Dingle then is partly constituted through a particular economic imaginary that seeks to develop the place as a tourist destination, and therefore manifests itself in an infrastructure of hotels, shops, restaurants, cafes, etc. Indeed, Dingle owes its emergence as a global tourist destination to the making of David Lean's famous film 'Ryan's Daughter', which transformed Dingle from a poor fishing port to one of Ireland's major tourist centres (see McCormack, 2005).

Doreen Massey (1995: 183) argues that we need to understand that "... places, in fact, are always constructed out of articulations of social relations (trading connections, the unequal links of colonialism, thoughts of home) which are not internal to that locale but which link them to elsewhere". Ryan's Daughter played on folk memories of Irelands struggle for independence that circulated through worldwide Irish diasporas, including those who emigrated from Dingle, sat in (easy/uneasy) relation to contemporary nationalist sentiments in the area, created conditions that enabled Dingle to be in-

5 Fáilte Ireland is the National Tourism Development Authority of the Republic of Ireland, providing strategic and practical support in developing and sustaining high-quality and competitive tourism in and for Ireland.

tegrated into global networks of cultural production, supply chains servicing the tourist industry, and migratory flows of seasonal workers. Place (Dingle) is constructed in conjunction with 'space' (Dingle as a space of cultural production or tourism). The concept of 'space' may be seen to refer to the interrelationship between processes of economy, culture and politics that extend beyond the material place of Dingle whereas 'place' can be conceived of as a 'throwntogetherness' (Massey, 2010), where Dingle is produced on a moment-to-moment basis, place as always in production, the collision of "microworlds [that] find themselves on the same proximate turf" (Amin, 2004: 39). As Massey suggest places are normally made out of the unspectacular interactions between people, ideas and values born out of 'throwntogetherness' but sometimes the mundane is disrupted and the private sentiments that might animate people are forced into forms of public politics. In these circumstances the politics of place, as represented by the cultural politics of language policy, become struggles over particular constructions of place, of which histories will come to define Dingle as a particular kind of place.

*Social and political*

Above I have discussed how identity (of place) is constituted relationally. Now I want to consider identity in relation to the political. I am concerned in this chapter with the cultural politics of place which infers the politics of identity. I deliberately avoid the language of 'identity politics' because I want to articulate a way of thinking and acting in relation to the politics of language without invoking the essentialism of identity. I want to maintain a certain degree of radical doubt in relation to identity. Later, when discussing 'public/private' I will develop the notion of identification as preferable to identity. For the moment let me elaborate on the importance of understanding the cultural politics of language and place in terms of both its social and political dimensions and the relevance of the relationship between the 'social' and the 'political'. For this I will draw extensively on the work of Chantal Mouffe.

Chantal Mouffe has contributed to the development of a view of political identity, and of the field of politics, as constituted relationally (Mouffe, 1993; 2007). This approach to political theory resonates strongly with Massey's development of space/place. In particular Mouffe has articulated the idea of political identity as consisting of a we/they relationship. This relates to an elaboration of Derrida's idea of 'difference', in particular that all identity is constituted in and through difference; the interior of the I/we requiring an exterior you/they. I have argued (Warren 2012 forthcoming) that the nation-seeking politics of the Irish anti-colonial struggle drew upon 19th Century discourses of the nation-state that organised politics around a particular chain of equivalences – that the political boundary mapped onto a linguistic boundary and that the basis for a national polity required the assumption of a unified 'people'. The founding politics of an independent Irish state was structured around difference, the constitution of a collective identity where "... the creation of a 'we' which can exist only by the demarcation of a 'they'" (Mouffe, 2007: 15), of a 'constitutive outside'. For Mouffe politics requires this 'we/they' relation as the ground upon which political practice can operate, politics requires agonistic relations, a politics of adversaries rather than enemies. Ash Amin (2004: 39) discusses this in relation to the politics of place as an arena for struggles over different visions of the local which means "... seeing the local political arena as an arena of claims and counter-claims'. Amin terms this a 'politics of connectivity' where political actors have to choose between 'different senses of place and place attachment on the basis of agonistic engagement between different coalitions of cultural and geographical attachment' (42). The perspective developed by Mouffe, Massey and Amin involves a conception of the real as contingent, relational and performative. It is not that this implies an instability of structures or meanings, but that the stability necessary to produce a regularity in social effects requires active political work. The constitution of the Gaeltacht as a space of 'national archive' required active political and cultural work, political discourses, and bureaucratic institutions to realise this particular imagination.

The contingent nature of any political settlement arises out of the tension between the 'social' and the 'political'. In Mouffe's approach the 'social' refers to our habituated responses and interpretations of the world, similar to Bourdieu's concept of the 'habitus' (see Hillier & Rooksby, 2002). The 'social' is therefore made up of sedimented practices that take on the character of 'commonsense'. Irish citizens regularly express a positive sentiment to the Irish language without translating this private sentiment into a public politics. The 'political' refers specifically to the contestation of visions of place, identity, the 'good life', the 'public good'. The historical construction of Dingle as a particular place partially organised around the politics of language, and the economic and demographic changes that have occurred create the conditions whereby the habitual orientations towards Irish can be disrupted and propelled into the domain of the 'political' where different visions of identity and place have to be contested and mobilised around.

*Public and private*[6]

The contemporary notion of the 'public sphere' as a space of democratic debate is linked with the emergence of arguments for a deliberative democracy associated with the work of political philosophers such as John Rawls and Jürgen Habermas. At the core of theories of deliberative democracy is the assertion that the two pillars of liberal democracy – the institutions of the rule of law defending individual human rights and the processes and procedures of popular sovereignty are compatible. This assertion arises from a recognised tension between individual rights and the formation of collective identity through democratic participation. Deliberative democracy seeks to overcome this tension through the construction of a 'public sphere' as a space where rational debate can be exercised by citizens on the basis of equality and impartiality. The aim is the achievement of consensus on the main issues affecting society. Thomas Risse (2010) notes that this perspective is central to contemporary debates about the European Union's democratic deficit. Indeed, Jürgen Habermas has been prominent as a public intellectual on this issue. So, these are not matters of abstract reflection.

I have argued for a relational and contingent understanding of identity, including that of space/place, and that the identity of space/place involves definitional struggles. Importantly I noted Massey and Amin's argument that the 'throwntogetherness' of place, of living in diversity forms the basis of politics. This idea was further extended in the discussion of Chantal Mouffe's conceptualisation of politics defined as the necessary

6 This title plays on C. Wright Mills' classic sociological work *The Sociological Imagination* where Mills discussed the iterative relationship between private concerns and public issues.

contest over different visions of the public good. It is this that leads Mouffe to critique notions of deliberative democracy. One of the fundamental limitations of this approach, according to Mouffe, is the central concept of 'consensus'. I argue elsewhere (Warren, forthcoming) that the dispute over the school's language policy can be understood as a conflict between individual and group claims, over different understandings of human rights. These are tensions between different notions of the public good and between different definitions of space/place. Mouffe argues that this contest between different sets of values is important and that a move towards consensus that suppresses the different values and visions at stake is unhealthy for democracy (Mouffe, 2009: 93). Another way of understanding this is that the deliberative approach conceives its central concepts as given. The alternative relational approach I am advocating here requires that these concepts themselves be the focus for debate and definition; that is politics is understood as a space of imminent contest. Drawing on Bourdieu (Bourdieu & Wacquant, 1992) and further developed by Rogers Brubacker (1996; 2004) we would need to approach concepts such as 'human rights', 'identity', 'place' and 'history' as objects of study, as the things that need explaining rather than the terms we use to explain.

Central to this discussion is the relationship between what we might call the private and the public. The impossibility of constituting a democratic politics based on a private realm of values and public realm of rational debate is core to Mouffe's challenge to deliberative democratic theory. The interesting point here is that of how private sentiment is translated into public political positions – that is how the social is transformed into the political. The struggle over the schools' language policy is a struggle over which language – Irish or English – is the legitimate public language. This entails definitional struggles over what kind of place Dingle is. By translating private sentiments about the Irish language into public positions in relation to the school's policy involves attaching these private sentiments to different sets of values and visions about the nature of modern Ireland and Dingle's place within this (Warren, 2012 forthcoming). This is not so much a process of people with similar identities grouping together as the forging of identity around the process of identification. Rogers Brubaker (1996; 2004) challenges the tendency within both political and academic discourse to view 'groups', ethnic, national or linguistic, as distinct bounded entities with agency and interests. He argues that this substantialist approach invokes a kind of primordial conception of ethnicity, suggesting that people belong to fixed ethnic or national groups that are characterised by common descent and language. Instead he argues that we need to view identity as an event, things that happen, as practices of group identification, similar to Massey's argument about place as event. Consequently we need to focus on the processes by which people come to form such identifications. Again, drawing on Brubaker's work, we need to take account of how private sentiments are translated, articulated and transformed. Brubaker discusses the role of ethnopolitical entrepreneurs in constructing certain issues as 'ethnic' conflicts, transforming private sentiments (about neighbours, etc.) into ethnic conflicts by constructing others as the constitutive outside, of constructing not just a 'we/them' relation around which a democratic politics could be mobilised but a 'friend/enemy' relation around which an exclusionary politics is conducted.

The role of organisations and the media in organising the translation of sentiment into public politics could be considered as significant in the struggle over the school's language policy. The 'Concerned Parents' group represented a position organised around antagonism to the school's Irish-medium education policy. However, support for the school's policy came from a number of language-based organisations including *Tuismitheoirí na Gaeltachta* (Parents of the Gaeltacht) and *Todhchaí na Gaeltachta* (Defend the Gaeltacht). The media played an important role in creating a space not just for reporting on the dispute but of providing space for comments from the different organisations and individuals. This ranged from the local media such as the regional *The Kerryman* newspaper and the *Dingle News* blog to English language national newspapers such as *The Irish Times*, The *Irish Independent*, and *The Irish Examiner* as well as the Irish-language media including *Foinse* (Irish-language national newspaper), Raidió na Gaeltachta and TG4 (Irish-language radio and television media). The dispute also featured in the *British Guardian* and *Times* newspapers. Sentiment and public position were organised but the range of sentiments were likely to be varied with some long-standing local families objecting to the schools' policy and new residents supporting it, from fluent and new Irish-speakers both opposing and supporting. So, the constituencies available to support one side or the other represent not only varied sentiments but also different kinds of affective attachment to place. The link between personal identity, language and place were unstable. In this sense an essentialist politics of place and identity would be unworkable when translating sentiment into public position.

## Conclusion – Re-imagining a Politics of Language, Place and Identity?

How are we to understand the two very different depictions of place outlined at the beginning of this chapter? And, can we conceive of a non-essentialist cultural politics of place and identity?

I have argued that in order to understand how two very different depictions of the same place can be produced simultaneously I have argued that we need to approach the constitution of place and identity through a relational framework. In particular I have argued that we can understand place and identity as being produced at the intersection of three dynamics – space/place, social/political, and public/private. We can understand places as constituted out of the interaction or collision of different trajectories of history, economics, culture and politics which are non-linear and so produce quite distinct imaginings of place that sit side by side with each other. Consequently Dingle can be imagined as a particular kind of space of natural beauty and linguistic heritage in a way that doesn't disrupt people's sentiments towards the Irish language. I have noted how elsewhere I have analysed the way the Gaeltacht has been produced as a particular linguistic space, as an 'archive of the nation' that refuses the dynamic nature of language use and linguistic identity and has failed to engage with the economic conditions that sustain language communities. This analysis also showed how public positions around the Irish language have made it a nodal point around which politics is conducted, making it possible for the cultural politics around the school's language policy to take the forms it did. Therefore people's private sentiments towards a language may remain in the domain of the social, making place through ordinary everyday practices of interaction; not just inter-subjective interaction but interaction with dynamics that are more global. The making of Ryan's Daughter was used as an example of the complex interaction of the local and global, of place and space. But sometimes, as with the school's language policy, private sentiments are transformed into public positions; private sentiments of disregard and love, hostility and accommodation are translated into organised political positions and mobilised in the realm of politics.

In the brief depiction of the cultural politics of language that arose in Dingle I suggest that it was structured around a conflict between two opposing conceptions of rights where the achievement of one set of rights appeared to negate the other set of rights. In other words, conceptualising bilingualism without accounting for the historical production of Irish as a threatened language could relegate Irish to the private domain because of the cultural power of English. Alejandro Portes et al. (1999: 225-6), in a discussion of transnationalism in historical perspective, have noted the tensions between adaptation to colonised cultures and the maintenance of transnational ties in the context of colonial settler communities. The struggles around identity and language can partly be viewed as traces of previous elite transnational formations. But this still leaves unresolved the relationship between Irish and how to belong in a region that has undergone demographic and cultural change and where attachment to the language as a public language has long been disputed. If identity is not fixed, and therefore the relationship between cultural identity and language and language and place is contingent, how can you construct a politics of place? The demographic changes in Dingle certainly attest to the contemporary movements of peoples as a result of European expansion. But does this constitute transnationalism, and if so what form? The focus on Irish-speaking Ireland is not a focus on the tradition objects of transnational research. Yet the fate of Irish can be understood as partially overdetermined by historical and contemporary transnational formations. As noted earlier the vulnerability of Irish speaking communities is a consequence of colonial transnational formation. In the contemporary moment the diasporic communities arising out of European expansion and global migration in Ireland are part of the normative process of transnationalism (Vertovec, 1999, 2001). Modern communication technologies and low-cost airlines make it possible to negotiate stretched out forms of sociality, and therefore engage construct diverse forms of engagement with place (Appadurai, 1996). So, while attention in transnational research has been given to the adaptations, negotiations, and complex identities by transnational communities, little focus has been given to the fate of vulnerable cultural or linguistic communities within wider host societies in relation to transnational formation. Doreen Massey and Ash Amin argue that the 'throwntogetherness' of place or the sharing of territory while living in diversity constitutes the basis upon which a politics of place can be constituted. Furthermore, this non-essentialist approach to the politics of place means that politics is not mediated through such binaries as 'modern and traditional', particular and cosmopolitan'. Instead, concepts such as 'belonging' can be opened up to interrogation and the nature of what it is to belong in places such as Dingle can become the focus of political debate. Therefore the opposition between an Irish-medium education and the installation of an English stream could be reconfigured into a debates over whether increased diversity necessitated the continued threat of Irish as a viable community language; how might new Irish speakers relate to the community of traditional Irish speakers; can the possession of Irish be considered a aspect of cosmopolitan identity?

If, as proposed, places are made through social practice, then the construction of a different cultural politics of place and identity can contribute to producing a different kind of place. At stake here, then, is the possibility of producing a place (Dingle) where increased diversity can sit alongside a strong and confident Irish language community.

## References


Amin, Ash (2004): Regions Unbound: Towards a New Politics of Place. In: Geographiska Annaler. No. 86B. pp. 33-44.

Appadurai, Arjun (1996): Modernity at Large: Cultural Dimensions in Globalization. Minneapolis: University of Minnesota Press.

Bourdieu, Pierre/ Wacquant, Loic (1992): An Invitation to Reflexive Sociology. Oxford: Polity Press.

Brubaker, Rogers (1996): Nationalism reframed: nationhood and the national question. In: The New Europe. Cambridge: Cambridge University Press.

Brubaker, Rogers (2004): Ethnicity without groups. Cambridge, Mass./London: Harvard University Press.

Creedon, Ted (2007): Parent's row breaks out over school's Irish language policy. In: The Kerryman. 12 September 2007. Tralee.

Dingle Peninsula Tourism (2011a): Bígí Linn. http://www.dingle-peninsula.ie/ [14.04.2011].

Dingle Peninsula Tourism (2011b): Culture, Heritage & Irish Language on The Dingle Peninsula/Oidhreacht, Cultúr agus Gaeilge ar Leithinis Chorca Dhuibhne. http://www.dingle-peninsula.ie/culture.html [22.04.2011].

Dingle Peninsula Tourism (2011c): The Dingle Peninsula Corca Dhuibhne. http://www.dingle-peninsula.ie/peninsula.html [22.04.2011].

Fáilte Ireland (2010): Tourism Facts 2009. http://www.failteireland.ie/FailteCorp/media/FailteIreland/documents/Research%20and%20Statistics/Tourism%20Facts/Tourism_Facts_2009_544KB.pdf [22.04.2011].

Hillier, Jean/ Rooksby, Emma (eds.) (2002): Habitus: a Sense of Place. Aldershot: Ashgate.

Irish Examiner (2007): Editorial: Language barriers – Irish at the expense of education? In: Irish Examiner. 17 October 2007. Cork, Ireland.

Massey, Doreen (1995): Places and their Pasts. In: History Workshop Journal. No. 39. pp. 182-192.

Massey, Doreen (2004): Geographies of Responsibility. In: Geographiska Annaler. No. 86B. pp. 5-18.

Massey, Doreen (2010): For space. London: Sage.

McCormack, Helen (2005): Ryan's Daughter: the inside story. In: The Independent. http://www.independent.co.uk/arts-entertainment/films/features/ryans-daughter-the-inside-story-510119.html [22.04.2011].

Mouffe, Chantal (1993): The return of the political. London: Verso.

Mouffe, Chantal (2007): On the political. Abingdon: Routledge.

Mouffe, Chantal (2009): The Democratic Paradox. London: Verso.

Portes, Alejandro and others (1999): The study of transnationalism: pitfalls and promise of an emergent research field. In: Ethnic and Racial Studies. No. 24. pp. 217-237.

Risse, Thomas (2010): A Community of Europeans? Transnational Identities and Public Spheres. Ithaca/London: Cornell University Press.

Vertovec, Steven (1999): Conceiving and researching transnationalism. In: Ethnic and Racial Studies. No. 24. pp. 447-462.
Vertovec, Steven (2001): Transnationalism and identity. In: Journal of Ethnic and Migration Studies. No. 27. pp. 573-582.
Warren, Simon (2012 forthcoming): The making of Irish-speaking Ireland – belonging, diversity and power. In: Ethnicities. Sage Journals. http://etn.sagepub.com/content/early/2011/09/08/1468796811419597.full.pdf+html [08.09.2011].
Warren, Simon (forthcoming): SÚIL EILE – A different perspective on migration, language acquisition, belonging and multicultural society. In: Lavia, Jennifer/ Mahlomaholo, Sechaba (eds.): Culture, Education, and Community: Expressions of the postcolonial imagination. London: Palgrave Macmillan.

# Propuesta Teórica en la Reconstrucción de las Cosmovisiones, Lenguas y Conocimientos de los Pueblos Originarios ante la Globalización

*Miguel Sánchez Álvarez*

## Resumen

*En esta exposición encontrará usted información de una de las múltiples culturas y numerosos pueblos originarios en la región Los Altos de Chiapas, México. Pese a la influencia de la globalización ideológica y económica en la República mexicana coexistimos más de 70 pueblos originarios y 68 agrupaciones lingüísticas (INALI, 2009a: 17; 2009b: 32) que compartimos el territorio mexicano junto con la sociedad ladina o mestiza, los pueblos originarios nos caracterizamos por nuestra forma de organización social, manera de relacionarnos con nuestro territorio, recursos naturales en apego a nuestras cosmovisiones, sistemas de conocimientos, lenguas y culturas heredadas desde diferentes etapas históricas: prehispánica, colonial, poscolonial o independencia, revolución y actual. De ahí que, tanto los pueblos originarios como la sociedad ladina o kaxlai mexicana[1], han desarrollado conocimientos científicos, tecnológicas, expresiones artísticas, literarias y valores sociales, que nos han dado identidad como una gran nación mexicana multicultural y multilingüe. Sin embargo, en el mundo existen intereses muy poderosos que pretenden imponer que las naciones, los estados y pueblos, practiquen modos de vida única, una sola economía basada en el mercantilismo y consumismo de productos industrializados que buscan nuevos espacios transnacionales, imponen una sola forma de conocimiento, hablar una sola lengua, practicar una sola religión, vestirse de una sola manera y explotar de manera irracional los recursos de la Tierra; estos intereses e imposiciones están disfrazados bajo distintos nombres y conceptos dentro de la teoría económica, se denominan como desarrollo económico, progreso económico y desarrollo social; nos han hecho creer que mediante el desarrollo económico mejorarían nuestras condiciones de vida, se superarían las diferencias entre ricos y pobres, pero los hechos nos demuestran que es todo lo contrario ya que se han generado distintos problemas en nuestras sociedades, culturas y ambiente.*

## Introducción

La presente propuesta resulta del análisis y síntesis de diversas investigaciones que vengo realizando bajo distintas metodologías[2] desde la década de los 80's, 90's del siglo pasado, hasta nuestro tiempo, se busca llegar a un estudio serio, profundo y holístico en el análisis, explicación de las condiciones socioculturales, territoriales y ambientales; para

1 Ladino o *kaxlan* (en lengua maya tsotsil y tseltal) se refiere a las personas que hablan la lengua castellana o española y que no hablan y no pertenecen a la cultura de los pueblos originarios.

2 La metodología utilizada en las investigaciones destaca la tradición oral, observación directa y participante, talleres participativos y entrevistas.

la construcción de la memoria histórica sobre los ideales y luchas para la continuidad biocultural de los pueblos originarios[3] y de los mexicanos, para generar las capacidades sociales en la toma de decisiones en la producción e innovación de sistemas de conocimientos. Resulta también de la necesidad de construir el puente de enlace entre las sociedades y culturas para entender esa otredad, del México de los pueblos originarios, que no se le ha querido reconocer sus cosmovisiones, lenguas y conocimientos, su derecho a la libre decisión, ante la imposición del sistema hegemónico que globaliza y occidentaliza los diversos modos de vida y culturas.

## Construir lo propio para contrarrestar lo ajeno

Los pueblos originarios del mundo nos enfrentamos con un enemigo invisible que se llama globalización, un proceso que comenzó antes de 1492, y tuvo un impulso tremendo con la conquista de América por las potencias europeas (Godelier, 1997: 9); desde entonces, el Occidente ha venido ampliando cada vez más su influencia en todo el mundo, aunque ha tenido que renunciar a sus colonias, el proceso de occidentalización a nivel mundial prosigue ininterrumpidamente. La occidentalización de ahora se caracteriza bajo una economía de mercado basada en el sistema capitalista que presupone la propiedad privada de los medios de producción y del dinero; la producción industrial en masa de bienes de producción y de consumo; una democracia parlamentaria, combinada con un sistema pluripartidista, a través de partidos políticos con ideologías que supuestamente buscan la democracia; la ideología de los derechos humanos que, según sea el caso, ha sustituido o complementado al cristianismo (Godelier, op. cit.).

En los territorios de los pueblos originarios, sentimos más los efectos de la globalización y occidentalización debido a la imposición económica e ideológica que trunca o cambia drásticamente nuestras formas de organización social comunitaria, los conocimientos, las formas de producción y de relacionarnos con nuestro territorio, por obligarnos a abandonar o cambiar nuestra cosmovisión, por explotar nuestros recursos naturales de manera irracional, por plagiar nuestros conocimientos, elementos simbólicos ancestrales y actuales. Como se puede dar uno cuenta, nos enfrentamos ante el enorme problema de ¿cómo hacer que los conocimientos y las culturas se enriquezcan y perduren?

Mi visión como maya tsotsil huixteco[4] y como antropólogo es que en México hay grandes oportunidades y grandes retos para mejorar nuestra situación social, cultural y ambiental. Pero veo también una nación dependiente, tanto en economía, ciencia y tecnología; un país donde los políticos y los planificadores de la administración pública han estado implantando modelos de desarrollo que no resuelven de fondo los problemas sociales, económicos y ambientales de nosotros los mexicanos.

Como acertadamente menciona Burgueño (2006: 80) todo indica que el potencial científico y tecnológico está concentrado en unos cuantos países: Estados Unidos, países de Europa y Japón, los cuales poseen la infraestructura científica, la mayor parte de

3 Hablaré en términos de pueblo originario, pueblos originarios o maya tsotsil, tseltal, en lugar de pueblo indígena o pueblos indígenas.

4 Nombre gentilicio que proviene del municipio de Huixtán, Chiapas.

los investigadores y los recursos financieros; ahí se definen los grandes rumbos de la investigación y las actividades primordiales de innovación. Son los centros de la economía global (Burgueño, op. cit.). En algunos países subdesarrollados se han realizado importantes esfuerzos y se usa considerablemente la tecnología moderna, pero no existe una generación endógena de tecnología, pues su conocimiento es reducido y menor su aplicación innovadora encaminada a la solución de problemas propios (Burgueño, op. cit.). Las tecnologías de la información y las comunicaciones han profundizado la división en el mundo de la globalización, no solamente entre quienes tienen o no tienen, sino entre los que saben y no saben, entre los que cuentan o no con acceso al conocimiento científico y tecnológico. Existe una brecha tecnológica en la globalización que divide las economías según su capacidad para la generación, asimilación y difusión del conocimiento (Burgueño, op. cit.).

De igual manera, hemos sido conducidos y mediatizados por ideologías que se expresan en partidos políticos, en corrientes religiosas, que lejos de ayudar a nuestra sociedad causan más problema, dependencia y mayor división social. Todos estos procesos están reproduciéndose al interior de la República mexicana y al interior de los pueblos originarios. Superar estos grandes retos no es nada fácil, pero tenemos que hacer un esfuerzo por reconstruir ese conocimiento desde al interior de nuestras comunidades y pueblos para un modo de vida justo, humano, equilibrado entre las sociedades; entender las cosmovisiones de nuestro pasado y presente para no olvidarnos que somos seres biológicos y culturales, que formamos parte de la naturaleza y del cosmos, este aspecto nos debe orientar para que nuestra ciencia y tecnología tenga grado de humanidad y sabiduría para ser más amigables con el ambiente y contrarrestar los problemas de desigualdad social y económica.

Debemos buscar cómo reconstruir, engrandecer nuestros conocimientos y cultura como mexicanos y como pueblos originarios, o como naciones multiculturales, es tiempo de generar ese cuerpo teórico-conceptual y metodológico desde nuestras visiones, tarea nada fácil después de tanto tiempo de opresión, discriminación y colonialismo, pero los mexicanos somos seres humanos dotados de inteligencia, sabemos observar, inventar, construir y buscar soluciones a nuestras necesidades; nuestra herencia cultural prehispánica, colonial, las creaciones científicas, tecnológicas, artísticas y las ciencias sociales así lo testifican. La reconstrucción de nuestros conocimientos y cultura deben girar y basarse en torno a la cosmovisión, lengua y los sistemas de conocimientos que poseemos sobre nuestro territorio y nuestra cultura, de ahí que las investigaciones de las ciencias sociales y de las ciencias naturales (ambientales) deben considerar los sistemas de conocimientos que nos dan forma, cuerpo y vida como pueblos originarios y como mexicanos.

Debo aclarar que con esta propuesta no se trata de tener como enemigo a la sociedad *kaxlan* o ladina, tampoco se trata de renunciar a los avances del conocimiento científico que ha desarrollado la humanidad, ni mucho menos pretende dejar de lado los aportes de las ciencias sociales y del desarrollo regional, sino todo lo contrario, se trata de explicar de manera crítica, propositiva, nuestra situación, para darnos cuenta de un enemigo que es creado por los intereses de los grandes capitalistas que ostentan el poder político, económico y tecnológico, que rompe con todos los diferentes modos de ser y de vivir.

Tampoco se intenta retroceder en el pasado y olvidar los avances, más bien tiene la intención de darnos cuenta de no caer en una sociedad inventada como la que se presenta en la novela de ciencia ficción de Aldous Huxley (1986): *Un Mundo Feliz*; en un mundo en el cual la sociedad altamente tecnificada, las personas carecen de sentimientos, no conocen dolor, no saben enfermarse, las mujeres dudan de la maternidad, la sociedad totalmente estratificada en clases no se da cuenta de su realidad de clase debido a que desde niños son condicionados de manera psicológica e ideológica en cómo deben ver y comportarse de manera natural en su mundo, lo que Huxley maneja como hipnopedia; por esta situación no se percatan ni se inconforman de su situación de clase y de explotación, ya que la clase social de alta jerarquía es la que gobierna, regula todos los aspectos de su vida social, económica y política. A semejante mundo y sociedad nos estamos aproximando, por eso la construcción de los conocimientos, la planeación y administración de nuestra herencia cultural y herencia natural (territorio, recursos naturales y agrobiodiversidad) debe ser desde el interior, no en la adopción de modelos de desarrollo que están fuera de nuestra realidad, de ahí que nos lleva a la necesidad de construir nuestros conocimientos, cultura, de manera analítica, crítica y propositiva. Es una necesidad que tenemos los mexicanos, los científicos sociales, para reorientar la ciencia, tecnología y la educación, para que estén al alcance y servicio de la gente, así como en la orientación epistemológica de los conocimientos para la base de un desarrollo desde el interior de esta gran nación mexicana multiétnica y multicultural.

Para contrarrestar la dependencia económica e ideológica es importante contar con bases hacia un modo de vida alternativo con sabiduría, y para esto, ilustraré como ejemplo que nosotros los mayas tsotsiles huixtecos tenemos una antigua tradición en buscar ocote,[5] con el cual nos iluminamos por las noches y también utilizamos una parte para intercambiar[6] y suministrarnos de los sagrados alimentos: frutas, verduras, tortillas, tamales u otros que se antojen. Pero antes, para obtener el ocote las personas se dirigían a las montañas donde buscaban los troncos y trozos viejos de los árboles de pino que han caído desde hace mucho tiempo; en los troncos se buscan las raíces y en los trozos el "corazón" para obtener la madera roja y dura que sirve para prender el fuego del fogón donde se calientan todos los miembros de la familia, y el que se utiliza para iluminarnos con antorchas cuando se viaja de noche y no hay luna. Para encontrar las raíces del viejo tronco de pino que servirá de ocote se tiene que escarbar la tierra hasta encontrar la vena gruesa y el corazón, quien lo encuentra tiene entonces suficiente combustible para iluminarse y suficiente material con que intercambiar productos para la alimentación que compartirá con su familia.

Así también, nosotros los investigadores y los estudiantes, tenemos que volver los ojos a nuestro territorio, cosmovisión, lengua y sistemas de conocimientos; a escarbar el pasado histórico y el presente, a conocer nuestro territorio con sus respectivos lugares históricos, sagrados y topónimos; ahí podemos conocer y adquirir conciencia de dón-

---

5 Ocote, madera colorada de árbol de pino, se le conoce con el nombre de *toj* o *taj* en la lengua tsotsil y tseltal.

6 Intercambio que se dio y se sigue practicando entre tsotsiles huixtecos y tseltales en los días de mercado en la cabecera municipal de Tenejapa, Chiapas. El intercambio o trueque, lo conocemos en la lengua maya tsotsil como *tukul, tukultajel*, que indica la acción de intercambiar un producto por otro.

de venimos, quiénes somos y cómo será nuestro futuro; a percatarnos de los peligros que nos acechan; tenemos que estar iluminados para emprender el viaje hacia el futuro, para que la oscuridad de la noche no nos desoriente, que el enemigo no nos gane, para que no vayan a robar más nuestro territorio, conocimientos, productos y riquezas como está ocurriendo en la actualidad en México y en el mundo.

## Fundamentos de las cosmovisiones, lenguas y sistemas de conocimientos de los pueblos originarios

Nuestros modos de vida, cosmovisiones, sistemas de conocimientos y espiritualidad mantienen formas alternativas en cómo relacionarnos con nuestro territorio (montañas, suelos, aguas, plantas, hongos y animales), a la vez, el territorio es nuestra base principal donde se despliega nuestro desarrollo sociocultural y es fuente de vida, por ello, decimos madre Tierra, jme' jkaxiltik en la lengua maya tsotsil y tseltal, ahí es donde nacemos, crecemos y adquirimos nuestra conciencia de ser, en esta parte debemos enfocar nuestra atención de manera analítica y propositiva, considerando al territorio, lenguas, cosmovisiones y los sistemas de conocimientos siguientes:

1. El sistema de organización social familiar, comunitario, intercomunitario y pluriétnico, que resultan de las relaciones socioculturales, productivas e ideológicas. Entre la sociedad maya tsotsil-tseltal y ladina o mestiza se establecen diferentes formas de relaciones sociales, económicas, ideológicas, gastronómicas e simbólicas. Estas a su vez, se reproducen en las prácticas y en los modos de vida cotidiana de cada grupo social. Existen redes de relaciones familiares que se ligan con las propias comunidades, es decir, en los aspectos intracomunitarios, pero también existen relaciones sociales de solidaridad y de cooperación que trascienden las fronteras comunitarias y municipales. En los sistemas de conocimiento social, destaca la educación familiar y el aprendizaje del medio natural que los padres-madres le inculcan a sus hijos e hijas. Destaca también los conocimientos que se transmiten a través de los sistemas de cargos político-religiosos y en la indumentaria tradicional (Sánchez, 2009: 388).
2. El sistema de lenguaje y de comunicación, resultan de las relaciones entre diferentes lenguas y culturas como mecanismos de transmisión de los conocimientos cuya base descansa en el territorio y cultura de las sociedades. Nuestras lenguas transmiten valores, ética humana y modos de vida; en cada lengua se transmiten palabras, conceptos, planos del entendimiento del mundo; por ejemplo, en las ceremonias se reproducen las oraciones y discursos especializados, la música, las danzas, los tejidos y bordados expresan diferentes lenguajes de comunicación (op. cit.).
3. El sistema de concepción o cosmovisión, son las relaciones socioculturales, simbólicas y espirituales que se ligan con el territorio y el universo, forma parte del ser y modo de vida de los pueblos y sociedades. Cada pueblo cuenta con un territorio que le sirve de base para el despliegue de los elementos socioculturales. En nuestros sistemas de concepción del mundo se presentan mediante palabras, conceptos, planos y niveles de entendimiento y relación del hombre con la madre Tierra y el Uni-

verso. Los asentamientos históricos, los lugares sagrados son fuentes de conocimientos y de sabiduría que nos heredaron nuestros antepasados, en donde plasmaron sus manifestaciones arquitectónicas, simbólicas y espirituales (Sánchez, 2009: 389).

4. Sistema de educación familiar y comunitaria, que se basa en el aprendizaje de los principios, normas y valores comunitarios; de igual manera, mediante la interacción y observación de la naturaleza, así como en las prácticas productivas se vuelve toda una universidad de aprendizaje. En las comunidades mayas los niños y niñas desde muy temprana edad empiezan a conocer el entorno natural y entran en contacto directo con el suelo, las plantas, animales y fuentes de aguas que les permiten desarrollar sus órganos sensoriales y su capacidad mental (op. cit.: 389).
5. Sistemas de apropiación del territorio y ecosistema, se basa en el conocimiento en la clasificación, uso y manejo de los suelos, bosques, fauna, minerales, hongos y aguas. El territorio es la base del despliegue sociocultural, en él se presenta y se desarrollan las manifestaciones espirituales, ahí se encuentran los lugares históricos y sagrados que se liga con la naturaleza humana y cósmica. Asimismo, en las comunidades de los Altos de Chiapas existen racionalidades productivas y de consumo que procuran satisfacer las necesidades básicas e indispensables. Por ejemplo, los hermanos tsotsiles de la comunidad Dos Lagunas, municipio de San Cristóbal, para abastecerse del agua para el consumo humano se raciona a cada familia con igual cantidad del vital líquido, nadie tiene derecho en consumir más agua[7], pero ante la influencia del sistema capitalista pone en peligro esta relación equitativa y racionalizada del uso de los recursos de la Madre Tierra (op. cit.).
6. Sistemas agropecuarios y de aprovechamiento forestal, se fundan en las estrategias productivas y las relaciones sociales de producción. Los sistemas productivos son prácticas sustentables que ha multiplicado y diversificado las semillas y productos agrícolas para mantener a la sociedad. En la agricultura tradicional de temporal tsotsil huixteca se basa principalmente en los múltiples conocimientos y estrategias de apropiación y arreglos del ecosistema para obtener resultados favorables de producción agrícola. El agricultor huixteco hace uso de seis a nueve sistemas de cultivos. La práctica de policultivos, asociación del maíz con frijoles, haba, papa, calabazas y verduras permite obtener diversos productos para la dieta familiar. Las formas de apropiación de la naturaleza ha permitido generar conocimiento para establecer diferentes sistemas y métodos productivos con los que generar agrobiodiversidad; de igual manera, los conocimientos en la producción de animales domésticos son básicos para satisfacer necesidades de alimentación y para complementar el ingreso económico (Sánchez, 2005).
7. Sistemas de seguridad y soberanía alimentaria, se basa en la satisfacción de necesidades elementales en alimentación, en la generación de una racionalidad productiva y de consumo, de intercambio de los productos agrícolas que garantiza la continuidad de la vida humana y de la agrobiodiversidad. Nuestras formas de producir, consumir, intercambiar los productos agrícolas y las formas de preparar los alimentos nos garantiza contar con los sagrados alimentos necesarios basado en productos

7 Observación en la comunidad Dos Lagunas, municipio de San Cristóbal de Las Casas, Chiapas, México, años 1994-2010.

naturales que benefician a la nutrición y a la salud humana, comparado con el consumo de alimentos chatarras que traen problemas de obesidad, diabetes, colesterol y gastrointestinales (Sánchez, 2005).

8. Sistema de conocimiento de atención a la salud físico, psicológico y espiritual, prácticas que se ligan en el conocimiento de la naturaleza humana, en el uso de plantas, animales, hongos, aguas y minerales que tienen propiedad medicinal. Los conocimientos tsotsiles y tseltales en los Altos de Chiapas en el uso de fauna silvestre van desde el uso alimenticio y medicinal para tratar diversas enfermedades (Sánchez, 2000). Autores como Enríquez, Mariaca, Retana y Naranjo (2006: 491, 493, 497), en el estudio sobre el uso medicinal de la fauna silvestre, encontraron 74 especies y 36 partes o productos de éstos que son empleados para tratar una o más enfermedades o padecimientos registrados, desde dolor de cabeza hasta cáncer o sida. La fauna silvestre utilizada en la medicina tradicional sirve como remedio tanto para enfermedades reconocidas por la medicina occidental, como para enfermedades culturales locales, reconociendo a 128 enfermedades.
9. Sistemas de conocimientos en las artes y técnicas: arquitectura, música, danza, cerámica, tejidos, bordados y otros. Este conjunto de sistemas de conocimientos representa un campo amplio y complejo que no han sido estudiados suficientemente, pero se siguen desarrollándose en las familias y comunidades.

Todos los sistemas de conocimientos tradicionales señalados, más los que resulten merecen nuestra atención en su entendimiento y comprensión profunda desde las cosmovisiones, lenguas y modos de vida de cada pueblo, porque ahí se encuentran los pilares de la ciencia y tecnología. Ahora, el reto es, ante tantos prejuicios, marginación y exclusión en la participación del desarrollo de la ciencia y tecnología, y el gran abismo que existe en el conocimiento de las diversas manifestaciones socioculturales ¿cómo se puede enriquecer nuestros sistemas de conocimientos?, a esta situación nos lleva a plantear el diálogo de saberes que religue los conocimientos de las ciencias sociales y de las ciencias naturales, y que sirva de puente para la interculturalidad.

## Interculturalidad e integración de saberes en la investigación y educación

El diálogo intercultural debe darse de manera bilateral, multidimensional y no de manera unilateral, debemos de despojarnos de la vieja idea de que los pueblos originarios son quienes se deben integrar en el modelo de desarrollo económico y político hegemónico, en el sistema capitalista. Implica también que la sociedad nacional se interese en los conocimientos que tenemos los pueblos originarios, deberá de actuar con los más altos principios y valores de la moral y ética humana para evitar imposiciones y despojos. En la figura 1, expongo gráficamente cómo entiendo que debe estar encaminado el diálogo intercultural y la integración de saberes para la investigación y educación, sin que implique imposición y pérdida de los elementos culturales de ambas partes.

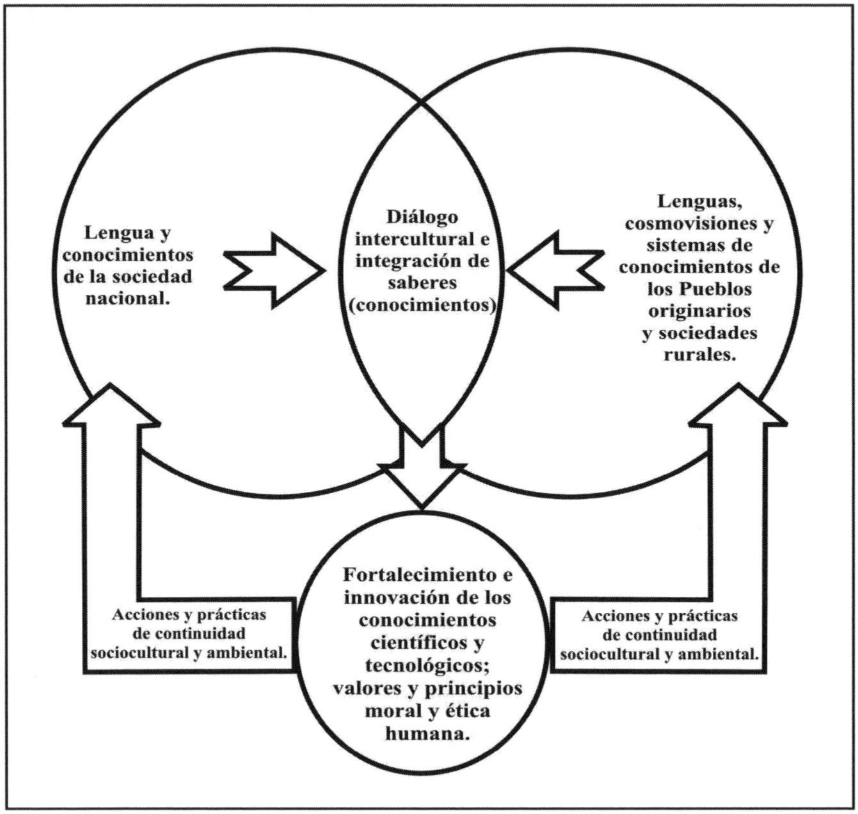


Figura 1: Diálogo intercultural e integración de saberes

Por ende, la integración de saberes representa la búsqueda y en muchos de los casos, la re-significación de nuestros modos de vida social, económica, ideológica y ambiental. Solamente vista y ejercida de esta manera podemos considerar que:

- El diálogo intercultural significa conocimiento y disfrute pleno de dos a más culturas y lenguas, pero también entre personas o individuos. Es una forma de vida y de relacionarnos entre distintas sociedades, culturas y lenguas.
- Nos lleva a la necesidad de generar e integrar conocimientos desde un enfoque holístico, sistémico basados en los principios, valores socioculturales y cosmogónicos existentes para encaminarse hacia una ética humana.

Los aspectos y pasos que debemos considerar en la integración de saberes (conocimientos con sabiduría) en la investigación y educación intercultural son diversos, pero destaco los siguientes:

*Primer momento*: En teoría y en práctica establecemos una interacción alumno, docente con las sociedades, pueblos originarios y comunidades rurales. Resultado: Alumnos, profesores e investigadores aprendemos, nos nutrimos de los conocimientos comunitarios en el ámbito sociocultural, productivo y ambiental de los pueblos originarios y sociedades rurales.

*Segundo momento:* Alumnos, profesores e investigadores generamos conocimientos teóricos-prácticos para interactuar y compartir con los pueblos originarios y comunidades rurales. Resultado: Las sociedades y pueblos originarios y no indígenas rurales fortalecen sus conocimientos teóricos-prácticos, mejoran su calidad de vida social y calidad de vida ambiental.

*Tercer momento*: Mejoramos nuestros conocimientos tanto en teoría y práctica de manera dialogada y con pleno conocimiento, establecemos así la integración y/o comprensión de saberes, establecemos vinculación de los conocimientos en ambas partes para la interculturalidad.

## Aspectos transnacionales

Como se puede percatar, la necesidad de establecer el diálogo intercultural se debe a que en pleno siglo XXI sigue habiendo una situación de colonialismo, las empresas de tipo capitalista industrial buscan nuevos espacios locales y regionales en las distintas naciones del mundo, aparecen como agentes transnacionales del modelo desarrollo hegemónico que recrea su propio mecanismo de reproducción material e ideológica al interior de las naciones. Esta situación significa mayor imposición en la producción de los bienes materiales, económicos e ideológicos (político y religioso) por parte del sistema hegemónico y globalizador hacia los pueblos originarios y de los distintos grupos sociales de las naciones; de igual manera, la influencia del modo de vida capitalista e industrial ha generado mayor explotación, saqueo, contaminación y destrucción de los recursos de la madre Tierra. En resumidas palabras, existe el grave riesgo que en los pueblos originarios y en los grupos sociales de las distintas naciones estemos perdiendo la capacidad en la toma de decisión social en la producción y reproducción de los bienes materiales y de los elementos identitarios y culturales propios.

Esta situación ha generado también distintas reacciones, por otra parte, encontramos movimientos sociales de resistencia, solidaridad y de cohesión social en el ámbito local, regional, estatal e internacional que refuerzan aspectos de cooperación comunitario, búsqueda y reconstrucción de los elementos identitarios étnicos y multiétnicos, son movimientos que rebasan las fronteras locales, regionales y de las naciones, esta situación nos lleva a la necesidad de entender las experiencias exitosas de los movimientos de grupos sociales transnacionales que buscan nuevas alternativas hacia un modo de vida sustentable.

Como señala, Velasco Ortiz, 1998, en la experiencia mexicana, existen las comunidades transnacionales que son uno de los resultados del flujo migratorio desarrollado en el siglo veinte entre México y Estados Unidos. Velasco señala que son muchos los cambios sociales y culturales que trajeron las migraciones a nivel local y nacional. En el proceso de construcción de las comunidades transnacionales de migrantes, los cambios pueden ser vitas en tres niveles.

> El primero, en las relaciones estructurales de la 'comunidad-territorio' local con el sistema social amplio, con la sociedad nacional y supranacional. Ello puede ser observado en el plano económico, vía la nueva relación de los migrantes con

los mercados locales, nacionales e internacionales de trabajo, y en el plano político en la nueva relación con los gobiernos regionales y nacionales, no sólo de su lugar de origen sino de los lugares de destino. El segundo, en el sistema de prácticas de la propia comunidad. En especial, las prácticas asociadas con la cohesión, prestigio y solidaridad que rearticulan a la comunidad en los territorios originales y de migración, y que pueden ser observadas en la dinámica de las redes de migrantes. Y un tercer nivel, en la conciencia comunitaria que expresa un sentido de pertenencia como proyecto cultural que desborda el territorio local y nacional, y que puede ser estudiado en las asociaciones pro-pueblos y otras formas más completas de organización que han surgido en diferentes lugares de destino (Velasco, 1998: 121).

Este conjunto de cambios permiten a estas comunidades transnacionales, como producto del proceso de des-reterritorialización de la identidad comunitaria. En esta nueva configuración cultural, la historia y el territorio del grupo siguen siendo fundamentales, pero ahora bajo la óptica de la experiencia migratoria y los nuevos lugares de destino de la migración. El cruce de fronteras locales y nacionales deriva en una resignificación del territorio original y una identidad socioterritorial cada vez más compleja y múltiple. Es difícil pensar a la comunidad transnacional sin mecanismos y agentes que permitan la cohesión y solidaridad en territorios tan distantes geográfica y políticamente (Velasco, op. cit.).

Velasco Ortiz, menciona que en su experiencia de investigación con migrantes transnacionales procedentes del estado de Oaxaca y asentamientos en la frontera mexicana en Tijuana, Ensenada y el Valle de San Quintín, en Baja California, y en Vista, Valle de San Joaquín y Los Ángeles, en California, del lado de la frontera estadounidense, distingue dos nuevos mecanismos presentes en estados comunidades transnacionales: las redes de migrantes y los agentes transnacionales. Las redes pueden ser vistas como entramados de relaciones sociales relativamente invisibles, pero al mismo tiempo reales, en la que están insertos individuos, familias o grupos de otro tipo, que funcionan como un campo relacional con una representación espacio-temporal. Las asociaciones de migrantes pueden ser analizadas como agentes transnacionales de la comunidad dispersa en varios territorios. En términos culturales las redes de migrantes se distinguen de las asociaciones de migrantes, porque las primeras son construidas como conjunto de prácticas con sentidos implícitos, en tanto que las segundas son construidas por el uso explícito de los sentidos de las prácticas. Desde el punto de vista de la relación territorio-identidad, las redes de migrantes pueden ser vistas como un mecanismo articulador, más que integrador, en la medida que resultan de la agencia social de los migrantes en su reproducción y producción de la sociedad. En tanto, las asociaciones, que son una especie de red politizada, surgen como un mecanismo "integrador" en la medida que constituyen un conjunto de prácticas concertadas en búsqueda de fines específicos y pueden desarrollar formas de solidaridad con fines explícitamente políticos (Velasco, 1998: 123).

Dichos mecanismos de articulación e integración de las comunidades transnacionales no es nada nuevo, la historia de los pueblos mesoamericanos y de la época colonial registra el alto grado de movilidad que tenían los grupos sociales por situaciones de migración y de política de reubicación de las poblaciones, especialmente cuando los pueblos originarios fueron concentrados de dos a más pueblos en una población para su mayor control por parte de la política de los colonizadores españoles, en estas concentraciones ocurrieron lazos de cooperación e integración, dando resultado final de mestizaje social, lingüístico y cultural, y desde luego que trajo nuevas formas de relación con el territorio y la naturaleza, surgieron nuevas formas de arreglos ecológicos generados por las actividades agropecuarias, así como en la reconfiguración de la comunidad y del territorio.

En la actualidad, la migración de los seres humanos en todas partes del mundo han generado poblaciones cosmopolitas, por mencionar un ejemplo, en la ciudad de San Cristóbal de Las Casas, Chiapas, históricamente estaba poblado por mayas, zoque, ladinos y mestizos que proceden desde la época prehispánica y colonial, pero en fechas recientes su composición poblacional se ve complementada por grupos de familias de distintas nacionalidades: españoles, alemanes, francés, ingleses, italianos, chinos, estadounidenses, entre otras, en esta nueva relación social, política y económica se establecen redes de cooperación y de integración que merece mayor atención en su estudio y comprensión al respecto.

Otro ejemplo, destaca el movimiento del Ejército Zapatista de Liberación Nacional en el año 1994, que en la actualidad aglutina distintos grupos sociales de distintas comunidades, municipios y estados en la República mexicana, pero esta situación no queda ahí, ya que en el movimiento se suman individuos y organizaciones de otras nacionalidades que luchan por ocupar espacios políticos y territoriales, por un modo de vida alternativo pero integrado por diferentes culturas, esta situación bien merece un estudio y análisis amplio y profundo al respecto, podemos decir, que estamos en frente ante movimientos sociales regionales y transnacionales que todavía desconocemos su situación futura.

## Conclusión

Las cosmovisiones, las lenguas propias y los sistemas de conocimientos tradicionales son los ejes fundamentos de la ciencia, tecnología y modos de vida de los pueblos originarios; de igual manera, las manifestaciones socioculturales se despliegan en la base territorial; los aspectos socioculturales y la base territorial son fundamentales para la continuidad social y biológica, de ahí la importancia en su conocimiento, desarrollo e innovación; a la medida que tengamos esa capacidad de generar los conocimientos le estaríamos dando un nuevo enfoque epistemológico de la investigación científica, tecnológica y de la educación para una vida alternativa más justa y humana.

La permanencia y dinámica sociocultural de los pueblos originarios en Chiapas y en México, más la presencia de los grupos sociales transnacionales nos lleva en la necesidad de reforzar los lazos de solidaridad y de cooperación con los hermanos de los pueblos originarios de Sur américa y con los hermanos mayas de Centro América que conforma la parte sureste de México, Guatemala, Belice, Salvador, Honduras y Nicaragua ya que culturalmente y territorialmente corresponde la gran nación maya prehispánica, de ahí la importancia de los lazos de solidaridad y cooperación transnacional en sentido y en las políticas para una vida alternativa o digna.

Así también, en el caso de México es necesario establecer lazos de cooperación con los hermanos de los pueblos originarios en los países de Canadá y Estados Unidos cuyos movimientos y luchas se encaminan de manera internacional por la búsqueda de un modo de vida alternativa, rebasando fronteras nacionales, esto no significa que estemos en la idea de una independencia local y regional, sino más bien en sentido de cooperación en la producción y reproducción de nuestros elementos materiales y culturales, en la convergencia de nuestros elementos identitarios como seres humanos culturalmente diversos o culturalmente similares pero territorialmente distantes, en otras palabras siendo transnacionales.

En cuanto a la importancia del diálogo intercultural reside justamente en la generación e integración de los conocimientos por parte de las comunidades, pueblos originarios y de la sociedad en general para la perfección y avance del conocimiento, que encamine en la construcción de la vida y no en la destrucción.

## Bibliografía


Burgueño Lomelí, Fausto (2006): Ciencia y desarrollo: tendencias actuales. In: Ciencia y tecnología en la frontera. Revista de divulgación científica del Consejo de Ciencia y Tecnología del Estado de Chiapas, Tuxtla Gutiérrez, Chiapas. V3 N4. pp. 59-63.

Enríquez Vázquez, Patricia/ Mariaca Méndez, Ramón/ Retana Guiascón, Oscar Gustavo y Naranjo Piñeira, Eduardo Jorge (2006): Uso medicinal de la fauna silvestre en los Altos de Chiapas. México. Interciencia, Julio. Año/vol. 32. núm. 007. Caracas Venezuela. pp. 491-499.

Godelier, Maurice (1997): El occidente, ¿espejo o espejismo de la evolución de la humanidad? In: Arizpe, Lourdes (ed.): Dimensiones culturales del cambio global. UNAM/CRIM. pp. 93-114.

Huxley, Aldous (1986): Un mundo feliz, Editorial Época. S. A., México, D.F.

INALI (2009a): Programa de revitalización, fortalecimiento y desarrollo de las lenguas indígenas nacionales 2008-2012 PINALI. Instituto Nacional de Lenguas Indígenas. México D.F.

INALI (2009b): Catálogo de las lenguas indígenas nacionales. Instituto Nacional de Lenguas Indígenas. México D.F.

Sánchez Álvarez, Miguel (2000): Los tzotziles-tzeltales y su relación con la fauna silvestre. Consejo Estatal para las Culturas y Artes (CONECULTA), libros de Chiapas: historia e historiografía, Talleres Gráficos, Tuxtla Gutiérrez, Chiapas, México.

Sánchez Álvarez, Miguel (2005): Sistemas y tecnología de producción agrícola en Huixtán, Chiapas, Centro Estatal de Lenguas, Artes y Literatura Indígenas, Gobierno del Estado de Chiapas, Talleres Gráficos, Tuxtla Gutiérrez, Chiapas, México.

Sánchez Álvarez, Miguel (2009): Los procesos y elementos de apropiación territorial de los tsotsiles-tseltales en el municipio de Huixtán, Chiapas. Tesis de doctorado en Ciencias en Planificación de Empresas y Desarrollo Regional; Instituto Tecnológico de Oaxaca, Oaxaca, México.

Velasco Ortiz, M. Laura (1998): Identidad cultural y territorio: una reflexión en torno a las comunidades transnacionales entre México y Estados Unidos. In: Región y sociedad, Colegio de Sonora, México, Vol. IX, No. 15, pp. 105-130.

# Teaching in Heterogeneous Classrooms: The Play of Reason and Unreason

*Neda Forghani-Arani and Anne M. Phelan*

## Abstract

*This study[1] is guided by the questions of what is involved and what is at stake in handling significant classroom situations in the transcultural space of urban classrooms with significant numbers of immigrant students. In an attempt to move beyond the frame of catalogues and criteria of teachers' diversity competencies, the authors set out to explore the experience of teaching in culturally, ethnically, nationally and linguistically heterogeneous classrooms characterized by transnational migration, in terms of practical wisdom, judgment and tact. The case study of a teacher in an urban secondary school in Vienna illustrates that there is more to pedagogic competence than teachers' knowledge of and commitment to diversity and social justice. The study suggests that the language of phronesis and tact can be immensely useful because it complicates the language of teacher efficacy. It can be concluded that any consideration of culturally responsive teaching must acknowledge the obligations that arise in the midst of practice, shaping teachers' responses.*

## Diversity Competence as an Element of Pedagogical Professionalism

Transnational migration has created spaces of tension in global cities and in urban classrooms. It takes place within fluid social spaces that are constantly reworked through migrants' simultaneous embeddedness in more than one society (Levitt/Glick Schiller, 2004; Pries, 2005; Smith, 2005). These "arenas" are "multi-layered and multi-sited", including not just the home and host countries but other sites around the globe that connect migrants to those with whom they share same national, ethnic, linguistic or religious memberships (Levitt/Jaworsky, 2007: 131). An urban classroom is one such social space constantly reworked through simultaneous cultural embeddedness of the

1 This case study is part of a larger collective case study of teachers teaching in classrooms with a sizable population of students with migration background in Austrian public secondary schools. The ongoing research project is conducted at the University of Vienna since 2006. Data is collected from teachers by obtaining descriptions of lived experience in form of anecdotal narratives in conversational interviews. The guiding question of the interview is: "What is it like for you to teach migrant pupils?" "Is it different to teach students with migration background? And if yes, how is it different?" Descriptions of lived experience in form of anecdotal narratives serve as the major source of data. Anecdotes are understood here as narrative accounts of incidents, situations, occurrences and episodes experienced by the interviewed teachers as they relate to the guiding question of the research, namely their pedagogical interactions with migrant pupils. After having identified and isolated a number of thematic aspects of the phenomenon on the basis of the transcribed lived experience descriptions related in the initial interview, data interpretation is continued in a second round of interviews with the interview partners engaging and including their interpretation of data in an attempt to examine and expand interpreted meanings. All interviews are audiotaped and transcribed.

immigrant students in interaction with their non-immigrant teachers and classmates. And as such, it is an intersection space of "collision of many layers, relations, perspectives and cosmologies" (Khagram/Levitt, 2008: 12).

What is it like for teachers to teach in these spaces of collision, tension, disagreement and rupture?

In recent years there has been an increasing interest in teaching and teacher efficacy in culturally diverse classrooms. The discourse is often embedded in multicultural or intercultural discourses, and more recently in the context of transnational or transcultural studies. Adick (2010) reviews the terminological boom of inter-, multi-, and transcultural studies in the field of education, primarily in the German language educational discourse, in reference to students with migration background in the school system of host countries. In the academic discourse she finds the term 'intercultural' usually used in a programmatic sense, the 'multicultural' as more descriptive (Gogolin/Krüger-Potratz, 2006: 110). In educational policy and public debates both terms are often used interchangeably. The multicultural describes and analyses a state of affairs, for example the multicultural society or the multicultural setup of a classroom. The intercultural is a normative stance in response to multiculturality. It has to do with the requisites of adequate pedagogical handling of multicultural setups. Transcultural approaches in education are often based on a conceptualization of culture as empirically and normatively "transcultural"; mutually delimiting, ethnically founded and socially homogenous cultures are in reality internally plural and externally transboundary (Adick, 2010: 107).

How do teachers who are predominantly socialized and trained in monocultural school settings experience the transnational or transcultural spaces of today's culturally diverse classrooms? How do they deal with the specific tensions of internally plural and externally transgressive classroom spaces? How do they know what is the right thing to do? How do they assess, judge and act in everyday classroom situations where (inter-, multi-, trans-)culturality seems to matter?

Literature on cultural competence of teachers is based on the premise that teaching efficacy in heterogeneous classrooms depends on the teachers' consciousness of their own enculturation, cultural identities, assumptions, perspectives and biases, as well as of the cultural identities of others (Gay, 2000; Guyton/Wesche, 2005; Ladson-Billings, 1995; Tucker et al., 2005). The literature suggests that teachers tend to introduce their own cultural beliefs into the curriculum and ignore the cultural heterogeneity of their students (Gay, 2000; Reed, 1996; Sleeter, 2008). When teachers become conscious of their own cultural identity, they become culturally efficacious individuals who can move between two or more cultures and also become advocates for those from cultures other than the dominant one (Bennett, 2007; Guyton/Wesche, 2005). Researchers and practitioners have developed tools such as the Multicultural Teacher Efficacy Scale (Guyton/Wesche, 2005) and the Multicultural Dispositions Index (Thompson, 2007) to assess culturally responsive teaching. More recent discourse takes a critical stance on the predominant praxis of intercultural communication and intercultural education. Training programs for intercultural competence are criticized for being limited to imparting culture-specific knowledge in an attempt to decipher the "foreign" and, therefore, for their "culturizing" and "ethnicizing" tendency (Auernheimer, 2002; Binder, 2005; Handschuck/Schröer, 2002; Gaitanides, 2003; Kalpaka, 1998; Leiprecht, 2002; Mecheril, 2002; Simon-Hohm, 2002).

Research has so far paid little attention to the normative nature of pedagogical decisions in the process of practicing intercultural effectiveness. How do teachers judge, decide and act? What is involved and what is at stake in handling the ambiguity and uncertainty of culturally significant situations? What vocabulary can articulate the process of judgment involved? Teachers are required to be discerning about what is appropriate and what is not and what is good and what is not in their interactions with students (van Manen, 1991, 2002). It is not simply a matter of identifying means to a particular end but deciding what constitutes a fitting end at a given moment for these students. Yet the vocabulary of moral perception and attunement seems to be missing from research on teachers' cultural competence.

Our core questions of 'what is involved and what is at stake' in handling culturally significant classroom situations, and our desire to move beyond the frame of catalogues, criteria and yardsticks of teachers' competencies, led us to a search for *another* vocabulary. Recalling Wittgenstein's caution (2003: 119) that "the limits of my language mean the limits of my world", we set out to examine the possibilities to be found in the languages of practical wisdom and tact.

## A Normative Turn

> Nearly everything that a teacher does while in contact with students carries moral weight. Every response to a question, every assignment handed out, every discussion on issues, every resolution of a dispute, every grade given to a student carries with it the moral character of the teacher (Fenstermacher, 1990: 134).

The neglect of the normative nature of pedagogical decisions and actions about cultural competence is related to a great extent to the prevalence of technical rationality in teaching and teacher education. The emphasis on instrumental reasoning, based on a conception of knowledge as episteme, whereby teachers and teacher educators are expected to identify the means for bringing about pre-determined ends, is evident in the pervasiveness of outcomes-based curricula and standardization throughout the Western hemisphere. The assumption persists that teachers need propositional expert knowledge consisting of a set of theoretically grounded assertions of a universal nature encapsulated in explicit formulae, procedures, rules and methods ideally derived from research. Knowledge of various cultures and lists of cultural key competences are examples. So-called factual and timeless knowledge then can be applied to different situations and problems, where the 'problem' is thought 'to be soluble by a straightforward application' of generalizable formulae (Dunne/Pendlebury, 2002: 197). Such extant knowledge is understood as inherently correct and coherent. Issues of applicability in the practice are usually attributed to the usage or the users of knowledge, in other words to failure in bridging the theory-practice gap (Korthagen et al., 2001).

And it is precisely the language of the theory-practice gap, and the assumption that theory is to be applied to practice, that denies a rich understanding of practice. Rooted in the particular, the practical realm invites a different kind of knowing that is not primarily concerned with the straightforward application of theory, but with bringing the particulars of specific, concrete situations into play with more general understandings. "Entering the practical means entering a realm of legitimate uncertainty, ambiguity, and disagreement" (Phelan, 2001: 42). It calls for a wisdom and an ethic of its own, that which Aristotle (1962) called *phronesis* or practical wisdom.

## Practical Wisdom as Discernment and Situational Appreciation

Practical wisdom, as we examine it in this paper, refers to teachers' capacity to discern particulars and make judgments about how to act in different situations and contexts (Phelan, 2009). The end in view is always human flourishing or *eudemonia*. Discerning teachers are sensitive to the particulars of students' lives and stories, to all the inconvenient complications and the competing demands of practice (Pendlebury, 1993). They respond to what is there before them "with full sensitivity and imaginative vigour" (Nussbaum, 1990: 84). While abstract knowledge and skills are necessary for the practical realm, they are insufficient for "the matter of the practical" which is essentially imprecise (Aristotle quoted in Korthagen et al., 2001: 26). It therefore calls for "responsiveness and yielding flexibility, a rightnesss of tone and a sureness of touch that could not be adequately captured in any general description" (Nussbaum, 1986: 304).

Teachers' adeptness at judgment relies on the extent to which they can enter into a play of thought between general understandings (e.g. of culture) and the particulars of the classroom, and on "bringing both into illuminating connection with each other"; this requires perceptiveness in one's reading of particular situations as much as flexibility in one's mode of "possessing" and "applying" the general knowledge (Dunne/Pendlebury, 2002: 198). If discerning teachers respect the particularity of the situation or case, they will find a way of bringing that particularity into some relationship with established norms or procedures in the area. To this end, teachers are keen students of knowledge (Phelan, 2009).

*Phronesis* has a different locus and justification of certitude than episteme. The certitude of episteme lies in a grasp of generalizable principles, whereas the fleeting certitude of practical reason eventually arises from knowledge of particulars (Korthagen et al., 2001). Practical wisdom requires a play of both kinds of knowledge: the general, in the light of the context-related particular.

## Pedagogical Tact and the Wholeness of the Child

There is an undeniable resonance between the interpretation of Aristotle's *phronesis* as situational appreciation and discernment and Johann Friedrich Herbart's understanding of pedagogical tact as that which slides in between theory and practice, completely voluntarily, namely a quick judgment and decision (Herbart, 1802).

The notion of tact was introduced into educational discourse in 1802 by Herbart, who is considered as the founder of pedagogy as a scientific discipline. He describes pedagogical tact as a mediator between educational theory and practice, the instantaneous assessment and decision-making of the educator to meet the necessities of the situation and the individual case at hand. Such pedagogical tact, developed in educational practice, has to do with the mind-set and the disposition of the educator, and is a result of thoughtfulness, genuine interest and moral commitment, which in turn leads to successful pedagogical practice and endeavour (Asmus, 1982; Benner, 1986; Blaß, 1972; Herbart, 1802; Metz, 1992, 1995; Müßener, 1983, 1991; Muth, 1961, 1962; Prondczynsky, 1993).

Herbart posited that tact occupies a special place in practical educational action. Tact is the immediate ruler of practice. It manifests itself in everyday teaching in the process of making instant judgments and quick decisions, and forms a way of acting which is first of all dependent on *Gefühl* (feeling or sensitivity) and only more remotely on convictions derived from theory. Tact alerts and informs the teacher of the moment the student is in a position to grasp or to perceive the significance of a truth (Herbart, 1913-1919, vol. I). "It tells the teacher which opinion of the student should be treated coldly, ignored, criticized, or encouraged" (Suzuki, 2010: 24). Pedagogical tact is sensitive to the requisites of the particular situation, and slips in to position the prevailing condition of the student within his or her entire growth process. Tact is a ruler of practice, which rules in response to the call of the moment moved by a concern for the long-term development and wholeness of the child.

Coupling the Aristotelian language of situational appreciation and discernment and the Hebartian concern for and sensitivity to the development of the child, we now explore a classroom vignette in an attempt to understand 'what is involved and what is at stake' in the pedagogical encounter with culturality, looking through what Khagram and Levitt call a "transnational lens" (Khagram/Levitt, 2008: 4). Levitt argues that "a transnational lens opens up the possibility of conceptualizing the local or the micro in non-territorial terms, such as an economic development project, the 'cell' of a broader criminal network", or – in the case of our vignette – a classroom moment in a public Viennese high school (Khagram/Levitt, 2008: 4).

## The Call of the Moment: Klaudia's Story

Klaudia[2] can be described as a mainstream, white, middle-class Austrian teacher in an urban high school in Vienna. The student body is diverse in terms of culture, religion, nationality, and language. In an interview, Klaudia described her school as one of the few public high schools with a bilingual program, namely, with both English and German as languages of instruction. She explained,

2 All names used in this paper are pseudonyms.

> [S]o I started this program at our school and we only accept one class every year. My students are the most colourful bunch. I have students from – let's say – 12 different nationalities. Many of them are from India, one from Iran – her father is from Iran, her mother is from Iraq, very interesting –, there is one from Sri Lanka, two from Croatia, from Poland, three from Nigeria, actually there are only two Austrians. Many of the parents work at the UN and it's a fact that, you know, they are very ambitious. Many of them are expats' kids, UN kids, or the parents are here on business. They are somehow connected to international organizations (2006, I-1).

Klaudia's new program is set against the larger educational context in Austria where intercultural education has been introduced as one of the thirteen cross-curricular educational principles. Cross-curricular principles are topics defined by the Ministry of Education, which teachers are recommended to take into account across the curriculum. The principle of intercultural education includes fostering understanding between students of different backgrounds and nurturing the values of tolerance, understanding and respect. The principle also states explicitly that teachers must recognize diversity and multilingualism as positive. Existing legislation concerning equity and migrant education policies is phrased in vague and non-binding terms, and implementation depends largely on teachers. While describing her efforts to recognize and include a diversity of cultural backgrounds in her curriculum, Klaudia relates the following story:

> A student of mine from Sri Lanka, he went to the (…), he went to Hajj, you know the Muslim pilgrimage, and I could tell he was different, when he came back. He was just so filled with faith when he came back from Mecca. Imagine, there are millions of people circumambulating the Kaaba, and you are part of it, I mean for a 13-year old. Shortly after that we were doing major religions, and I said: 'Well, tell us about it, you were there' (...) and then he took his Koran, stood in the corner of the class and chanted a prayer for us with all the movements that go with the phrases. Everything turned so quiet. Then he told us about his religious beliefs. He made it very clear that he would never ever marry a girl who doesn't wear a headscarf, and that he persuaded his mother and his sister to wear the hijab after he came back. He said: 'otherwise a woman's hair would catch fire'. That's when I said: 'Let's change the topic'" (2006, I-1).

When asked to share the reasoning behind her decision to "change the topic", Klaudia explains,

> This is always extremely sensitive. As a teacher, if I contradict him, I'd create resistance and opposition on his part. I would end up shoving him into a corner and that is exactly what I want to avoid as a teacher. That's not my job, that's not what I'm here for, that's not my role. If I let it pass and let the other kids take over the discussion (…) well actually I didn't even think of that option. You have absolutely no idea what would turn out. You never know, someone could get up and say: 'rubbish' or 'that's nonsense' or something like that. So (…) I simply turned it off. I said: 'That's enough for now' because it was getting out of hand, it

was actually kind of scary. I was somehow perplexed. You have to be so careful. It's like walking in a minefield (2006, I-2).

Klaudia literally draws the transnational landscape of her classroom, and posts the sites around the globe that connect her students to those with whom they share same national, cultural or religious memberships: Austria, Croatia, India, Iran, Iraq, Mecca, Nigeria, Poland, Sri Lanka, and beyond that their cross-border affiliations; UN kids, expats' kids, international organizations. Her classroom is neither global nor national nor local. Her students are transnational because they live across various cultural and territorial borders, and because as children of immigrants they have always been at the "interstices of symbolic and political boundaries" (Khagram/Levitt, 2008: 11). She shares the story of a potentially explosive collision of perspectives and cosmologies as one of her "transnational actors" involved in physical movement across national, cultural and religious borders, and under strong influence of transnational social fields affects not only his own private sphere but the public space of the classroom (Levitt/Waters, 2002: 4). This is one of the many instances where the fluid social space of Klaudia's transnational classroom is reworked through her immigrant students' simultaneous embeddedness in more than one society, continuously re-inventing the space in unpredictable ways.

How does she know how to judge, decide and act at such intersections?

Bill Green (2009) writes that *phronesis* or practical wisdom – and we would add tact – is essentially an aporetic state wherein the ethics of undecidability confronts the politics of decision making. While the moment calls for a response, and in the urgency and drama of the moment, tact slips in to provide one, the swiftness of the teacher's action may belie what hides beneath. Fear, wondering, and imagining characterize the moment of undecidability; "I was somehow perplexed" (2006, I-2), Klaudia explains. What makes the decision even more difficult is the knowledge that the results may not fully satisfy; "[Y]ou never know (...) it's like walking in a minefield" (2006, I-2), she ponders. The teacher makes two key decisions: 1) to invite the student to speak, and the reverse, 2) to put an end to the student's speech.

The teacher's first decision – to include – appears to be reasoned and reasonable. Klaudia notices that Kulasiri, a student from Sri Lanka now living in Vienna, has just returned from the Muslim pilgrimage, the *Hajj*. She discerns a difference in the young man, one she explains with reference to the impact of the pilgrimage, describing the boy as now "filled with faith." Seeing an opportunity, perhaps, to further intercultural understanding in the context of a history class on world religions, Klaudia calls on Kulasiri to tell his classmates about the pilgrimage. What she expects, however, is unclear. Is Kulasiri to relate information about the pilgrimage based on his empirically-derived authority – "[Y]ou were there" (2006, I-1) – or is he to bear witness to what she deems a transformative faith experience? Instead of relating information or giving an account of his experience, the student "took his Koran, stood in the corner of the class and chanted a prayer with all the movements that go with the phrases" (2006, I-1). "Everything turned so quiet" (2006, I-1) and an atmosphere of prayer, or study as a prayerful act, pervaded the classroom. No longer an 'objective' account or illustration, religion as an object of study becomes much more – a subjective experience and an embodied belief. It is not clear, however, if the chanting of the Koran troubles the teacher or the other students. There is a sense of watchfulness conveyed in the teacher's remarks as the class witnesses the faith practice of another. However, as Kulasiri begins to relate "his religious beliefs" regarding women, Klaudia becomes uneasy. The difference he introduces cannot be contained within the assumed rationalism of the study of world religions in a history lesson – as an example of one of many religions and their associated practices. Perhaps, the plurality initially sought by the teacher can no longer be managed as a curriculum resource intended to animate the topic of 'major religions.' The potential response from the other students to Kulasiri's expressed concern about preventing women's hair from catching fire renders the event sufficiently 'scary,' in the teacher's view, to shut down the discussion before it becomes ignited. Therein appears Klaudia's second judgment.

Klaudia's second decision to "change the topic", stems from her stated concern that some harm could befall Kulasiri or his classmates. If the topic prevails, she assumes that the only option available is that she contradicts the student's statement. She fears, however, that harm could result from telling him that he is wrong. To do so, in Klaudia's view, would be to create resistance, "shoving him into a corner" – an awkward or difficult position. Klaudia wants to avoid diminishing the student in such a manner. She is adamant: "[T]hat is exactly what I want to avoid as a teacher. That's not my job, that's not what I'm here for, that's not my role" (2006, I-2). Harm could also result, Klaudia believes, from letting the conversation continue in the hands of the other students because, "You have absolutely no idea what would turn out. You never know, someone could get up and say: 'rubbish' or 'that's nonsense' or something like that" (2006, I-2). In fact, she admits never having considered the option of relinquishing control of the conversation: "If I let it pass and let the other kids take over the discussion (…) well actually I didn't even think of that option" (2006, I-2). One may wonder why she didn't feel that she could trust either herself or the children with Kulasiri's remarks. To do so would be paramount to "walking in a minefield" – something could blow up and someone could get hurt. The teacher's capacity to imagine the harm that might be endured by her students is enough to usher in the imperative to stop the session from continuing – "you have to be careful" (2006, I-2) she insists.

Klaudia appears moved to act beyond thinking of all the practical or intellectual options before her. To be moved, in this instance, is akin to obligation or that which binds the teacher to a sense of responsibility and the necessity of particular judgements. Obligation cannot be legislated by codes of ethics, ministerial educational principles or professional standards of practice; it is unlike a contract that can be reviewed and agreed on. Rather, obligation is a feeling that "comes over me and binds me" (Caputo, 1993: 7). Obligation enables humans to respond to "real lives and events" but it points to the difficulties of defining responsibility in advance of encountering others (Smits et al., 1997: 193). "Obligations are strictly local events, sublunary affairs, between people (…). They happen" (Smits et al., 1997: 227). While the teacher's decision to invite the student to speak may have been shaped by the play between general principles (e.g. diversity and intercultural education are desirable) and particulars (e.g. a child who has just been to Mecca in a class on the history of major religions), her decision to "change the topic," thereby silencing the student and the difference he introduces, appears almost instinctual, less reasoned but not unreasonable. Sound the alarm: Do no harm!

While it is difficult to argue with Klaudia's sense of obligation to do no harm, some complex questions emerge about obligation that arises in the midst of practice: What are the sources of obligation? What is lost and gained in the call of such moments?

There seem to be several sources of obligation at play in this classroom moment: the obligation to plurality or difference, the obligation to be open to newness or natality, the obligation to care; and the obligation to repair. One might say that the teacher's felt obligation was to care, in the form of having no harm done to students. Obligation is imposed upon the teacher by the imagined suffering face of the other, standing there in front of her. Suffering in this instance does not take the form of bodily pain or material deprivation but the potentially harmful exclusion or marginalization of a student. Moreover, given the teacher's impulse to contradict Kulasiri, there seems to be an underlying though unspoken concern about students' exposure to religious fundamentalism or an unfounded belief or a non-empirically derived proposition. The moral obligation that Klaudia *feels* towards the students in front of her, and their immediate and long-term wellbeing, overrides her responsibility to promote intercultural understanding in that moment. In a state of "perplexity" and undecidability, Klaudia's capacity to imagine the impact of the pilgrimage on a teenage boy is paralleled by her capacity to imagine the impact of student or teacher reactions on her students. She feels the need to protect Kulasiri from herself and his peers even as she wants to protect her students from Kulasiri. Conjuring up an image of an innocent youth under threat from comments such as "rubbish," the teacher foregoes the more abstract principle of plurality and closes down the topic, for now. Difference, though initially welcomed, appears to have gotten out of hand, and thus becomes potentially dangerous. However, to maintain the aura of a classroom where no harm can be perpetrated (despite the inability to anticipate what might follow) means that the teacher may have to establish herself as in control of the classroom discourse and yet compassionate at the same time. Compassion, however, may be the new face of conservatism. To be moved by the potential suffering of a child is also "to be elevated to a place that remains untouched by other others whose suffering cannot be converted into my sympathy or admiration" (Ahmed, 2004: 192). Does the teacher's compassion for the potential suffering of students allow her to sidestep a greater responsibility?

One concern perhaps is that by taking control of the discourse, the teacher prevents students from engaging with one another about the nature and substance of belief. The manifestation of belief in this classroom moment could be understood in terms of testimony, on the part of Kulasiri, as "a pledge beyond concrete evidence" (Farley, 2010: 15), "[f]or one can testify only to the unbelievable. To what can, at any rate, only be believed; to what appeals only to belief and hence to the given word, since it lies beyond the limits of proof, indication, certified acknowledgement [le constat], and knowledge" (Derrida, 1998: 20). And yet to read only Kulasiri's contribution in terms of belief is, perhaps, to succumb to a secularization of schooling and an understanding of the classroom as home to knowledge, proof and the evidential, a place devoid of mere belief. But belief of all kinds permeate classroom engagements. Klaudia's belief in the teacher's capacity to prevent harm creates a satisfying substitution which replaces the lost gratification of plurality as an educational principle. As a result, youth, who are often on the outside, or the underside, of democracy miss the chance to take their place in their classroom, a process that prepares them to make judgements for themselves in the light of hearing other perspectives as well as testimonies.

Moreover, as a result of Klaudia's decision to contain the conversation, a particular set of affective relations is established as the norm within the classroom; the latter can only be a place where harm is prevented, never repaired or healed. Such an understanding of the classroom is in keeping with the idea that adults cannot expect the young to shoulder the burden of and even repair conflict wrought in the wider society. Such an understanding, however, prevails against promise and forgiveness as activities that characterize life lived among others and which could be cultivated in the classroom.

None of this suggests, of course, that the teacher should have gone with the conversation, trusted the students and herself to engage with sensitivity with one another and even risk the hurt to provide more room for diversity. What it may suggest is the complexity of the moment of pedagogy and the difficulty in knowing for sure whether one is right in one's judgements, whether one has weighed all possibilities for action. It is this 'not knowing for sure' and acting nonetheless that breathes heroism into teaching and equates practice, as Klaudia expressed it, with "walking in a minefield."

## Implications and Conclusion

Summing up and looking ahead, we return to the questions with which this chapter began: How do teachers who are predominantly socialized and trained in monocultural school settings experience the transnational or transcultural spaces of today's culturally diverse classrooms? How do they deal with the specific tensions of internally plural and externally transgressive classroom spaces? How do they know what is the right thing to do? How do they assess, judge and act in everyday classroom situations where (inter-, multi- and trans-)culturality seems to matter?

We are interested in the situational, context-related particular, in the 'what is involved and what is at stake' of significant intercultural encounters in pedagogical contexts, where cultural difference makes a difference. In an attempt to test new grounds we take a turn – a normative turn – from the instrumental reasoning and propositional knowledge predominant in teacher education and research to a practical reasoning and situational discernment, thus entering a play of both kinds of knowledge: the general, in the light of the context-related particular. Intrigued by the resonance between the interpretation of Aristotle's *phronesis* as situational appreciation and discernment and Herbart's construct of pedagogical tact as the quick judgment, decision and action that slides in as teachers discerningly respond to pedagogical situations, we draw on the vocabulary of practical wisdom and tact to illuminate the complexity of moments of undecidability calling for a judgement to be made and an action to be taken.

The classroom vignette we chose to explore is situated in a European context, more specifically in the context of Austrian schools, which is characterized by a growing disparity between an increasingly diverse student population and a largely homogenous, native Austrian teaching force.[3] We set out to map the grounds of the minefield of transcultural tensions where difference is experienced as explosive. What have we learned?

The language of *phronesis* and tact is immensely useful because it complicates the language of teacher efficacy in heterogeneous classrooms. A teacher may be conscious of her own enculturation and the cultural identities of her students; she may even fully appreciate her responsibility in culturally diverse classroom settings, but each classroom requires situational appreciation and discernment. As such, knowledge, though crucial, is insufficient; teachers require experience and the opportunity to consider their interpretations of experience so that they can cultivate wise judgements.

However, not even the language of *phronesis* and tact is enough. While this language allows us to focus on the play of general understandings and particular events in classrooms, it does not help account for the less reasoned responses of teachers. Any consideration of culturally responsive teaching must acknowledge the obligations that arise in the midst of practice, shaping teachers' responses. Obligations cannot be predetermined in advance of practice but they are encountered in the call of particular moments. Obligation is not reasoned; it is a feeling that overcomes one. In the case under consideration, the obligation to care for the child, to prevent harm, overrides the obligation to engage with cultural difference. A greater good, in the teacher's view, is at stake.

In the light of this discussion, one wonders if teaching for diversity can, or should be held as an ideal good in every case. Teacher education can do much to cultivate practical wisdom and tact; it can even help teachers to think in terms of their obligations. However, in the end, teachers, immersed in their practice, must be trusted to respond to the call of particular moments.

## References


Adick, Christel (2010): Inter-, multi-, transkulturell: über die Mühen der Begriffsarbeit in kulturübergreifenden Forschungsprozessen. In: Hirsch, Alfred/ Kurt, Ronald (eds.): Interkultur – Jugendkultur, Bildung neu verstehen. Wiesbaden: Springer. pp. 105-133.

Ahmed, Sara (2004): The Cultural Politics of Emotion. New York: Routledge.

Aristotle (1962): Nicomachean Ethics. Translated by Martin Ostwald. Indianapolis: Bobbs-Merrill.

Asmus, Walter (ed.) (1982): Pädagogische Schriften. Bd. 1. Stuttgart: Klett-Cotta.

Auernheimer, Georg (2002): Interkulturelle Kompetenz/ ein neues Element pädagogischer Professionalität? In: Auernheimer, Georg (ed.): Interkulturelle Kompetenz und pädagogische Professionlität. Opladen: Leske-Budrich Verlag. pp. 183-205.

Benner, Dietrich (ed.) (1986): Die Pädagogik Herbarts, eine problemgeschichtliche Einführung in die Systematik neuzeitlicher Pädagogik. Weinheim: Juventa.

Bennett, Christine L. (2007): Comprehensive multicultural education: Theory and practice (6th ed.). New York: Pearson Education.


---

3 The disparity between an increasingly diverse student population and a largely homogenous (native Austrian) teaching force looks set to continue in the near future: only 3.5 % of students in teacher training institutions compared to 17.7 % of the student population at Austrian schools have another mother tongue than German (BMUKK, 2011).

Binder, Susanne (2005): Interkulturelle Kompetenz: die neue Herausforderung im Klassenzimmer. In: Erziehung und Unterricht. 3-4/05. pp. 284-292.

Blaß, Josef L. (1972): Pädagogische Theoriebildung bei Johann Friedrich Herbart. Meisenheim am Glan: Hain.

BMUKK, Bundesministerium für Unterricht, Kunst und Kultur (2011): SchülerInnen mit anderen Erstsprachen als Deutsch, Statistische Übersicht Schuljahre 2002/03 bis 2009/10. Informationsblätter des Referats für Migration und Schule. Nr. 2/2011. http://www.bmukk.gv.at/medienpool/8953/nr2_11.pdf [25.07.2011].

Caputo, John D. (1993): Against ethics: Contributions to a poetics of obligation with constant reference to deconstruction. Bloomington, ID: Indiana University Press.

Derrida, Jacques (1998): Monolingualism of the Other: Or, the Prosthesis of Origin. Translated by Patrick Mensah. Stanford: Stanford University Press.

Dunne, Joseph/ Pendlebury, Shirley (2002): Practical reason. In: Nigel, Blake and others (eds.): The Blackwell Guide to the Philosophy of Education. Oxford: Blackwell.

Farley, Lisa (2010): The reluctant pilgrim: Questioning belief after historical loss. In: Journal of the Canadian Association for Curriculum Studies. 8(1). pp. 6-40.

Fenstermacher, Gary D. (1990): Some moral considerations on teaching as a profession. In: Goodlad, John I./ Soder, Roger/ Sirotnik, Kenneth A. (eds.): The Moral Dimensions of Teaching. San Francisco: Jossey-Bass. pp. 130-151.

Gaitanides, Stefan (2003): Interkulturelle Kompetenz als Anforderungsprofil in der Jugend- und Sozialarbeit. In: IZA Zeitschrift für Migration und Soziale Arbeit. 3-4. pp. 44-50.

Gay, Geneva (2000): Culturally responsive teaching: Theory, research, and practice. New York: Teachers College Press.

Gogolin, Ingrid/ Krüger-Potratz, Marianne (2006): Einführung in die Interkulturelle Pädagogik. Opladen: Barbara Budrich/ UTB.

Green, Bill (2009): The (im)possibility of the project. In: Australian Educational Researcher. 37(3). pp. 1-17.

Guyton, Edith M./ Wesche, Martin V. (2005): The multicultural efficacy scale: Development, item selection, and reliability. In: Multicultural Perspectives. 7(4). pp. 21-29.

Handschuck, Sabine/ Schröer, Hubertus (2002): Interkulturelle Orientierung und Öffnung von Organisationen. In: Neue Praxis. 32(5). pp. 511-521.

Herbart, Johann Friedrich (cit. 1802): Erste Vorlesungen über Pädagogik. In: Asmus, Walter (ed.) (1982): Pädagogische Schriften. Bd.1. Stuttgart: Klett-Cotta.

Herbart, Johann Friedrich (1913-1919): Pädagogische Schriften. In: Willmann, Otto (ed.): Johann Friedrich Herbarts Pädagogische Schriften. Osterwieck/ Harz, Leipzig: Zickfeldt.

Kalpaka, Annita (1998): Interkulturelle Kompetenz – Kompetentes (Sozial)pädagogisches Handeln in der Einwanderungsgesellschaft. In: IZA Zeitschrift für Migration und Soziale Arbeit. 3-4. pp. 77-79.

Khagram, Sanjeev/Levitt, Peggy (Eds.) (2008): The Transnational Studies Reader: Intersections & Innovations. New York: Routledge.

Korthagen, Fred A.J. and others (2001): Linking Practice and Theory: The Pedagogy of Realistic Teacher Education. Mahwah, NJ: Lawrence Erlbaum Associates.

Ladson-Billings, Gloria (1995): Culturally relevant teaching. In: Theory into Practice. 34(3). pp. 159-165.

Leiprecht, Rudolf (2002): Interkulturelle Kompetenz als Schlüsselqualifikation aus der Sicht von Arbeitsansätzen in pädagogischen Handlungsfeldern. In: IZA Zeitschrift für Migration und Soziale Arbeit. 3-4. pp. 87-91.

Levitt, Peggy/ Glick Schiller, Nina (2004). Conceptualizing simultaneity: a transnational social field perspective on society. In: International Migration Review 38(3). pp. 1002–1039.

Levitt, Peggy/ Jaworsky, Bernadette N. (2007): Transnational Migration Studies: Past Developments and Future Trends. In: Annual Review of Sociology 33(1). pp. 129-156.

Levitt, Peggy/ Waters, Mary C. (2002): The Changing Face of Home: The Transnational Lives of the Second Generation. New York: Russell Sage Foundation.
Mecheril, Paul (2002): "Kompetenzlosigkeitskompetenz". Pädagogisches Handeln unter Einwanderungsbedingungen. In: Georg Auernheimer (ed.): Interkulturelle Kompetenz und pädagogische Professionalität. Opladen: Leske-Budrich Verlag. pp. 15-34.
Metz, Peter (1992): Herbartianismus als Paradigma für Professionalisierung und Schulreform: Ein Beitrag zur Bündner Schulgeschichte der Jahre 1880 bis 1930 und zur Wirkungsgeschichte der Pädagogik Herbarts und der Herbartianer Ziller, Stoy und Rein in der Schweiz: Frankfurt a. M.: Peter Lang.
Metz, Peter (1995): Interpretative Zugänge zu Herbarts Pädagogischem Takt. In: Zeitschrift für Pädagogik. 41(4). pp. 615-631.
Muth, Jakob (1961): Pädagogischer Takt – eine unplanbare erzieherische Verhaltensweise. In: Bildung und Erziehung. 14. Jahrgang. pp. 261-271.
Muth, Jakob (1962): Pädagogischer Takt: Monographie einer aktuellen Form erzieherischen und didaktischen Handelns. Heidelberg: Quelle & Mayer.
Müßener, Gerhard (1983): Pädagogischer Takt qua ars iudicandi. Ein historisch systematischer Beitrag zu einem hochschuldidaktischen Obligatum in der Lehrerausbildung. In: Vierteljahresschrift für wissenschaftliche Pädagogik. 2/83. pp. 159-170.
Müßener, Gerhard (ed.) (1991): Didaktische Texte zu Unterricht und Erziehung. In: Wissenschaft und Schule, Johann Friedrich Herbart. Wuppertal: Deimling. pp. 135-147.
Nussbaum, Martha C. (1986): The Fragility of Goodness: Luck and Ethics in Greek Tragedy and Philosophy. Cambridge: Cambridge University Press.
Nussbaum, Martha C. (1990): Love's Knowledge: Essays on Philosophy and Literature, New York: Oxford University Press.
Pendlebury, Shirley (1993): Practical arguments, rationalization and imagination in teachers' practical reasoning: a critical discussion. In: Journal of Curriculum Studies. 25(2). pp. 145-151.
Phelan, Anne M. (2001): The death of a child and the birth of practical wisdom. In: Studies in Philosophy and Education. 20(1). pp. 41-55.
Phelan, Anne M. (2009): The ethical claim of partiality: practical reasoning, the discipline, and teacher education. In: Journal of Curriculum Studies. 4(1). pp. 93-114.
Pries Ludger (2005): Configurations of geographic and societal spaces: a sociological proposal between 'methodological nationalism' and the 'spaces of flows'. In: Global Networks. 5(2). pp. 167-190.
Prondczynsky, Andreas (1993): Pädagogik und Poiesis. Eine verdrängte Dimension des Theorie-Praxis-Verhältnisses. Opladen: Leske u. Budrich.
Reed, Charlotte (1996): Overcoming prejudices: An invitational approach. In: Urban Review. 28(1). pp. 81-93.
Simon-Hohm, Hildegard (2002): Interkulturelle Kompetenz in der Sozialen Arbeit. In: Neue Praxis. 32(2). pp. 39-45.
Sleeter, Christine (2008): An invitation to support diverse students through teacher education. In: Journal of Teacher Education. 59(3). pp. 212-219.
Smith, Michael P. (2005): Transnational urbanism revisited. Journal of Ethnic and Migration Studies. 31(2). pp. 235-244.
Smits, Hans and others (1997): Encountering Obligation in Qualitative Educational Research: A Postmodern Perspective. In: Alberta Journal of Educational Research, 43(4). pp. 192-206.
Suzuki, Shoko (2010): Takt in Modern Education. Münster/ New York/ München/ Berlin: Waxmann.
Thompson, Franklin (2007): Multicultural teacher dispositions and the development of the multicultural dispositions index. Omaha: University of Nebraska at Omaha.
Tucker, Carolyn M. and others (2005): Promoting teacher efficacy for working with culturally diverse students. In: Preventing School Failure. 50(1). pp. 29-34.

Van Manen, Max (1991): The Tact of Teaching: The Meaning of Pedagogical Thoughtfulness. Ontario: The Althouse Press.
Van Manen, Max (2002): The Tone of Teaching. Ontario: The Althouse Press.
Wittgenstein, Ludwig (2003): Tractus Logico-Philosophicus: Logisch-philosophische Abhandlung (originally published 1922). New York: Barnes & Noble.

# The Confluence of Global and Local Currents in Brazil's Municipal Schooling

*Steven Hales*

## Abstract

*Public school reform in Brazil since the 1990s has been shaped by a confluence of transnational neoliberal and national non-neoliberal currents. The thrust of this reform has been twofold: to enhance Brazil's economic competitiveness in the global market and redress societal problems. A number of educational decentralization/centralization policies have been implemented to achieve these aims. These policies reflect tensions between global forces and local needs. Although policy texts advocate curricular and pedagogical autonomy to municipal school systems along with the critical engagement with pressing societal issues, accountability mechanisms align Brazil's public primary education system with neoliberal quantitative conceptions of quality. These characteristics of public schooling in Brazil are not a replication of a global model but rather a locally forged variation. This chapter draws on the author's 2008 ethnographic study of municipal elementary school curricula in Brazil's Northeast to deconstruct the "hybrid" facets of Brazilian public schooling, unveil an associated paradox, and raise a connected research implication of global significance.*

## Introduction

"It is now increasingly difficult to understand education in any context without reference to the global forces that influence policy and practice" (Crossley, 2000: 324). Yet global influences are "intermeshed" with local features in each system (Marginson/Mollis, 2002: 587). This merging constitutes heterogeneous processes of *glocalization*: "the interplay between globalizing and localizing forces" (Jungck/Kajornsin, 2003: 35). Public schooling in Brazil since the 1990s has been shaped by the interplay of transnational neoliberal and national non-neoliberal currents. The former have focused on enhancing Brazil's economic competitiveness while the latter have been most concerned with rectifying urgent societal issues. To this end, a host of seemingly contradictory educational decentralization/centralization policies have been instituted. The mixture of neoliberal and non-neoliberal interests in these policies is a local variation of global tendencies. One that harbors priority disputes between local societal needs and global economic aspirations.

This chapter draws on a portion of the author's ethnographic research on municipal schooling in Northeast Brazil. That research relied on critical educators' conceptualizations of the nexus between curriculum, knowledge, and pedagogy as a theoretical framework for examining policy texts and teaching practices across two municipal elementary schools. That inquiry also presented critical educators' views of neoliberalism and educational decentralization/centralization. This chapter begins by depicting these views in order to make sense of a few multilevel dimensions of the research findings. Such multilevel analyses yield a better understanding of the complexities of education systems as well as help to comprehend the "dynamic interactions between global trends and local responses" (Arnove, 2003: 3; Bray/Thomas, 1995). Moreover, the perspectives of those who put policy into practice in schools are instrumental for illuminating discrepancies between policy rhetoric and curriculum realities as well as understanding the dynamics between the transnational and the local in the realm of public education. This chapter enriches the education literature's portrayal of "hybrid" facets of Brazilian public schooling in this regard.

## Neoliberalism and Educational Decentralization/Centralization

Neoliberalism, what Torres (2009) refers to as "neoliberal globalization," has arguably been the defining transnational force affecting education systems worldwide in recent decades (Apple, 2006; Klees, 2008). Arnove (1997: 79) outlines the etymology and multifaceted aspects of neoliberalism:

> The term neoliberal derives from the neoclassical economic theories expounded by major international donor agencies like the World Bank and the International Monetary Fund (IMF) and their consultants. The theories are based on work of classical economists Adam Smith and David Ricardo, who believed that the role of the state consisted in establishing the conditions by which the free play of the marketplace, the laws of supply and demand, and free trade based on competitive advantage would inevitably rebound to the benefit of all. Government policies, based on these notions, have led to a drastic reduction in the state's role in social spending, deregulation of the economy, and liberalization of import policies.

Critical educational scholars understand neoliberalism as an "economic/political paradigm", yet one that emphasizes an economic rather than a political conception of democracy (Apple, 2006: 14). Neoliberalism defines "profit making and market freedoms as the essence of democracy" (Giroux, 2004: 31). Neoliberal ideology also preaches that society should function according to the principles of the economic market (Apple, 2006; Arnove, 1997; Stromquist, 2003; Torres, 2002). The "market economy" is therefore seen as a "market society" through a neoliberal lens (Giroux, 2004: 32). Whereas proponents of neoliberalism argue that free markets benefit all, critics maintain that the notion of free markets is delusional. That is to say, although the state yields to market forces in certain respects, "markets are marketed" by state regulatory measures (Apple, 2006: 58). Critics also hold that the focus on economic growth disregards social justice concerns like inequality (Chomsky, 1999; Davis, 2007). Critical scholars hence contend that neoliberalism is neither inevitable nor neutral (Apple, 2006; Hursh, 2009).

Neoliberalism has become a "common sense" recipe for nation rebuilding (Apple, 2006: 15; Davis, 2007). In Latin America this reorganization has been marked by structural adjustment policies dictated by international agencies along with privatization, deregulation, and decentralization measures (Arnove, 1997; Fischman/Ball/Gvirtz, 2003; Schugurensky, 2003). The World Bank and the International Monetary Fund in particular have profoundly affected this restructuring (Arnove, 1997; Derqui, 2001). Selcher (1998) provides a detailed account of how such neoliberal tides pushed 1990s reforms in Brazil.

Neoliberalism has also impacted education policy and practice in Brazil and beyond in recent decades. Numerous scholars have documented this (Apple, 2006; Arnove, 1997; Basu, 2004; Beech, 2009; Canen/Grant, 1999; Derqui, 2001; Fischman/Ball/Gvirtz, 2003; Gandin, 2007; Giroux, 2004; Henales/Edwards, 2002; Hypolito/Vieira/Pizzi, 2009; Kempner/Jurema, 2002; Klees, 2008; Lopes/Macedo, 2003; Marcondes, 1999; Rivarola/Fuller, 1999; Schugurensky, 2003; Stromquist, 2003; Torres, 2009). For neoliberals, schools are envisioned less as institutions for promoting political democracy as they are for their alignment with national economic production, global economic competitiveness demands, and associated labor needs (Apple, 2006; Canen/Grant, 1999; Fischman/Ball/Gvirtz, 2003; Stromquist, 2003). In short, "the school becomes an institution that must serve the economy" (Stromquist, 2003: 200). Consequently, school systems globally are more and more resembling a "competitive market" (Apple, 2006: 2). As part of this, there has been a growing obsession with education system rankings, standardized testing, and accountability (Broadfoot, 2000; Hursh, 2009). Broadfoot (2000: 359) summarizes:

> In today's increasingly globalised, fluid and fragmented world, the pressure for education to provide the international currency which will form the basis for trade in the knowledge society becomes daily more explicit. As a result, those aspects of educational activity that do not lend themselves to explicit and quantifiable measurement are increasingly difficult to sustain.

And Arnove (2003: 4) similarly states:

> The belief that there is a causal relationship between the 'excellence' of a school system, as measured by national standardized examinations, and the economic success of a country in global competition has revived the interest in the relationship between education systems and national productivity.

As well, neoliberalism has propelled a worldwide surge of educational decentralization/centralization policies (Astiz/Wiseman/Baker, 2002; Bjork, 2003; Bray, 2003; Derqui, 2001; Gvirtz/Beech, 2004; Hypolito/Vieira/Pizzi, 2009; Karlsen, 2000; Meade/Gershberg, 2008; Mukundan/Bray, 2004; Narodowski/Nores, 2003; Rivarola/Fuller, 1999; Schiefelbein, 2004; Schugurensky, 2003; Whitty/Power/Halpin, 1998). Educational decentralization/centralization is "inherently a political process concerned with specifying who rules in particular settings" (Samoff, 2003: 426). It involves shifting authority, autonomy, and accountability for educational financing, governance, and provision between the central state, provinces or states, municipalities, and schools (Derqui, 2001). Moves toward greater decentralization may include a *delegation* of functions and responsibilities to sub-national levels, which may or may not result in increased local authority and autonomy (Bray, 2003; Karlsen, 2000). Alternatively, in the case of *devo-*

*lution* local levels (allegedly) gain authority and autonomy in certain respects such as curriculum in relation to a central body (Bray, 2003; Karlsen, 2000).

Decentralized autonomy and authority cannot be dissociated from centralization, however. Educational decentralization/centralization is therefore a "double and concurrent dynamic" (Schugurensky, 2003: 58). Decentralization in Brazil for instance is hinged to national goals, evaluations, and standards. Additionally, as research from India suggests, a multitude of factors wedge a gap between decentralization "rhetoric" and "reality" (Mukundan/Bray, 2004). A principal reason is that, like all education policies, decentralization/centralization is molded by "relationships and tensions between groups in society" (McGinn/Street, 1986: 472). Educational decentralization/centralization in Brazil is indicative of this contestation. Brazil's case also shows how, in spite of neoliberal rhetoric permeating education in Latin America, policies are reconfigured across national boundaries and at sub-national levels (Ball, 1998; Beech, 2009).

## "Hybrid" Schooling in Brazil

Since the 1990s Brazil has undergone a decentralization of financial, administrative, and curricular autonomy to municipal and school levels together with a centralization of national education plans, curriculum standards, exams, and rankings (Derqui, 2001). This concert of educational decentralization/centralization policies reflects neoliberal and non-neoliberal elements. Five examples showcase this hybrid characteristic of schooling in Brazil. These are the *Lei de Diretrizes e Bases da Educação Nacional* (LDB, or Law of Guidelines and Foundations for National Education), national and municipal evaluations and ranking systems, the *Parâmetros Curriculares Nacionais* (PCNs, or National Curriculum Parameters), the municipalization of public school systems, and school decentralization.

Regarded as the "Constitution of Education" in Brazil, the LDB underscores the decentralization/centralization alliance and the blend of neoliberal and non-neoliberal influence. It advocates a national core curriculum for primary schooling and federal responsibility of assessment via national tests, yet it also calls for the devolution of governance to and curricular autonomy at sub-national levels (Brasil, 1996; Gandin, 2007; Valente/Arelaro, 2002). The emphases on access to schooling and municipal curricular autonomy are a "compromise" between neoliberal and non-neoliberal interests (Gandin, 2007: 188). On the other hand, since the LDB was created in a political context that favored a diminishing role of the state as a provider of basic social services and the submission of facets of education to market forces, it led to decentralization according to neoliberal rationale (Valente/Arelaro, 2002). This has included the "transfer of federal resources to states and municipalities" as well as "reductions in spending per pupil" (Wong/Balestino, 2003: 74).

National and municipal evaluations and rankings also epitomize the relation between neoliberalism and educational decentralization/centralization in Brazil. National exams such as the *Prova Brasil* (Brazil Exam) and the *Sistema Nacional de Avaliação Básica* (SAEB, or National Exam for Basic Education) are a core component of education reform there. They are designed to ameliorate educational quality by providing quantifiable performance benchmarks (Fischman/Ball/Gvirtz, 2003). Despite being ostensibly diagnostic, these tests prioritize the results of schooling (Crespo/Soares/Mello e Souza, 2000; Valente/Arelaro, 2002). They also stimulate competition among schools and municipal systems (Valente/Arelaro, 2002). Such competition is viewed as a recipe for educational quality, and it is pegged to an elaborate ranking system (Valente/Arelaro, 2002). Exam scores and figures such as student passing rates are factored into the *Índice de Desenvolvimento da Educação Básica* (IDEB, or Index of the Development of Basic Education). The IDEB is a nationwide ranking system that monitors the quality of municipal school systems. Municipal exams and rankings in turn play a prominent role and are tied to funding. For instance, in Teresina, Piauí municipal exams are used to rank each school in the city. The schools with the highest rankings receive a monetary reward.

Brazil's PCNs likewise represent educational decentralization/centralization as well as an ideological tug of war over curriculum. The PCNs are a compilation of pedagogical orientations, evaluation criteria, objectives, and contents for public primary schooling. The PCNs were meant to guarantee quality with national curriculum standards (Moraes, 2003). They were also created to implement the national evaluation and ranking system (Gandin, 2007; Hypolito/Vieira/Pizzi, 2009; Marcondes, 1999; Valente/Arelaro, 2002). Some thus regard the PCNs as neoliberal attempts of curriculum control (Canen/Grant, 1999; Gandin, 2007; Hypolito/Vieira/Pizzi, 2009). Conversely, streams of critical educational thought permeate the PCNs. A quality education is defined in the PCNs as a practice that develops "autonomous, critical and participatory citizens" (Brasil, 1997a: 27). In this vein the PCNs endorse the need to engage with pressing societal issues in the curriculum (Brasil, 1997b; Moraes, 2003). As well, the PCNs are meant to provide an impetus for the formulation of municipal and school curricula (Brasil, 1997a; Fischman/Ball/Gvirtz, 2003). These localized curricula are considered essential for societal transformation, including the construction of a more democratic society (Brasil, 1997a).

Municipalization has been another central aspect of education reform in Brazil in recent decades. Hailed from a neoliberal standpoint as a more "cost-effective way" of "delivering education," the basic premise with respect to primary public schooling is decentralizing governance from federal and state to municipal levels (Azevedo, 2002; Derqui, 2001: 565; Sarmento, 2005). At the same time, municipalization has been promoted for expanding democratic participation in political processes, ensuring greater municipal autonomy in overseeing schooling, and leading to the creation of municipally distinct curricula (Sarmento, 2005; Souza/Faria, 2004). For instance, the curriculum of Curitiba in Brazil's South region is expected to differ from the curriculum of Belém in the nation's North. Even municipalities in the same region have developed unique curricula. This curriculum contextualization is exemplified in Brazil's Northeast with Salvador, Bahia's and Teresina, Piaui's curriculum guidelines that champion the integration of local realities in the curriculum (Hales, 2011).

Municipal decentralization in Brazil has been complemented by more recent calls for greater school autonomy (Derqui, 2001). Such autonomy is illustrated by the community-driven school governance models in some municipalities (Borges, 2008; Gandin, 2007; Gandin/Apple, 2002). These models are symbolic of the sub-national variation of policies due to political party sway and other factors (Beech, 2009; Borges, 2008). The decentralization of autonomy to schools is also evidenced by pedagogic proposals – essentially curriculum guidelines – that schools elaborate (Monfredini, 2002). For example, the proposal of a municipal elementary school in Salvador stresses the school's role in transforming the surrounding neighborhood by addressing critical issues in the curriculum.

Curriculum contextualization indicates the influence of critical theoretical thought on Brazilian education. It also marks the agency of local actors there to create alternatives to neoliberal globalization. Accordingly, while the transnational current of neoliberalism is regarded as the "major thrust in educational policy in Brazil," the terrain of Brazilian public schooling is far from a homogenous landscape (Gandin, 2007: 186). It "must be understood not as a simple reproduction of a global trend in education, but as a hybrid process, with local characteristics and peculiarities" (Gandin, 2007: 180). In line with this book's theme then, public schooling in Brazil – from policies in text to the pedagogical practices in the in-class curriculum – is both a transnational space and a site of regional localization.

## Policies in Practice: The Enacted Curriculum

This chapter highlights how policies at the document level are implemented in classrooms. It does so by providing a snapshot of findings derived from semi-structured and informal interviews with municipal public elementary school pedagogic staff during the author's 10-month ethnographic research in Northeast Brazil in 2008. One semester was spent at Sabiá, located in the neighborhood of Sol in Salvador, Bahia. A second semester was spent at Tucano, located in the neighborhood of Triunfo in Teresina, Piauí. In line with these fictitious S and T names for the schools and neighborhoods in Salvador and Teresina respectively, pseudonyms were chosen to protect participants' identity: S names for Sabiá staff and T names for Tucano staff. These accounts delineate several strands of the multilevel web of transnational neoliberal and national non-neoliberal contradictions spanning Brazilian public schooling.

Even though pedagogic staff in each context deemed the PCNs as flexible pedagogic guidelines for the formulation of locally relevant curricula, teachers from both schools asserted that there isn't a discrepancy between what they teach and what the PCNs specify should be taught. Tânia from Tucano cited the case of a student who arrived in the middle of the year. This student affirmed that she was learning the same content at Tucano that she had been studying at a municipal school in Brasília. Simone from Sabiá likewise remarked:

> We follow a curriculum that is already determined. Even the textbooks, they are based on these PCNs. We follow this, we follow the already made curriculum (...) because there is a law that tells you what you must do in order for students to achieve. (...) So, you must follow those PCNs (Interview with Simone, 2008).

Teachers in both schools brought up tests and textbooks in reference to this. Thaís stated, "If we don't follow this scheme, when the test comes around (...) if most of the students do poorly it is because the teacher isn't following the curriculum" (Interview with Thaís, 2008). Thaís also mentioned that school administrators have questioned her when she's taught content not found in textbooks. She referred to this link between tests, textbooks, the PCNs, and the municipal curriculum as the "quality that I have to guarantee" (Interview with Thaís, 2008). Simone shared a related perspective that teachers are pressured to teach and test the same content. She associated this with accountability. "You are always being held accountable, you have to fill out lists of abilities that you've taught, whether you've taught that ability, regardless of whether the student has learned or not. You have to follow the script" (Interview with Simone, 2008).

An array of figures and rankings are emblematic of related accountability pressures and quantitative notions of public school quality in Brazil. The pedagogic coordinator at Tucano, Tiessa, spoke to this concerning statistics such as attendance and homework completion figures municipal schools are required to submit to the Teresina Municipal Secretary of Education (SEMEC). This information is then forwarded to the Ayrton Senna Institute in São Paulo, which publishes comparative data of the nation's municipal systems. Other participants contested this pressure. Several Tucano teachers viewed quantitative indicators as "makeup" that conceals qualitative realities. One of them declared that SEMEC does not care how they teach, "they just want to see the results" (Interview with Tatiana, 2008). Tatiana worded this as the emphasis on "quantity" at the expense of "quality" and added that teachers and schools are held accountable for meeting predefined target numbers set by SEMEC. Another teacher volunteered a supporting anecdote that she was questioned why only six of her students answered a question correctly on the diagnostic Ayrton Senna Institute math exam. Tatiana concluded, "Either you obey the system, or you are swallowed by this system" (Interview with Tatiana, 2008).

Pedagogic staff in both contexts spotlighted the connections between test scores and rankings. Simone divulged that the municipal exams are designed to raise students' scores in order to yield a better municipal system ranking. She said the rankings in turn spark competition for notoriety between schools in Salvador. She continued that the scores imply that students are doing well, "but in reality they aren't" (Interview with Simone, 2008). Two participants from Tucano also touched on the prominence of the municipal Portuguese and math exams – the only subject areas that factor into official measures of quality – and their connection with rankings. They elucidated that these exams are used to rank each school in each municipal system and each system in the country.

Pedagogic staff at Sabiá and Tucano associated the weight given to such numbers with the pressure to pass students. Simone recalled one year when a teacher failed 80% of a class and was reprimanded by school administrators, "You can't fail them" (Interview with Simone, 2008). She recollected another instance when she failed students, but later discovered the administration passed them. She attributed this to the fixation with school and municipal scores on the IDEB rankings. Tucano staff complemented these views. Tatiana shared that teachers who do not pass 90% of their students are interrogated. As a consequence, she said that teachers pass students as long as they attend class. The school principal Teresa also acknowledged such challenges. Nonetheless, she argued it's better to keep students in school than "on the street" (Interview with Teresa, 2008). Two Sabiá teachers spoke critically of Brazilian public schooling in these regards. Sara expounded:

> There are predetermined contents along with abilities to acquire and develop for each year. What happens in our reality (...) students pass from one year to the next without the minimal abilities necessary to be at that level. The challenge is to (...) teach the mandatory contents but according to the level of the students. We have to find a methodology that attends to both the pre-syllabic and the literate. (...) What we learned in theory doesn't work (Interview with Sara, 2008).

Simone added, "I fight about passing students just to pass (…) so that the school scores high on the IDEB ranking. It's a crime" (Interview with Simone, 2008). Pedagogic staff's perspectives are consistent with critiques of accountability. Decentralization is a prescription of the market-centered neoliberal paradigm, yet neoliberal motives of enhancing national economic competitiveness in global markets have also sprouted state regulatory measures (Apple, 2006; Basu, 2004; Fischman/Ball/Gvirtz, 2003). Gvirtz and Beech (2004) and Tatto (1999) for example disclose how, amidst the alleged devolution of curriculum authority to provinces and states in Argentina and Mexico respectively, exams and textbooks have been used as accountability instruments to sustain centralized control over curricula. So, in spite of the decentralization of responsibility for public schooling to sub-national levels in Brazil and elsewhere in the Americas, federal accountability mechanisms curtail local autonomy (Azevedo, 2002; Fischman/Ball/Gvirtz, 2003; Hypolito/Vieira/Pizzi, 2009; Mazurek/Winzer/Majorek, 2000; Schugurensky, 2003; Tatto, 1999; Valente/Arelaro, 2002). This literature supports the contention that the devolution of authority is "one of the illusions created by neoliberalism" (J. Portelli, personal communication, July 20, 2010).

Participants' perspectives also parallel arguments against neoliberal quantitative conceptions of educational quality. One criticism is that statistics such as enrollment figures, failure rates, test scores, the amount of money spent on each student, and the length and number of school days are misleading quality indicators (Aranha, 2008; Sands, 2008; Santos, 2002; Torres, 2002; Valente/Arelaro, 2002). An overlapping assertion is that such notions of quality disguise qualitative facets. Aranha (2008) and Sands (2008) profile telling cases in this respect in Brazil. Additionally, the emphasis on continuous progression through school supposedly ensures access to a quality education and reflects an inclusive educational system in which the state fulfills its democratic role (Valente/Arelaro, 2002). Yet such touted improvements have at times been justified solely for cost-saving rationale (Valente/Arelaro, 2002). Furthermore, others maintain that the obsession with what Schugurensky (2003: 59) calls "standardized outcomes" disregards classroom practices and realities (Arnove, 1997; Klees; 2008). Indeed the accentuation on exams diverts attention from societal matters that influence the curriculum and other conditions needed to improve school quality (Kempner/Jurema, 2002; Santos, 2002). A major tension for Brazilian teachers therefore is between devoting class time to exam preparation or, as championed in curriculum documents, engaging with critical local issues (Santos, 2002).

## Concluding Remarks

This chapter's focus is limited to a few strands of the web of contradictions spanning the global-local dynamics of municipal public schooling in Brazil. Even so, it exposes a noteworthy paradox: The implemented education policies negate the aims of schooling touted in policy texts. Public school pedagogic staff's perspectives uncover interconnected layers of contradictions embedded in this paradox. First, centralized aspects of educational decentralization/centralization policies override decentralized ones as neoliberal quantitative barometers of quality gauged by rankings based on statistics such as national exam scores take precedence. Second, accountability to such centralized mechanisms inhibits local curricular autonomy and undermines the alleged devolution of authority. Third, the critical engagement with students' lived realities and local issues do not factor into official measures of quality. Instead, the global neoliberal current pushing education policies trumps the critical theoretical principles infusing Brazil's curriculum documents.

This chapter also partially reveals how the confluence of global and local currents forges a divide between education policy rhetoric and practice in municipal elementary schools within a region of Brazil. It does so through the perspectives of policy-makers at the ground level: school pedagogic staff. On this note and, concerning the broader theme of transnational spaces and regional localization, municipal public schools in Brazil are spaces of tension between the global and local. Most notably, the transnational torrent of neoliberalism is colliding with local waves of critical educational thought. The educational decentralization/centralization alliance exhibits this: There is a conflict between reaching standardized quantitative outcomes and addressing pressing local qualitative issues such as violence.

This chapter's analysis of the bridge between education policies and the enacted curriculum offers a gateway for further inquiry into the intersection of neoliberalism, public schooling, and society in Brazil and other locales. The urban periphery contexts that are home to the majority of public schools and youth in Brazil are also the epicenters of this violence and additional acute societal problems nationwide. A prominent research implication then is examining whether and how global neoliberal ideologies redefine schooling and marginalize such contexts in Brazil and elsewhere. This is particularly significant given that urban periphery spaces comprise the greatest percentage of the world's population growth and the planet's socio-economically poor, together with evidence that neoliberal policies are connected with global inequality and exclusion (Davis, 2007).

## References


Apple, Michael (2006): Educating the "Right Way": Markets, Standards, God, and Inequality. 2nd edition. New York: Routledge.

Aranha, Ana (2008): O Que os Números Não Mostram. In: *Época*. 527. http://revistaepoca.globo.com/Revista/Epoca/0,,EMI6359-15228,00.html [20.06.2009].

Arnove, Robert (1997): Neoliberal Education Policies in Latin America: Arguments in Favor and Against. In: Torres, Carlos/ Puiggrós, Adriana (eds.): Latin American Education: Comparative Perspectives. Boulder: Westview.

Arnove, Robert (2003): Introduction: Reframing Comparative Education. In: Arnove, Robert/ Torres, Carlos (eds.): Comparative Education: The Dialectic of the Global and the Local. 2nd edition. Lanham: Rowman & Littlefield.

Astiz, Fernanda and others (2002): Slouching Towards Decentralization: Consequences of Globalization for Curricular Control in National Education Systems. In: Comparative Education Review. 46-1. pp. 66-88.

Azevedo, Janete (2002): Implicações da Nova Lógica de Ação do Estado para a Educação Municipal. In: Educação e Sociedade. 23-80. pp. 49-71.

Ball, Stephen (1998): Big Policies/Small World: An Introduction to International Perspectives in Education Policy. In: Comparative Education. 34-2. pp. 119-130.

Basu, Ranu (2004): The Rationalization of Neoliberalism in Ontario's Public Education System, 1995-2000. In: Geoforum. 35. pp. 621-634.

Beech, Jason (2009): A Internacionalização das Políticas Educativas na América Latina. In: Currículo sem Fronteiras. 9-2. pp. 32-50.

Bjork, Christopher (2003): Local Responses to Decentralization Policy in Indonesia. In: Comparative Education Review. 47-2. pp. 184-216.

Borges, André (2008): State Government, Political Competition, and Education Reform: Comparative Lessons from Brazil. In: Bulletin of Latin American Research. 27-2. pp. 235-254.

Brasil (1996): Lei de Diretrizes e Bases da Educação Nacional. Brasília. www.ufrpe.br/download.php?endArquivo=noticias/4248_LDB.pdf [22.01.2008].

Brasil (1997a): Parâmetros Curriculares Nacionais: Introdução aos Parâmetros Curriculares Nacionais (1ª a 4ª série). Brasília. Ministério da Educação e do Desporto/Secretaria de Educação Fundamental (MEC/SEF).

Brasil (1997b): Parâmetros Curriculares Nacionais: Apresentação dos Temas Transversais (1ª a 4ª série). Brasília. Ministério da Educação e do Desporto/Secretaria de Educação Fundamental (MEC/SEF).

Bray, Mark (2003): Control of Education: Issues and Tensions in Centralization and Decentralization. In: Arnove, Robert/ Torres, Carlos: Comparative Education: The Dialectic of the Global and the Local. 2nd edition. Lanham: Rowman & Littlefield.

Bray, Mark/ Thomas, Murray (1995) (eds.): Levels of Comparison in Educational Studies: Different Insights from Different Literatures and the Value of Multilevel Analyses. In: Harvard Educational Review. 65-3. pp. 472-490.

Broadfoot, Patricia (2000): Comparative Education for the 21st Century: Retrospect and Prospect. In: Comparative Education. 36-3. pp. 357-371.

Canen, Ana/ Grant, Nigel (1999): Knowledge for Equity in the Mercosul Countries: Limits and Potentials in Educational Policies. In: Comparative Education. 35-3. pp. 319-330.

Chomsky, Noam (1999): Profit Over People: Neoliberalism and Global Order. New York: Seven Stories Press.

Crespo, Manuel and others (2000) (eds.): The Brazilian National Evaluation System of Basic Education: Context, Process, and Impact. In: Studies in Educational Evaluation. 26. pp. 105-125.

Crossley, Michael (2000): Bridging Cultures and Traditions in the Reconceptualisation of Comparative and International Education. In: Comparative Education. 36-3. pp. 319-332.

Davis, Mike (2007): Planet of Slums. New York: Verso.
Derqui, Jorge (2001): Educational Decentralization Policies in Argentina and Brazil: Exploring New Trends. In: Journal of Education Policy. 16-1. pp. 561-583.
Fischman, Gustavo and others (2003): Toward a Neoliberal Education? In: Ball, Stephen, Fischman/ Gustavo E./ Gvirtz, Silvina (eds.): Crisis and Hope: The Educational Hopscotch of Latin America. New York: RoutledgeFalmer.
Gandin, Luís (2007): The Construction of the Citizen School Project as an Alternative to Neoliberal Educational Policies. In: Policy Futures in Education. 5-2. pp. 179-193.
Gandin, Luís/ Apple, Michael (2002): Challenging Neo-liberalism, Building Democracy: Creating the Citizen School in Porto Alegre, Brazil. In: Journal of Education Policy. 17-2. pp. 259-279.
Giroux, Henry (2004): Critical Pedagogy and the Postmodern/Modern Divide: Towards a Pedagogy of Democratization. In: Teacher Education Quarterly. 31-1. pp. 31-47.
Gvirtz, Silvina/ Beech, Jason (2004): From the Intended to the Implemented Curriculum in Argentina: Regulation and Practice. In: Prospects. XXXIV-3. pp. 371-382.
Hales, Steven (2011): Legitimacy in Brazil's Public School Curricula. In: Schröttner, Barbara/ Hofer, Christian (eds.): Looking at Learning. Higher Education. Language. Place / Blicke auf das Lernen. Hochschule. Sprache. Ort. Münster/New York/München/Berlin: Waxmann.
Henales, Lidia/ Edwards, Beatrice (2002): Neo-liberalism and Education Reform in Latin America. In: Current Issues in Comparative Education. 2-2. pp. 120-129.
Hursh, David (2009): The World is not Flat: Challenging Neoliberal Policies. In: Hill, Dave (ed.): The Rich World and the Impoverishment of Education: Diminishing Democracy, Equity and Workers' Rights. New York: Routledge.
Hypolito, Álvaro and others (2009) (eds.): Reestruturação Curricular e Auto-Intensificação do Trabalho Docente. In: Currículo Sem Fronteiras. 9-2. pp. 100-112.
Jungck, Susan/ Kajornsin, Boonreang (2003): "Thai Wisdom" and Glocalization: Negotiating the Global and the Local in Thailand's National Education Reform. In: Anderson-Levitt, Kathryn (ed.): Local Meanings, Global Schooling: Anthropology and World Culture Theory. New York: Palgrave Macmillan.
Karlsen, Gustav (2000): Decentralized Centralism: A Framework for a Better Understanding of Governance in the Field of Education. In: Journal of Educational Policy. 15-5. pp. 525-538.
Kempner, Ken/ Jurema, Loureiro (2002): The Global Politics of Education: Brazil and the World Bank. In: Higher Education. 43-3. pp. 331-354.
Klees, Steven (2008): A Quarter Century of Neoliberal Thinking in Education: Misleading Analyses and Failed Policies. In: Globalisation, Societies, and Education. 6-4. pp. 311-348.
Lopes, Alice/ Macedo, Elizabeth (2003): The Curriculum Field in Brazil in the 1990s. In: Pinar, William: International Handbook of Curriculum Research. Mahwah: L. Erlbaum Associates.
Marcondes, Maria (1999): Teacher Education in Brazil. In: Journal of Education for Teaching. 25-3. pp. 203-213.
Marginson, Simon/ Mollis, Marcela (2002): The Door Opens and the Tiger Leaps: Theories and Reflexivities of Comparative Education for a Global Millennium. In: Comparative Education Review. 45-4. pp. 581-615.
Mazurek, Kas and others (2000): The Americas: Struggles for Equality and Quality in a Diverse Hemisphere. In: Mazurek, Kas and others (eds.): Education in a Global Society: A Comparative Perspective. Boston: Allyn & Bacon.
McGinn, Noel/ Street, Susan (1986): Educational Decentralization: Weak State or Strong State? In: Comparative Education Review. 30-4. pp. 471-490.
Meade, Ben/ Gershberg, Alec (2008): Making Education Reform Work for the Poor: Accountability and Decentralization in Latin America. In: Journal of Education Policy. 23-3. pp. 299-322.

Monfredini, Ivanise (2002): O Projeto Pedagógico em Escolas Municipais: Análise da Relação Entre a Autonomia e Manutenção e/ou Modificação de Práticas Escolares. In: Educação e Pesquisa. 28-2. pp. 41-56.
Moraes, Silvia (2003): In Search of a Vision: How Brazil is Struggling to Envision Citizenship for its Public Schools. In: Pinar, William (ed.): International Handbook of Curriculum Research. Mahwah: L. Erlbaum Associates.
Mukundan, Mullikottu-Veettil/ Bray, Mark (2004): The Decentralisation of Education in Kerala State, India: Rhetoric and Reality. In: International Review of Education. 50. pp. 223-243.
Narodowski, Mariano/ Nores, Milagros (2003): Searching for 'Neoliberal' Education Policies: A Comparative Analysis of Argentina and Chile. In: Ball, Stephen and others (eds.): Crisis and Hope: The Educational Hopscotch of Latin America. New York: RoutledgeFalmer.
Rivarola, Magdalena/ Fuller, Bruce (1999): Nicaragua's Experiment to Decentralize Schools: Contrasting Views of Parents, Teachers, and Directors. In: Comparative Education Review. 43-4. pp. 489-521.
Samoff, Joel (2003): No Teacher Guide, no Textbooks, no Chairs: Contending with Crisis in African Education. In: Arnove, Robert/ Torres, Carlos (eds.): Comparative Education: The Dialectic of the Global and the Local. 2nd edition. Lanham: Rowman & Littlefield.
Sands, Joseph (2008): Education Funding in a Recentralizing Democracy: A Cautionary Tale of Four Brazilian Cities. In: Latin American Politics and Society. 50-3. pp. 93-120.
Santos, Luciola (2002): Políticas Públicas Para o Ensino Fundamental: Parâmetros Curriculares Nacionais e Sistema Nacional de Avaliação (SAEB). In: Educação e Sociedade. 23-80. pp. 346-367.
Sarmento, Diva (2005): Criação dos Sistemas Municipais de Ensino. In: Educação e Sociedade. 26-93. pp. 1363-1390.
Schiefelbein, Ernesto (2004): The politics of Decentralisation in Latin America. In: International Review of Education. 50-3/4. pp. 359-378.
Schugurensky, Daniel (2003): Two Decades of Neoliberalism in Latin America. In: Ball, Stephen and others (eds.): Crisis and Hope: The Educational Hopscotch of Latin America. New York: RoutledgeFalmer.
Selcher, Wayne (1998): The Politics of Decentralized Federalism, National Diversification, and Regionalism in Brazil. In: Journal of Interamerican Studies and World Affairs. 40-4. pp. 25-50.
Souza, Donaldo/ Faria, Lia (2004): Reforma do Estado, Descentralização e Municipalização do Ensino no Brasil: A Gestão Política dos Sistemas Públicos do Ensino pós-LDB 9.934/96. In: Ensaio: Avaliação e Políticas Públicas em Educação, 12-45. pp. 925-944.
Stromquist, Nelly (2003): While Gender Sleeps: Neoliberalism's Impact on Educational Policies in Latin America. In: Ball, Stephen and others (eds.): Crisis and Hope: The Educational Hopscotch of Latin America. New York: RoutledgeFalmer.
Tatto, Maria (1999): Education Reform and State Power in Mexico: The Paradoxes of Decentralization. In: Comparative Education Review. 43-3. pp. 251-282.
Torres, Carlos (2002): The State, Privatization and Educational Policy: A Critique of Neo-liberalism in Latin America and Some Ethical and Political Implications. In: Comparative Education. 38-4. pp. 365-385.
Torres, Carlos (2009): Education and Neoliberal Globalization. New York: Routledge.
Valente, Ivan/ Arelaro, Lisete (2002): Educação e Políticas Públicas. São Paulo: Xamã.
Whitty, Geoff and others (1998): Devolution & Choice in Education: The School, the State and the Market. Buckingham: Open University Press.
Wong, Pia/ Balestino, Ramon (2003): "Prioritizing the Education of Marginalized Youth in Brazil", In: Ball, Stephen and others (eds.): Crisis and Hope: The Educational Hopscotch of Latin America. New York: RoutledgeFalmer.

# The Development of Transcultural Third Spaces by International and Transnational Students

*Dave Burnapp, Yan Feng and Wei Zhao*

## Abstract

*The social and academic adaptation of international and transnational students is shown to be facilitated by the students' creating online spaces. From these, using their own local networks, they can take support to help succeed in the new transnational spaces they are encountering. This can be conceived of as the creation of virtual 'Third Spaces', a way of mobilising and even deepening local identity as a tool for better negotiating transnational spaces. It is therefore possible for universities to create such virtual third spaces as a means of enabling students from different cultures to remain in their own country whilst benefitting from sharing learning opportunities with students in other countries.*

## Introduction and Background

This chapter brings together an emerging understanding of the adaptations, both social and academic, required of international and transnational students within the rapidly changing context of the internationalisation of higher education. Any form of international learning activity involves interfacing different cultural scripts of learning (Welikala and Watkins, 2008), and recognising how such interfaces are experienced is essential in order to design successful international and transnational collaborations. The changes within this field are many. There are changes related to the new forms of international and transnational education which students may experience as a result of ever-changing types of mobility and collaborations. There are changes of the intended student learning outcomes from higher education, which relate to new skills and competences for an increasingly globalised world. In addition there are changes related to the growth of information and communications technology (ICT), especially concerning ever-changing types of social networking platforms. These new online communities redefine the contacts and groups which students identify with and in part take their identity from. The very concepts of local, regional, national, international, and transnational are in fact problematized by online communities. Burnapp and Feng (2007) have listed the features necessary of any model that attempts to encapsulate the transcultural experiences of change of international students: such a model would need to recognise that although identity is linked to culture it is not fixed by culture; that although students are influenced by their original cultures of learning they are not completely constrained by them; that students willingly explore new cultures of learning; and that they strategically employ any resources available in order to succeed.

The distinction between international and transnational students, which is used throughout this chapter, needs early definition. *International* students are being defined as those students who physically move across borders to follow courses offered in other countries, which is to say that in these cases it is the students themselves who are mobile. In contrast *transnational* students are those who remain in their home country and follow a programme offered by a foreign provider, which is to say that in these cases it is the programme which is mobile, a form of provision which is also known as cross-border education (OECD, 2005).

This chapter will trace the authors' research over several years which links this emerging understanding to several theoretical frameworks, and this understanding is also informed by the authors' own experiences of themselves being international students (the Chinese authors studying in the UK, and the UK author studying in China), as well as being researchers and teachers. The topic hence relates to our own individual narratives and identities, our own identities of being rooted in a local place of origin yet negotiating transnational spaces, and also to our ongoing reflective professional development. Our stance concerning this topic, therefore, is not detached and objective but instead is engaged and often subjective. Our emerging understanding should be seen to be within the paradigm of reflective practice, as our attempts to comprehend the changes that international and transnational students experience are motivated by a desire to improve our professional activities, as all of us work in fields concerning the international experiences of students. This chapter draws on the research, both quantitative and qualitative, which the authors have previously published, as well as presenting data from new research carried out in order to bring the previous findings up to date.

It is predicted that transnational programmes will soon dominate international higher education provision (Bone, 2008). Taking just the UK as an example, Drew et al. (2008) researched the UK higher education sector "to identify the scale and pattern of current and planned trans-national education" (Drew et al., 2008: 4) and found that 65% of the 135 UK institutions in their study had transnational programmes in 2007, totaling over 1,500 programmes involving more than 275,000 students, that being 12% of the total number of students in UK higher education.

Drew *et al.* (2008) supply a classification of ten different models of transnational education, divided between two large categories depending on the institution with which the students have a contract: this may *either* be a contract with a local partner institution, *or* it may be with the foreign institution directly. The six different types of transnational education partnership within the general category where the students' contract is with a local partner of a foreign university or institution are: validation, articulation, franchise, joint awards, dual awards, and partial credit. In the second category, where the students have a contract directly with an institution in another country, there are four further types of provision: in-country/flying faculty; distance learning; blended delivery; on-campus provision overseas. It should be remembered, however, that there is considerable blurring and mixing amongst these categories.

Both transnational and international programmes promise intended outcomes which can be thought of as combining pragmatic and idealistic features: with the potential of not just broadening a student's skills base but also of being more profoundly transformational for those who participate. Hence the potential benefits of transnational programmes which are set out in the OECD (2005: 9) guidelines can be seen as bridging local and global, and these include:

> These new forms of cross-border higher education offer increased opportunities for improving the skills and competencies of individual students and the quality of national higher education systems, provided they aim at benefiting the human, social, economic and cultural development of the receiving country.

As an example of international rather than transnational education, the largest mobility programme within Europe is ERASMUS, which at one time was incorporated as part of the Socrates programme, and now (2007-2013) is part of the European Union Lifelong Learning Programme as the programme concerning the higher education sector. Currently, according to the European Commission's Education and Training website 'more than 4,000 higher education institutions in 33 countries participate' (European Commission Education and Training, 2010). The motivations for such international mobility presented on that site similarly include both the pragmatic and the idealistic:

> Many studies show that a period spent abroad not only enriches students' lives in the academic and professional fields, but can also improve language learning, intercultural skills, self-reliance and self-awareness. Their experiences give students a better sense of what it means to be a European citizen. In addition, many employers highly value such a period abroad, which increases the students' employability and job prospects (European Commission Education and Training, 2010).

The first two sections of this chapter will examine the adaptation of students who do physically move internationally, by firstly reviewing research carried out by one of the authors relating to the creation of a 'Third Space', a concept which will be shown links a person's local resources to much wider spaces. The second section will review later research conducted by the authors, which explored students' increased use of the internet as a source of support, and so suggested the creation of a 'Virtual Third Space'. This will be supplemented with recent findings of a repeat study, suggesting that this virtual support is of growing importance. The third and fourth sections focus more on transnational modes: the third section examines the experiences of students in China who are studying UK validated courses, who, although remaining in their home country, do still need to adapt to the requirements of a different culture of learning. The final section of the chapter will describe the creation of an innovative transcultural module, which uses mixed online communities of Chinese and UK students collaborating with each other in their learning, as a demonstration of how this emergent understanding of transcultural adaptation can help in the development of new forms of learning.

## The Creation of a Third Space

All people who leave their home to encounter new cultures can be thought of as undertaking a movement from a known place to somewhere which is at first unknown to them: in other words a space. Experience, though, helps transform unknown space to familiar place. Using the terminology of Tuan (1977), over time and with increased familiarity "what begins as undifferentiated space becomes place as we get to know it better and endow it with value" (Tuan, 1977: 6). In this understanding, using concepts from the phenomenology of geography, a place is far more than a location; it encompasses everything associated with it that can be thought of as meaningful (Relph, 1976). By examining the experience of adjustment – how the sojourners themselves perceive their transcultural experiences – the adaptation can be connected to another theoretical framework, one taken from cultural studies: "the Third Space", which Bhabha (1990) developed concerning the experiences of migrant communities.

In his study of adaptation of international students and their views of themselves as learners, Burnapp (2006) combined the theories taken from phenomenological geography with the descriptions of identity within the third space. The third space should not be seen simply as an over-lapping of two cultures, the local culture of origin and the new culture of the destination, as in a Venn diagram, it is best thought of as a fertile opportunity, an ability to draw on two systems or codes, with the potential of creating something new and generative from this synergy of cultures. Burnapp (2006) described seminars, as they are conducted in UK universities, as existential places with demands and expectations which newly arrived international students were at first unfamiliar with. Cortazzi proposes that educational researchers can use narratives to "explore participants perspectives on events and to see what their experience means" (Cortazzi, 2002: 196). Hence, by examining the reflective accounts produced by the students, it was possible to see how their narratives both recorded and helped to create their varying feelings of identifying with the epistemological requirements of the seminars. This can be illustrated with extracts from the students' accounts published in that article:

> Another interesting aspect of the education in the English universities is the participation. Students are encouraged to participate in seminars, to discuss, to say what they think. Even if the teacher is not right, is wrong in what he says, the student can take part to say 'Yes, I see that differently'. I find this very nice, very interesting, very different from Switzerland (Burnapp, 2006: 86).

Another student reported:

> Before I attended this course, I had thought discussing ideas in small group is useful, but I had no idea about how useful it is. When I took part in the group discussion, … I found out every member in the group contributed a little bit idea, this made the work easier and more interesting, just like many calm streams flowed together and become one larger noisy river. Discussion is really a great method to learn, it makes students enjoy learning, it also gives students a chance to communicate, organise and cooperate (Burnapp, 2006: 89).

In their adaptation to these new requirements the students did not abandon their earlier approaches to learning. So, rather than complete adaptation to the new scripts and the new needs, a more likely outcome was within the third space; a generative hybridisation of previous and new expectations.

## Virtual Third Spaces

Later this theoretical framework was extended to explore the possibility of a virtual third space (Burnapp/Feng, 2007). This term was devised to describe a strategy which international students may have developed to succeed in a culture of learning which is new to them, by exploiting new information technologies which allow people who are physically distant to share experiences and resources. The first research involved a cohort of Chinese students studying at a UK university, and set out to determine whether, by using the internet for social networking, the students were able to gather information and to form virtual communities of learners, and so to meld resources from their original culture of learning with the demands of their new location. The research employed mixed methods; initially a focus group of six students was conducted to identify these students' different uses of ICT, then the findings of that discussion allowed the development of a quantitative attitude survey to gather information from a wider sample.

For this survey 30 items were initially written, including categories of using the internet for communication, entertainment, shopping, formal education, and informal education. These survey items were piloted with 40 students and an item analysis was carried out using alpha coefficients to reduce the number of items to be included in the amended survey to 16, with some items worded to indicate a positive attitude and some a negative attitude. The resulting survey consisted of eight items in each of two major categories: social uses (including communications, entertainment, and shopping) and education (including formal and informal education). The education category consists of four items relating to formal uses (meaning those prescribed by the students' courses) and four items for informal uses (meaning those instigated by the students themselves). Of these four informal items, two relate to what can be thought of as general third space activities (i.e. exploiting Chinese resources in order to achieve better in their UK education) but which are not necessarily reliant on ICT:

*I do not think it is possible to combine Chinese and English resources in my study.*
*I think that discussing with Chinese friends gives me a deeper understanding of my courses.*

The two other items in this sub-category specifically relate to web/Internet, i.e. they can be thought of as clearly virtual third space activities:

*I do not use Web/Internet communications to get support for my courses from Chinese friends.*
*I often look for online Chinese information sources to support my courses in the UK.*

The eventual alpha coefficient for the eight items in the social category was in excess of (.7), and for the eight items in the education category in excess of (.6). The final instrument therefore consisted of 16 attitude statements, some positive and some negative, to which the students were asked to respond using a Likert scale; 4 = strongly agree, 3 = agree, 2 = disagree, 1 = strongly disagree.

The survey was presented bilingually in Chinese and English (see Appendix) to 58 students known to the researchers, hence this was not a probability sample and the findings should therefore be viewed as only exploratory. For these students, using ICT is a regular feature in their daily lives, and the only two items for which a negative attitude was found (that is a mean of less than 2 after inverting the negatively worded items) were:

*I often play online games.*
*I think the Web/Internet is now an essential part of education.*

Surprisingly, the students' uses of ICT for education were even more than uses for social activities. The suggestion that these students might synthesise Chinese and UK approaches to knowledge creation was supported, as they blended use of Chinese and of English resources. They reported that discussions with other Chinese students gave them 'deeper understanding', and many achieve this deeper understanding by making use of online resources and communications: a 'virtual third space'.

The authors were then able to repeat the use of this survey in 2010 with a different cohort (n = 53) of students also from China, but who had a very similar profile in terms of age and previous educational experiences to the 2007 cohort. There were several striking differences in the findings between the earlier and the more recent cohorts, which seem to indicate a growing role for the virtual third space. As was to be expected, given the wider social changes throughout this period, the newer cohort were even more integrated into internet uses than the earlier cohort, both socially and educationally, including formal and informal educational uses. Using independent samples t-test for equality of means, significant differences between the two samples were found for the following eight items (using a 95% confidence interval), within every case the 2010 cohort rating their attitudes more positively than the 2007 cohort:

*I feel I am a member of an online community of friends.*
*I think that discussing with Chinese friends gives me a deeper understanding of my courses.*
*I often look for online Chinese information sources to support my courses in the UK.*
*I use some form of online entertainment every day.*
*I regularly use the online resources supplied by my courses.*
*I use online methods of communication almost every day.*
*I value the online support supplied by my courses.*
*I think the Web/Internet is now an essential part of education.*

It is important not to over-claim the value of these findings from two opportunity samples in a single institution, but it seems that it is worth further exploring the role of virtual contacts, virtual support, and online information sources which were reported by these students in their attempts to come to terms with, and succeed within, a new transcultural learning space.

## The Experiences of Transnational Students

Within the emerging model of transnational education, where students remain in their home country whilst following a course provided by a foreign institution or agency, the learning materials are often supplied in the form of flexible and distributed learning. Some forms of transnational education deliver programmes by distance learning, for example via a Virtual Learning Environment (VLE). Examples of transnational programmes include Higher National Diploma (HND) level courses which have been validated by UK-based organisations and institutions but which are delivered in other countries such as China, India, Malaysia, and Singapore, at times using collaborating partner institutions. In the UK educational system these HND courses are one year short of a full degree. Such programmes are taught and assessed using English language, and may allow the students to progress abroad, for example to the UK or Australia, to take final year top-up programmes entitling them to full undergraduate degrees, and then to move onto Masters courses. In this model the students begin their full programme at home as transnational students, then may sometimes progress to become mobile international students at a later stage.

For transnational students the adaptation necessary to succeed in their courses may at first seem to be less, and to be easier to achieve, than that required of international students, as their adaptation needs may be assumed to be only academic and linguistic without requiring social adjustments. Burnapp and Zhao (2009), however, set out to investigate these assumptions, suspecting that the dislocation of academic and social conventions may itself be problematic:

> it is possible that the academic adaptation required, including what Welikala & Watkins (2008) describe as cultural scripts of learning, may be more difficult because cultures of education are likely to reflect to some extent the prevalent ideologies which are exhibited daily in such things as how the news is reported (for example whether several views are presented or just one official view), or how decisions are made in workplaces (using either horizontal or vertical decision making structures), or expectations of whose voices have the right to be heard in certain scenarios (Burnapp/Zhao, 2009: 32).

In this research the authors examined online postings which had been created by Chinese institutions and students to discuss their transnational education experiences; hence this is a form of non-participant observation in a naturalistic setting producing secondary qualitative data (Hewson et al., 2003). This research was facilitated by the participation of a Chinese researcher as these online postings were in Chinese, but the findings were presented and published in English.

The examination of these online discussions revealed various themes which were the main concerns of the students in the transnational programmes, including: differences in theories of education between previous courses and the students' current HND courses; the need to acquire different study methods such as autonomous learning, group work, and applications of theories; as well as personal issues relating to choice, change, and self-development. Permeating all these concerns were mentions of the challenges of studying in English language. These issues can be thought of both as resulting from chronological differences between students' previous and current study experiences, and as resulting from situational differences between the expectations of the students' current social environment (conventions associated with being in China) and their current educational environment (conventions associated with studying a UK-style programme). The extract below presents a similar pattern of adaptation to that described by the international students in the extracts reported earlier, seeming to suggest that for both international and transnational students adaptation should be seen as a longitudinal process rather than a single event, and that the process can be supported by online sharing of experiences and resources:

> I could not get used to the new way of studying when I first started the HND course. In the Chinese high school, I have not developed the self-study habit. My study method was to listen to what the teacher said and to make notes. I adopted self-learning method after half year of the HND programme. (…) In the class, the teachers use discussions, presentations and role play teaching methods to demonstrate the theories, and then group work to connect the theories and real situations together. This kind of study method and environment makes me become more outgoing and confident (Burnapp/Zhao, 2009: 35).

It should be noted that these discussion forums (online communities where Chinese participants seek and offer support concerning UK educational programmes) often display threads of discussion and argument, indicating social construction of attitudes and understandings. Once again the students were drawing on Chinese resources and contacts to succeed in their programmes. The authors concluded that this research suggested: "further evidence of a virtual third space created by students engaged in the crossing of educational systems (and the implicated cultural systems) using the internet to share and develop opinions and feelings" (Burnapp/Zhao, 2009: 38).

## University-created Virtual Third Spaces

This section reports on the most recent work carried out by the team, a developmental project set within the paradigm of reflective practice and action research. This will demonstrate how the authors have created a novel form of learning to make use of a virtual third space in transnational education. The project concerns the creation of an online programme to link collaborative learning groups, which include students in a university in China and students in a university in the UK. Reflections on this project explore many levels of sharing which is necessary in transcultural educational projects of this kind. These include managerial aspects relating to how projects and programmes should be established and operated; epistemological aspects relating to understandings of knowledge and how it is achieved; and technical aspects relating to the ICT requirements of online learning programmes which bridge different countries.

The project received funding from 'China Connect', a strand of a UK government strategy aimed to strengthen the UK's position in international education. This project was primarily concerned with engendering employability and entrepreneurship, particularly related to the globalised economy (Burnapp *et al.*, 2010). Hence the project aimed to create an on-line training module for students in the UK and Chinese universities. The intended learning outcomes for the *students* were to develop cross-cultural communication skills; knowledge of the business environment of other countries; entrepreneurship competences for the globalised world; and the ability to work with partners of different cultures. There were matching intended outcomes for the *teachers* from the two universities, including: experiencing cross-cultural educational collaboration, interaction with students in different cultures, and development of new pedagogic skills.

The development of the module, which involved an iterative process of exchanging ideas amongst a team of teachers drawn from the two countries, needed several stages of refinement: developing an e-learning platform, designing teaching materials, and evaluating a pilot programme with volunteer students. It was recognised from the beginning that in such collaborations it is necessary for the on-line materials to be both academically acceptable and to be technically accessible, to staff and students in two distinct cultures of learning, and with familiarity of different virtual learning environments. The process which was followed was informed by the authors' previous explorations into virtual third spaces, and the process exposed several distinct but related areas which should be addressed by any other academics intending to create such transcultural courses.

The process of planning the programme and preparing the materials took over one year, with the team members visiting each other in China and the UK, as well as constant contact by email and file sharing. Students from the two participating universities took part in trialling the materials, and other stakeholders, including careers staff and IT specialists, needed to be involved. It was found that such schemes are complex, with several levels of interfacing differences, but that transcultural solutions are achievable.

The institutional stakeholders who needed to be convinced of the worth of the programme included managers, students and staff. Taking one fundamental aspect, the overall approach to learning on which the programme would be based needed to be discussed and agreed within the team. Put simply, there was an expectation amongst the Chinese teachers that the programme should be heavy in theoretical content, whereas the UK staff proposed a lighter theoretical load but a higher degree of group interactivity and application of theory. Therefore the materials needed to be rewritten several times to achieve mutually agreeable goals. The eventual materials therefore typically include online source materials which the students must consult in order to establish a theoretical base, which is then used for interactive group activities requiring sharing of viewpoints, sharing of personal reflections, and the production of collaborative outputs such as components of a business plan. The teaching materials provide a balance of activities relating to enterprise and to inter-cultural communication.

Turning to a technical aspect, the institutional virtual learning environments, and the social networking tools which the students were familiar with, were different in the two countries; hence it was found that technical audits were necessary to check accessibility of the materials as they were developed. Again this required re-designing learning materials so that they were accessible with limited band-width and different versions of software, for example slideshows, and an open-access platform was chosen to carry the course content. Various methods of online interaction were included in the course materials, but in fact the volunteer students established their own channels of communication to supplement them. One learning aspect from the project is that staff should expect and accept that in such things the students will always be ahead of them.

The project from its inception was based on a desire to elicit views from all participants, and not to impose expert solutions from one side, and it is suggested that any such collaborative projects need to accommodate alternative expectations of the learning content, and different experiences of using e-learning. The project teams had bilingual Chinese-English speakers, but the teaching materials are in English, and recognising the opportunities and the constraints of using English as a global language has been a challenge for all concerned.

The following three learning points are suggested as being transferrable to other collaborative educational projects which intend to create learning activities within the virtual third space.

Firstly, take time to establish and share a vision of the aims and methods of your project: as the project is being developed it is essential to move slowly to work through differences, as even with bilingual team members and existing friendships in place, it was found that repeated contacts were necessary to achieve clarification of differences as they emerged. The bridging of different local expectations into a shared transnational space is possible, but needs time and caution, it is an activity which needs to be worked towards with conscious effort. Secondly it is essential to ensure that there are clear communication channels, this does not just require technical considerations such as emailing, file sharing, and online discussions, but also requires time to allow for team members to reflect on proposals. Attitudes towards time, it should be remembered, are culturally variable. The communication plan needs to acknowledge this variability. Thirdly, if the project funding body allows flexibility, then adopt a 'Sliding Planning Window' approach to project management: it is the nature of intercultural working that the unexpected will occur, so flexible responses will allow these differences to be recognised as being opportunities as well as threats.

The piloting of this project has now been completed, and it is expected that the programme will begin to be offered from the autumn of 2011 involving the same two universities but with an intention to extend to other partners.

In conclusion, this chapter describes the longitudinal development of a concept over several iterations of investigation, reflection, and communication amongst a team of researchers who themselves needed to develop a shared understanding. The research reported here in the different sections both produce and are produced by insights arising from cultural differences; hence this paper is itself an example of the development of third space thinking.

## References


Bhabha, Homi K. (1990): The Third Space – Interview with Homi Bhabha. In: Rutherford, Jonathan (ed.): Identity: Community, Culture, Difference. London: Lawrence and Wishart.

Bhabha, Homi K. (2004): The Location of Culture. Abingdon: Routledge.

Bone, Drummond (2008): Internationalisation of HE: A Ten-Year View. Department for Innovation, Universities & Skills. London: DIUS.

Burnapp, Dave (2006). Trajectories of adjustment of international students: U-curve, learning curve, or Third Space. In: Intercultural Education. 17(1). pp. 81-94.

Burnapp, Dave/ Feng, Yan (2007): Exploring Digital Third Spaces – an inquiry into the use of digital support systems by Chinese students in a British university. Paper presented at The 5th International Conference on ELT in China & the 1st Congress of Chinese Applied Linguistics. Beijing. May 16-21.

Burnapp, Dave/ Yan, Zigang/ Ahmedmia, Omar/ He, Shaowei/ Zhao, Wei (2010): Collaborative capacity building: a case study of the development of an on-line module concerning employability and entrepreneurship. Paper presented to: International Association for Development of the Information Society (IADIS) International Conference on International Higher Education, Curtin University of Technology. Perth/Australia. 29 Nov.-01 Dec.

Burnapp, Dave/ Zhao, Wei (2009): Voices from the chat rooms: research into the experiences of Chinese students participating in transnational education programmes as reported on internet social networks. In: Enhancing the Learner Experience in Higher Education. 1(1). pp. 30-43.

Cortazzi, Martin (2002). Analyzing narratives and documents. In: Coleman, Marianne/ Briggs, Ann. R. J. (eds.): Research Methods in Educational Leadership and Management. London: Paul Chapman Publishing.

Drew, Sue/ McCaig, Colin/ Marsden, David/ Haughton, Peggy/ McBride, John/ McBride, Denise/ Willis, Ben/ Wolstenholme, Claire (2008): Transnational Education and Higher Education Institutions: Exploring Patterns of HE Institutional Activity. DIUS Research Report 08 07. http://www.bis.gov.uk/assets/biscore/corporate/migratedd/publications/d/dius_rr_08_07.pdf [27.04.2011].

European Commission Education and Training (2010): The Erasmus Programme – studying in Europe and more. http://ec.europa.eu/education/lifelong-learning-programme/doc80_en.htm [26.07.2011].

Hewson, Claire/ Yule, Peter/ Laurent, Dianna/ Vogel, Carl (2003): Internet Research Methods. London: Sage.

OECD (2005): Guidelines for Quality Provision in Cross-border Higher Education. http://www.oecd.org/dataoecd/27/51/35779480.pdf [27.04.2011].

Relph, Edward (1976): Place and Placelessness. London: Pion.

Tuan, Yi-Fu (1977): Space and Place. London: Edward Arnold.

Welikala, Thushari/ Watkins, Chris (2008): Improving Intercultural Learning Experiences in Higher Education. London: Institute of Education.

## Appendix

**Questionnaire**

The aim of this research is to discover the different uses of the web/internet and different study methods amongst Chinese students at the University of Northampton. We would like you to answer the following questions about these topics. We would be grateful if you could spend just a few minutes to complete this questionnaire.
Many thanks

| **Item:**<br>*[Note, for the purposes of this research the term 'Web/Internet' will be used throughout the survey.]* | **4 = strongly agree**<br>**3 = agree**<br>**2 = disagree**<br>**1 = strongly disagree** |
|---|---|
| **Example** | 4 3 2 1 |
| 1. I often play online games | 4 3 2 1 |
| 2. I expect my use of the Web/Internet for shopping will increase greatly in the future | 4 3 2 1 |
| 3. I never watch streamed TV online | 4 3 2 1 |
| 4. I never contact my tutors electronically | 4 3 2 1 |
| 5. I do not think that it is possible to combine Chinese and English resources in my study | 4 3 2 1 |
| 6. I feel I am a member of an online community of friends | 4 3 2 1 |
| 7. I think that discussing with Chinese friends gives me a deeper understanding of my courses | 4 3 2 1 |
| 8. I do not trust sites for online shopping | 4 3 2 1 |
| 9. I regularly use the online resources supplied by my courses | 4 3 2 1 |
| 10. I use online methods of communication almost every day | 4 3 2 1 |
| 11. I do not use Web/Internet communications to get support for my courses from Chinese friends | 4 3 2 1 |
| 12. I often use the Web/Internet for shopping | 4 3 2 1 |
| 13. I often look for online Chinese information sources to support my courses in the UK | 4 3 2 1 |
| 14. I think the Web/Internet is now an essential part of education | 4 3 2 1 |
| 15. I use some form of online entertainment everyday | 4 3 2 1 |
| 16. I value the online support supplied by my courses | 4 3 2 1 |

Thank you very much for completing this questionnaire.

# Notes on Contributors

**Dave Burnapp** was born in 1950 in the UK and holds an EdD. He has worked in education and development in Vanuatu, Zambia, Algeria and China. He is currently a senior lecturer at Northampton Business School, where he researches and publishes on topics relating to the internationalization of higher education. He is a National Teaching Fellow and has managed several projects involving international collaboration.
E-mail: dave.burnapp@northampton.ac.uk

**Rudolf Egger** holds an MPhil and a PhD in pedagogy and sociology. He is a professor with the Department of Education at the University of Graz. His special research interests include qualitative analysis in social sciences, biographical research and didactics in adult education.
E-mail: rudolf.egger@uni-graz.at

**Yan Feng** was born in 1965 in China and holds an MA and a PhD in Education as well as a Postgraduate Diploma in English Language Instruction. She serves as the Deputy Director of the International Office of Shaoxing University (China), where she also works as an associate professor in the School of Education. Her research interests include international collaboration in higher education and teacher education to promote inclusion.
E-mail: fengyan@usx.edu.cn

**Neda Forghani-Arani**, born in 1961 in Tehran (Iran), holds an MA and a PhD in Education. She is a research associate and senior lecturer in the Department of Education at the University of Vienna (Austria). Her current teaching and research is focused on intercultural education, global education and teacher education research.
E-mail: neda.forghani-arani@univie.ac.at

**António Fragoso** holds a PhD in Pedagogy. He works at the University of Algarve, where he oversees the masters program in Social Education. He is convenor of the ESREA research network "Between Global and Local: Adult learning and development". His research focuses on adult education, community development and social change.
E-mail: aalmeida@ualg.pt

**Teresa Gonzáles Gómez** holds an MA in Sociology from the University of Granada in Spain and an MA in Social Sciences (Baltic Studies) from the University of Tartu in Estonia. She is an associate professor of Sociology at the University of Huelva (Spain). Her research is focused in the areas of social capital and cross-border cooperation. Currently she is doing a PhD.
E-mail: teresa.gonzalez@dstso.uhu.es

**Estrella Gualda** holds a PhD in Sociology and an MA in Politics and Sociology from the Complutense University in Madrid. She is a professor in Sociology at the University of Huelva (Spain) and director of the Social Studies and Social Intervention Research Center. Her research interests: migration, cross-border issues, social networks, social capital and research methods.
E-mail: estrella@uhu.es

**Steven Hales** was born in 1973 in Florida (US) and holds an MA in Teaching English to Speakers of Other Languages from the Monterey Institute of International Studies and a PhD in Curriculum Studies, Teacher Development and Comparative, International & Development Education from the Ontario Institute for Studies in Education of the University of Toronto. He has worked as a teacher in Asia, North America and South America.
E-mail: steven.hales@utoronto.ca

**Marc Hill** was born in Germany. He holds an MPhil in Education at the University of Cologne. He is a research associate at the Institute for Education and Educational Research at the Department of Intercultural Education at the University of Klagenfurt (Austria). Research interests: migration, urban development, marginalization, diversity, education, training and urban competencies. Currently he is doing a PhD.
E-mail: Marc.Hill@aau.at

**Elke Krasny** is a cultural theorist, curator and project-based artist. Her appointments include senior lecturer at the Academy of Fine Arts Vienna, visiting researcher at the Hong Kong Community Museum in 2011, visiting artist at the Audain Gallery Vancouver in 2011 and visiting scholar at the Canadian Centre for Architecture in 2012. In 2011 she received the Outstanding Artist Award in the category Women's Culture from the Austrian Ministry of Education, Arts and Culture.
E-mail: elke.krasny@gmail.com

**Fergal Lenehan** was born in Ireland and received a BA and an MA from University College Dublin and a PhD in Cultural Studies from the University of Leipzig. He teaches cultural history and cultural theory at the Department of Intercultural Studies and Business Communications at the Friedrich Schiller University of Jena (Germany).
E-mail: fergal.lenehan@uni-jena.de

**Emilio Lucio-Villegas** holds a PhD in Pedagogy. He works at the University of Seville and is the head of The Cátedra Paulo Freire at the University of Seville, a member of the Steering Committee of Esrea and a convenor of a network called Between Global and Local: Adult learning and development. His research is focused on literacy, local development of citizenship and participation.
E-mail: elucio@us.es

**Carmen Márquez** holds an MA in Social Work from the University of Huelva in Spain and two additional masters degrees, one in Gender Studies and one in Migration Studies. Currently she is writing her doctoral thesis. Her research is in the area of social networks, education and migration.
E-mail: carmen.marquez@dstso.uhu.es

**Germán Martínez Velasco** es Doctor en Ciencias Sociales y investigador titular de el Colegio de la Frontera Sur. El es especialista en el estudio de las migraciones centroamericanas a México, y recientemente de chiapanecos a los Estados Unidos. Su ultima publicacion consiste en la coordinación de un libro denominado una aproximacion a las migraciones internacionales en la frontera sur de México. También ha realizado estudios sociológicos sobre la dinámica de la marginacion en el sur de México, especialmente en el caso de las poblaciones indígenas. Es miembro del sistema nacional de investigadores del conacyt.
Correo electrónico: gmartine@ecosur.mx

**Vània Martins** has earned a first degree in Social Education at the University of Algarve in Portugal. She is currently completing her masters degree in Social Education. Since February 2010 she has been working at the University of Algarve, and since 2009 she has been working on international research in the area of cross-border identities in southern Europe. She has also begun working with the Theatre of the Oppressed.
E-mail: v.dmartins@hotmail.com

**Jennifer M. Murphy** was born in 1976 in California (US). She holds a Masters of Arts and a European Doctorate in Peace, Conflict and Development Studies from the Universitat Jaume I (Spain) and the University of Leeds (England). She is professor of the International Masters Program in Peace, Conflict and Development Studies and Personal Investigadora Contratada Doctora for the Instituto Interuniversitario de Desarrollo Social y Paz at the Universitat Jaume I in Spain. Her research interests include Peace, Conflict and Development Studies, with a special focus on the Western Saharan/Moroccan conflict, self-determination and nonviolent conflict transformation, postcolonial studies and political theory.
E-mail: murphysan@hotmail.com

**Sidi M. Omar** was born 1970 in Western Sahara and has a BA in Criticism and Dramatic Literature from the Higher Institute of Dramatic Arts in Syria and an MA in Peace and Development Studies, an MPhil and a European Doctorate in Peace, Conflicts and Democracy from the Universitat Jaume I, Spain. He is a member of the Diplomatic Service of the Sahrawi Republic (SADR). He is currently the SADR Ambassador to Ethiopia and the African Union. He is a visiting professor at the International Masters in Peace, Conflict and Development Studies of Universitat Jaume I.
E-mail: sidi1@yahoo.com

**Anne M. Phelan,** born 1959 in Waterford (Ireland) holds an MA in Education and EdD in Education. She is a professor in the Department of Curriculum and Pedagogy and a research associate with the Centre for the Study of Teacher Education at the University of British Columbia, Vancouver (Canada). Her interests lie in the relationship between language, subjectivity and power; the dynamics of judgment and responsibility and the paradoxes of autonomy (creativity and resistance) in professional life.
E-mail: anne.phelan@ubc.ca

**Angela Pilch Ortega** holds an MPhil and a PhD in Education. She works as an assistant professor at the Department of Educational Science, specifically in Applied Learning World Research, at the University of Graz. She is co-convenor of the ESREA network on Migration, Ethnicity, Racism and Xenophobia. Her research fields are based on qualitative-interpretative methods: biographical research in the area of social inequality, migration and social movements.
E-mail: angela.pilch-ortega@uni-graz.at

**Miguel Sánchez Álvarez**, nació 1963, en Jok'osik, Chiapas, México. El obtuvo su grado de Doctor en Ciencias en Planificación de Empresas y Desarrollo Regional, del Instituto Tecnológico de Oaxaca. Se formó como antropólogo social en la Universidad Autónoma de Chiapas. Es Profesor en la Universidad Intercultural de Chiapas. Es miembro del Cuerpo Académico Patrimonio, Territorio y Desarrollo en la Frontera Sur de México. Forma parte del padrón de Profesores del Programa de Mejoramiento del Profesorado (PROMEP). Sánchez Álvarez ha realizado y realiza diversas investigaciones antropológicas y ambientales de los pueblos originarios de México.
Correo electrónico: miguesanalvarez@gmail.com

**Barbara Schröttner**, born 1972 in Austria, holds an MPhil in Education, a Master of Arts in Peace, Conflict and Development Studies and a PhD in Education. She works as an assistant professor with the Department of Education, specifically the Institute of Continuing Education, at the University of Graz. Her research fields include adult and continuing education, globalization and development studies, postcolonial research and India. She has been involved in qualitative ethnographic research in India since 1999. She has lectured in Europe, Asia and the US.
E-mail: barbara.schroettner@uni-graz.at

**Alexander Unger** holds a PhD in Educational Science. He studied Pedagogy and Philosophy at the University of Darmstadt and worked as an assistant professor at the University of Magdeburg. Since 2011 he has been a junior professor in Educational Science and Media Education at the University of Hamburg (Germany). His main research interests are theory of space, media literacy and productive media cultures.
E-mail: alexanderunger@gmx.de.

**Simon Warren** holds a PhD in Education. He is a lecturer in Critical Policy Studies within the School of Education at the University of Sheffield (UK). His research explores multicultural, political and social belongings in a number of areas including the politics of language policy, language learning and multicultural society.
E-mail: s.a.warren@shef.ac.uk

**Erol Yildiz** was born in Samsun (Turkey) and holds an Mphil and a PhD in Education and has completed postdoc work in Sociology. He is a professor of Intercultural Education at the Faculty of Cultural Sciences, University of Klagenfurt (Austria). His research interests include migration studies, intercultural education, urbanity and globalization.
E-mail: Erol.Yildiz@uni-klu.ac.at

**Wei Zhao** was born in 1982 in Nanning, in Guangxi Zhuang Autonomous Region in southern China. He has spent ten years as a student, teacher, and researcher in the UK and holds a masters degree in Marketing. He currently teaches Chinese at the University of Northampton, and coordinates an educational project which links UK and Chinese students.
E-mail: wei.zhao@northampton.ac.uk